William James Roe

Inquirendo Island

William James Roe

Inquirendo Island

ISBN/EAN: 9783743327337

Manufactured in Europe, USA, Canada, Australia, Japa

Cover: Foto ©ninafisch / pixelio.de

Manufactured and distributed by brebook publishing software
(www.brebook.com)

William James Roe

Inquirendo Island

BY

HUDOR GENONE

———•─•——

NEW YORK:
TWENTIETH CENTURY PUBLISHING CO.
1890

PREFACE.

THE following pages contain certain things which, unless considered in connection with the whole narrative, may possibly be misinterpreted, and I will especially ask my readers not to overlook the concluding chapter which I have called my Postface.

While the story may be termed a satire, it will, I trust, not be found wanting in a spirit of full reverence for the essential truths of God's universe.

Between the pestilential marshes of superstition and the cold glaciers of reason, lies the fertile table-land of common sense, and it is there I have endeavored to take my stand.

CONTENTS.

INQUIRENDO ISLAND.

CHAPTER I.

THE WRECK OF THE SPEEDWELL.

I T was quite early in the morning that I set out alone
from Far Rockaway in one of my father's pleasure
boats. The wind being fair and not too brisk, I ventured
to steer out through the inlet upon the open sea. I
tacked about all day along the coast, trolling for blue-fish,
and about noon, happening to strike a school of Spanish
mackerel, I delayed my return until almost nightfall.

At last, long after sunset, the head of the *Speedwell* was
turned towards the land ; but a fog had come rolling in
from the east, and the shore was wholly hidden from view.
There was no compass on board, and stars and moon were
hidden overhead. With all the judgment I possessed, the
course was kept in that direction in which the inlet was
supposed to lie. An hour passed, and then the breeze,
which had held fair, began to die out. The fog became
denser and denser, and the wind at last failed altogether.

I became alarmed. It grew darker and darker, and the
palpable mist wrapped itself about me, cold, and clammy,
and comfortless, although the night was in June, and the
day had been warm. The boat was an open one, and I
was soon wet through. At least two hours must have
passed during which the *Speedwell* lay like a log on the

ocean, rolling gently as the lazy waves rose and fell, the
sail flapping, and the mast and rudder creaking. Then
with the lifting of the fog the wind freshened. I thought
with joy that I should now probably be able to see the
stars, and by their aid steer for home. But the fog only
lifted from off the sea to hang in the shape of a dense
cloud between the friendly stars and me, and the wind
rising rapidly, threw the sea into so great a turmoil that,
even had I known the course towards the inlet, there was
no safety except in keeping the boat's head to windward.
So, cold, wet, sleepy, and comfortless, I was forced to
keep the tiller all that unhappy night. The morning
broke at last. I scanned the horizon in every direction,
but all around was nothing but a waste of savage waters,
and the wind all the time due west. I knew now that
every moment I was leaving home further and further
behind. Still I did not despair, for upon my course
lay the track of the many steamships that cross the Atlantic. After the second nightfall the wind again went
down; but the clouds continued to hang low, and worn
out, I clung to the tiller for all the weary hours of the
daylight. With painful eagerness my eyes rested upon
the misty horizon; but the night folded itself again about
me, and not a sail was seen. Still all through the dark,
the wind held west, and the waves angrily heaved onward
my little craft. I clung despairingly to the helm, and
again the morning broke. Another day passed and
another night. Sleep I could not while the wind was
high. There was a sufficient supply of water in the
locker, but a few crusts of bread were all that was left of
the lunch that had been provided. These I ate ravenously, and then from time to time cast longing glances at
the fish that I had caught. Famished, I at last was driven

to the extremity of thus satisfying my hunger. This was
on the fourth day when the winds had died out, and a great
calm had overspread the sea. Then, too, it was that I
could sleep, waking at frequent intervals in hope of
rescue; but the sun beat pitilessly down, the *Speedwell*
drifted eastward, and far and near no sail. The sixth
night fell in clouds and darkness; again the waters rose,
and the wind, always from the west, blew fast and furious.

Another night of terror and despair, the angry ocean
gnashing its white teeth of foam astern, and all else dark.

Driving through the night, gripping the rudder, suddenly I heard through the gloom the sound of surf breaking ahead. But as yet there was no sign of land, and
while trembling with apprehension, the sound of the
breakers grew nearer and nearer, and in an instant the
boat, plunging forward, struck upon a sunken ledge of
rock, over which the sea dashed with great fury.

My expertness as a swimmer was of little avail in those
savage surges. Stabbed and mangled by the thrusts of
the keen ledge, the poor boat sank gurgling to its death,
while the same monster wave, having perfidiously betrayed
my companion, cast me, gasping and stunned, upon a
sloping beach beyond. There I lay, just beyond the
waters, till my strength returned. I staggered to my feet.
The dawn was just breaking; the fog was lifting; the
wind was lowering. By the dim light I saw above me
a towering precipice of granite, and on the shore, here
and there, interspersed with narrow patches of mud, jag-
ged swords of rock, and farther out, rising up through
the foaming billows, merciless nature held aloft her
sharp dirks in bared brown hands.

With them she had stabbed my *Speedwell*. It happens
often to men that when the brain is dullest the soul is

most thoughtful ; or perhaps 'tis then that, pitying our
weakness, our guardian angel thinks for us. Whether it
was I or my angel that thought, the idea came to me
thus, cold and wet and miserable as I was, how nature
continually is at war with itself. Brooding over this
thought I dragged myself wearily along the sands, seeking
some way of ascent in the line of precipitous rocks above
me. It was some time before I was successful in discovering a way, and when at last an opening was found, and
by dint of rough climbing I mounted upward, the effort
so exhausted me that I sank down upon the soft short
grass that covered the ledge, and with the sun shining
brightly, fell asleep.

It was noon when I awoke. I was stiff and sore, but
the sleep had refreshed me, and had, moreover, dried my
sodden clothes. I got up, and walked about vigorously.
I had lost my hat, but this I did not regard as important.
My fatigue over, curiosity naturally asserted itself. Where
was I ? What land was it upon which I stood ? My first
thought was that it was one of the Bermuda Islands, and
yet on reflection I knew that this could not be. According to the best calculation I could make, having due regard to the fact that I had merely drifted with the wind,
the *Speedwell* must have averaged over five knots an
hour. The island was therefore at least seven hundred
miles from the coast. As I gazed about me it may be imagined with some considerable astonishment, I perceived
that where I was appeared to be the highest land in any
direction. There was a slight mist that bounded the
view at a distance of perhaps half a mile ; but the mist
lay like a fleecy veil along the ground, while overhead it
was perfectly cloudless. Had there been mountains or
any considerable elevation they would have been plainly

visible. I went to the edge of the cliff and looked down :
except in the spot by which I had ascended, and in one
or two other places north and south, where gaps and fis-
sures appeared, the rock was a perpendicular wall. With
my returning strength came appetite. I had eaten nothing since the day before, and then only the stale fish, from
which I now revolted with a great loathing. I was as yet
in doubt whether or not the island was inhabited ; but I
felt assured that, if inhabitants there were, they must be
civilized, and therefore friendly ; so I set out on my way
inland without any special apprehension of any kind.
The mist gradually lifted, and the prospect widened.
The turf upon which I trod was soft, and the grass such
as one sees upon a well-kept lawn, interspersed with the
blossoms of white clover. At a distance a number of dun-
colored and tawny cows were grazing, and a few birds,—
orioles, sparrows, and thrushes,—flew about at the verge of
the bluff. There was not a tree in sight, nor a bush, and
no signs of vegetation of any sort, except the short mat of
grass and clover. The sight of the cows revived my
spirits, convincing me that the land upon which evil fortune had cast me was by no means desolate. Then, too,
I was thirsty, and forthwith began casting about to procure a drink of milk from one of my friends the cows.
The idea was an excellent one ; but like many other noble conceptions of the human mind, quite valueless until
put into actual operation. In this case it was all theory
and no practice, for the cattle were shy, and would not
suffer me to approach. Having lost my hat in the sea,
my only resource in the way of a milk pail was my leather
wallet, a birthday gift from my mother.

However, not that it mattered much. If I had possessed
the best milk pail in the world it would have been all the

same ; the cows were shy, and although I chased one
or two till tired out, I could not get near them.   I solaced
myself with the reflection that the smartest man living
cannot milk a cow at a distance ; and while I was walking on, meditating, I almost stumbled over the figure of a
man lying at full length upon the grass.   He got upon
his feet directly when he perceived me and stared in
mute astonishment.

He had an air that appeared to me to be foreign.   I
could not tell, however, by his gait or his appearance, to
what nationality he belonged ; so I resolved to try a few
European languages, of which fortunately I possessed a
smattering.

"Comment s'appelle ce pays ci?" I enquired, trying to
infuse into my voice at least as much suavity as his
stony stare invited.

He stared at me in gruff silence.

"Come si chiama questa isola?"

He grunted, but still said nothing.

"Was—" I began, making another attempt.   Then he
found his voice.

"Shut up, ye blamed fool!" said he in unmistakable
English, which had in it a burr that sounded even a trifle
Milesian.   "What ye mane onyway wid yer gibberish?"

I need not say that I was delighted ; not so much at
the strange being's rudeness, as at the very strong evidence his speech gave me that we should have little difficulty, so far as language went, in becoming better acquainted.   In my pleasure at hearing the sound of his
voice I smiled, and would have spoken, but the man
broke in :

"Come, now ; be aff out o' this."

" Won't you be kind enough to tell me the name of this place ? " I said, polite for two.

" Be aff out of this," he repeated, at the same time pointing very emphatically across the field. Instinctively I looked in the direction his fat, horny hand indicated ; and, walking leisurely towards us, I saw another individual, who—so far as the distance enabled me to judge—appeared to be of the same species as the first.

I waited no longer, but assured that it was better to fly to an ill I knew not of than to bear the one I had, I walked rapidly away, instigated to this course by further imperative summons to " be aff."

On approaching the new stranger I discovered that although he was undoubtedly of the same species as the first I had met, yet he evidently belonged to quite a distinct variety. In short, I detected in his gait and carriage, and in the expression of his face, that peculiar sign of gentlehood which no garb can hide or reveal.

His dress I also saw, though of a similar pattern to the other's, was of a rich material, and his hat was several inches higher.

I smiled and bowed.

The stranger returned my salute with grave civility ; and made as if to pass on, but a question of mine detained him.

" Will you be kind enough to tell me," I said, this time having the address to speak English, " what the name of this place may be ? "

" Inquirendo Island," he answered, fixing his eyes upon me with what was undeniably a peculiar expression.

" Pardon me if I detain you a moment," I continued, " but I find myself in a most unfortunate dilemma. I was blown off from the coast several days ago, and last night had the misfortune to be wrecked on the rocks directly below us. Although my education was not neglected I find myself at this moment quite unable to recall the precise location of this island. I assume it to be in the Atlantic Ocean somewhere to the north of the Bermudas. Am I right?"

The gentleman shook his head, and smiled in a sad way that appeared to me to be very strange. "Doubtless you are right," he said, with a sigh.

"Surely you know its latitude and longitude?"

"No, I do not, I confess; nor do I wholly understand your meaning. However, I cannot wait here. I have important business—"

"But, sir," I pleaded, as he moved on a few steps, "I only wish to ask a few questions. I am a shipwrecked stranger, and should feel greatly obliged for a little information."

The man paid no more attention to me; but began walking away, with some dignity, but also with great agility. I felt incensed, thinking that my usual quick perceptions had been at fault in so quickly accounting him a gentleman. I turned and strode after him.

CHAPTER II.

THE instant he heard me coming he increased his pace to a very fast walk indeed, and from that, as I still strove to overtake him, to a pompous trot; a very queer kind of a trot, in which one foot was always deftly planted before the other was lifted. It seemed a comical gait to go at; but nevertheless the gentleman contrived to get over the ground very quickly.

I was considerably irritated at this peculiar and perverse method of responding to my very courteous requests for information, and being irritated, and moreover a fast runner, I made after him at all speed. On he went, now puffing and panting with his exertions, and when I bade fair to overtake him he began to bawl at the top of his exhausted lungs: "Mike! Mike! Mike!"

Scarce had the words left his lips before, just over a knoll in front of us, appeared the Milesian, full tilt, ambling along in an uneasy fashion, head down. As soon as he espied me he roared like a young steer, and lifting up one brawny arm hurled a cobble-stone at me so deftly that if I had not seen the arm go up, I should infallibly have myself gone down, at the very least with a sorely bruised head. As it was, the stone whizzed past my ears, and the sensation I experienced was in its way a compliment to Mike's marksmanship. I stopped instantly, out of prudence.

The other arm went up, and another missile at Mike's instigation sought to claim my acquaintance. I remonstrated at this treatment with my heels. I am no coward, but I did not regard it as at all essential that I should stay and bandy paving-stones with one so evidently dexterous in using them; besides, I was very hungry. As I went Mike cried out : "Be aff, now, out o' this," more viciously than ever.

Without at all knowing in what direction to go in order to procure something eatable I nevertheless proceeded straight on, till to my amazement, rounding one of the numerous knolls, I came upon an iron fence; not a flimsy barbed concern, but a good, solid, substantial post-and-picket fence, some four feet or more in height. I was sufficiently observant, notwithstanding my hunger, to note that there were no evidences of the iron having been painted. On the contrary, it appeared to be quite fresh from the foundry. This was all the more singular to me as I had dealt in iron largely in the course of business, and knew very well that in that salt atmosphere one damp night on our own seaboard would have sufficed to rust it.

Another discovery that I made almost at the same time pleased me even more than this : it was that on the other side of the fence and parallel to it was a well-worn footpath. To leap the fence was the work of a moment, and the chance that in one direction the path led down hill, determined me to proceed that way. Soon I encountered other fences intersecting the first, all however of a similar pattern and material; but the path kept right on, almost in a bee-line, due north, up hill and down, over stiles, and through narrow openings. Here and there in the several fields through which I passed were cattle grazing, of the same peculiar breed that I had first seen, and in one was a large flock of sheep. With these were two men or half-grown boys ; but I judged it prudent to keep to the path rather than go out of my way on their account.

At last the foot-track led into a field of corn, tall and now just in the ear. I was by this time so ravenously hungry that I did not stop to consider whether or not my plucking an ear or two might be considered a trespass, or even a felony. I availed myself of the right of nature to provide for one's necessities, and never in my life did anything taste so good. I munched on, feeling at every mouthful in better humor, until I had eaten my fill, all the time, however, strolling leisurely along. As I threw my last cob away the path emerged from amid the tall stalks, and I stood on the crest of a very considerable elevation.

Astonishment and delight stayed my footsteps. I found myself on the verge of a most singular landscape. Immediately at my feet lay what appeared to be a vast garden, laid out with the utmost regularity in long parallel beds, between which were narrow paths, crossing each other at intervals. The ground sloping to the north and east was covered with vegetation, but here, as in all my journeying thus far, there was no sign of either tree or shrub. At the foot of the slope, beyond the garden, rose a number of spires and turrets and sharp-pointed gables. There at last certainly was some sort of civilization. The main path now crossed the cultivated ground, and I went on, intent only upon reaching the village. Vegetables of all kinds abounded in the garden. There were beds of beets and carrots, turnips and radishes, cucumbers and melons, and here and there, busy at work, were men and women, the latter clad in short tunics and wearing caps of a peculiar pattern. As I passed them they all rose up and looked with bulging eyes, as if I had dropped from the

clouds, while they nudged one another, and made remarks
to themselves in low tones.   I went on towards the clus-
tering houses, disregarding the staring eyes.   Men and
women alike seemed possessed with the most profound
but silent amazement at my personal appearance.   As I
walked on I could not help musing upon the very evident
fact that my attire must seem to these islanders striking
if not peculiar.   I was hatless in the first place, and my
checked suit was certainly very different from the cos-
tumes of any whom I had as yet encountered.

Silent astonishment among the laborers gave way to
some rather boisterous demonstrations from sundry urchins and half-grown boys whom I met loitering around
in the village street when at last I came among the
houses.   Their manners were not essentially different
from those of an equal number of young fellows of the
baser sort in any small place in my own country, and
bearing in mind the glassiness of our own house, I shall
attempt no description of their rudeness.   It might well
be, you understand, that when communication is established between the island and New York, the Inquirendians might revenge themselves by retorting in kind.

Not only did these youths accost me, but when I passed
on in dignified silence, they followed ; keeping, it is true,
at a considerable distance, but being no less annoying on
that account.   I wandered on, however, doing my best to
preserve an air of composure, and being continually on
the lookout for a place where I could procure a sufficiency
of something further to stay my appetite, which now indeed began to be ravenous.

Strange as it may appear, the entire village was built
altogether of iron ; not only was there no wood used anywhere in construction, but there was not a sign of a tree,

nor even a shrub, in any direction ; and I will here state the fact that, with a single exception, the nearest approach to anything wooden that I saw while on the island, was a particularly stout corn-stalk.*

The houses seemed to be all dwellings, and at the windows were seated females apparently engaged in some sedentary occupation. They were of all ages and varying degrees of comeliness ; but all had eyes, and all stared their best at me. This of course added to my embarrassment, but I strode on, trying to feel as little like a dog with a tin-can attachment as possible.

The string of hoodlums gathered accretions as I progressed, and when I turned into what proved to be the main business thoroughfare, I had full two score of followers ; and the grown people, stopping as I came up, stood on the iron curb-stones and stared ; while up went the sashes, bang went the blinds, click went the door fastenings, and young and old, male and female, at windows and doors, in dwellings and shops, stood and stared at me for dear life.

I was very much mortified.

Shops there were a plenty, but as yet no restaurant or bakery. I had passed one butcher's stall, where two or three whole carcasses were exposed for sale ; but I had not yet arrived at that state of desperation which impelled me to try raw flesh.

Seeing an establishment bearing the sign " Hats and Caps " I put on a bold front,—mindful of my bare head,— and approached the proprietor, who stood, like half the street, hands on hips, eyeing me.

---

* I may as well also at this point except from this statement the heads of certain of the inhabitants, as will more fully appear further on.

"I should like to purchase a hat," I said.

The man, a stalwart person of mature years, looked at me for an instant with grave suspicion plainly written on his features, and then letting his hands drop to his side, he turned about and entered the shop. There was no counter or anything like it; down the centre of the store was a narrow aisle, and piled up on the floor, and hanging on a multiplicity of hooks, were hats similar in shape to those I had seen on the heads of the inhabitants, of varying sober hues, and of an infinite number of sizes.

"Fit yourself," said the man, sullenly. Then casting a glance out of the open door he called, "John!" Instantly a dapper young chap appeared.

"Go out and tell that crowd to leave. If they won't, call the watch."

John obeyed, and the hoodlums fled over to the opposite side of the street, and stood there in row watching while I fitted myself with one of the hats. "I guess this will do," I said at last; "how much is it?"

I was enabled to be confident in respect to my ability to purchase, for it so happened that in my wallet were some half-eagles and a lot of silver change. I had also several bills of the Highland National Bank of Newburgh and of the Herkimer Bank of Rome, N. Y., but these I knew would probably be of no value, and were not included as available assets.

"Thrippence hapenny," responded the man.

Thinking that this was certainly very cheap I produced my change, and selecting a ten-cent piece tendered it to the hatter.

"What's this?" he asked, contemptuously.

"Ten cents."

"Fakens!" he retorted with a snort, holding it out. "What do I want with that?"

"Ain't it good?" said I—"won't it pass here?"

"See here, young man," he exclaimed, in a tone of considerable decision, "I'm getting tired of your pranks. Just you pay for that there hat without any more nonsense. If you don't, I'll call the watch."

"Call the town clock, if you like," said I, with some show of indignation; "but if you can't change ten cents perhaps you will take gold?"

This seemed to mollify him.

"I'll take gold, of course," he answered, promptly.

I showed him a five-dollar piece. He examined it critically, rung it on the floor, and bit it.

"It's gold, certainly," he remarked, "but for all that it's no good."

At this, of course, I remonstrated.

"What's the matter with it?" I said.

"It hasn't got our stamp on it." Then he added, looking at me with a curious expression, "See here, young man, what part of the island are you from, anyway?"

I tried to explain that I was a stranger, and had been cast ashore on the coast not very far from the village; but to this he listened with a pitying smile. I suppose if I had told him that I had dropped down from the clouds he could not have been more disdainful. He stood looking at me with a most peculiar expression on his face, and the other man who had been addressed as John also stood and stared. "What'll you take for this?" said the shop-keeper at length, balancing the coin on his finger.

"It ought to pass for a pound," said I, "if you use English money."

"You're from the east, ain't you?" said the man, when he had finished replying to my questions.

"No," I answered, "I am from New York."

"Where?"

"New York."

He shook his head.

"Poor fellow," he said, compassionately, "how long have you been away from your friends?"

I was beginning to get irritated, not liking his tone.

"I was six days at sea," I answered, a little crossly. "You don't appear to believe me when I tell you that I was wrecked on the coast."

"At any rate, I feel very sorry for you," he remarked, placidly. A kind heart and thievish palm sometimes go together.

Then the door opened and John came in with the change. This was counted out to me in silver and some coppers. The silver was very small and the copper very large, and the devices on all the coins were quite unfamiliar to me, although I was well acquainted with English money. However, I put it all in my pocket, and strolled on up the street.

When I emerged from the hatter's shop I again became an object of curiosity; but I disregarded the impertinence of the populace, and at the proper place, which I had no difficulty in finding, had the satisfaction to partake of an abundant repast. The beefsteak was excellent and my appetite enormous, notwithstanding the corn; but all the time I was eating the proprietor and his assistants regarded me furtively. I paid for my breakfast from the change that the hatter had given me, and was immensely surprised at the very moderate charge.

At the door I was accosted by two persons in a sort of

uniform, who, with an affectation of politeness, begged to know from what part of the island I came. I was now getting used to this question, but the manner of it in this instance appeared to me to be somewhat peremptory. I am not in the habit of permitting impertinence, and my resentment caused me to reply with some heat.

"There! you hear him," said a voice. I looked around and saw that it was my acquaintance, the hatter. This increased my wrath tenfold, for I could not see what business it was of the hatter's.

I therefore shook my fist at him with some vehemence. He forthwith fell back, and the assembly of urchins began to hoot, and crow, and make a variety of unseemly noises.

My demonstration in respect to the hatter was no doubt unwise. It certainly seemed to determine the action of the two uniformed men, whom, from their proceedings, I now judged to be policemen. With one accord they stepped forward, and each taking an arm, I was summarily hauled along the street. I struggled and remonstrated, but all in vain. I was threatened with a club if I persisted, and so discreetly forbore further resistance.

We came at last, having been followed the entire distance by the noisy crowd, to a low, unpretentious building, over whose door was set a curious quartered shield, on either side of which were two eccentric carvings of ferocious nondescript animals, half lion, half bull, blazing with shining gilt.

Behind a rail at an elevated desk sat an elderly individual of a benevolent appearance, who was forthwith addressed as "Judge" by my conductors. A few whispered words passed. I heard the judge say "asylum," and then the two policemen marched me out again. I protested

2

vigorously ; but to all my appeals the judge was not only pitiless, but absolutely indifferent. He paid no attention at all to me, and after his instructions had been given, went on writing as if he had done all that humanity as well as duty demanded.

Again in the street I was lugged back down the thoroughfare, followed as before by the noisy and boisterous urchins. The windows again went up, the heads popped out, and there was the same scene of staring and amazement.

Some one had, I suppose, been sent on ahead, for when we arrived at the extreme end of the town, in fact almost in the fields, we found in front of what appeared to be a stable, a peculiar vehicle, to which were harnessed a couple of lank and bony steers.

In this conveyance I was harshly bidden to take my place, and then, seated between the two policemen, we bounced and jolted over a poorly macadamized road out into the country.

Though uncomfortable and irritated, I could not avoid seeing that the country was well cultivated, and in the succession of hills and vales, with watercourses at frequent intervals, was surpassingly lovely. We drove on, up hill and down, at a lively gait, the little oxen trotting along unconcernedly, while I preserved an indignant, and my conductors a stoical, silence. After a fatiguing drive we came in sight of a large building, several stories in height, with turrets at the angles, the whole surrounded by a high wall of solid masonry.

CHAPTER III

A S we drove up two immense iron gates swung inward in response to a whistle from one of the policemen, and with a bang and clatter we wheeled into a great court-yard all paved with cobble stones laid in a mosaic pattern.

I was called upon peremptorily to alight, and several strapping young men issued from a door in one of the corner turrets, and to the care of one of these I was consigned—a tall, burly, black-browed, sinister fellow, to whom I felt at once and instinctively the strongest aversion. I had the dissatisfaction to overhear a remark from one of the blue-coats that I had better be carefully guarded, as I had already manifested some belligerent proclivities.

This speech had the effect to arouse my wrath, hitherto restrained from very hopelessness. I gave vent to my feelings in an indignant outburst of remonstrance.

" What have I done," I demanded, " to be treated in this way ? "

To this no response was made. The black-browed turnkey (for that this was his occupation I became speed-ily satisfied) vouchsafed no information, and only grinned in a horrid, odious way. A whispered consultation followed, and bidding me follow him the man strode on into the building.

I was conducted into a small apartment and told to sit down. After waiting half an hour or so three old men

came in and asked me questions, to all of which I replied
truthfully. They asked me from what part of the island
I came, and I repeated the story of my fortunate landing.
They shook their heads very much over this, and having
looked at my tongue and felt my pulse they all retired as
gravely as they entered, not deigning to acquaint me with
the result of their deliberations, nor to reply to my pro-
tests. However, I was not left very long in doubt, for
two stout fellows soon after appeared, and unceremoniously taking each an arm they marched me between them
through a long passage-way and up a flight of steps and
along a corridor. They stopped in front of a small
room, the door of which was open. It was lighted by a
narrow window, through which I caught a glimpse of the
verdant country. Into this room I was introduced forthwith in spite of my protestations. " What was it I had
done ? " I asked indignantly ; but to this sensible question
I received no reply. The men not unkindly bade me be
still, and then going out locked the door and bolted it securely. I peered after them through the grated opening,
and even tried the effect of remonstrance, but it was all
without avail. They went away and the corridor was
empty. I soon found that I was by no means solitary,
for as I clung to the grating I observed here and there,
at similar openings in doors up and down the hallway,
hands grasping the bars, and eyes gazing at me through
them.

I ventured to make a remark, not addressed to any particular pair of eyes, but appealing in a forlorn, purpose-
less way to a common humanity that appeared to abound
about me.

" What place is this ? " I asked.

At first silence ; then one or two rattlings of doors

followed, and at last a hollow voice snapped out: " This is hell ! "

" Pithy but not comforting," I thought ; but undismayed, and with an ardent desire for information, I persisted with interrogations ; to all of which receiving more or less incoherent answers, I became convinced that the unknown with whom I was conversing was a lunatic. Not until then did the idea—a horrible one indeed— occur to me that I also was kept in durance as a maniac.

So dreadful were my feelings then that even now I cannot recall them without a shudder.   I believe in my heart that for a time I was in some degree deranged. Certain it is that an unutterable woe and agony unspeak- able possessed me.   Famished, I could not eat, though food—palatable food—was brought me.   Athirst all the time, I could not drink.   In dire distress I paced mo- notonously back and forth from window to grating day after day ; at times fretting furiously, at others apathetic, at all despairing.

I know not the length of time that elapsed before I was in a measure restored to myself.   The three wise- visaged old men, whom many a time I cursed to their teeth, and whom I now know were mad-doctors, came singly at intervals, and made a pretence of conversation. With the lapse of time I waxed wise, discovering, as all must sooner or later, whether in Inquirendo or else- where, that temper is the very poorest possible refuge in any sort of distress.   At first I took refuge in sullen- ness and obstinacy, giving over my fits of fury ; then, finding that silence and scorn had no effect in softening the obstinate hearts or the crusty intellects of my keepers, I resorted to the stratagem of feigning satisfac- tion, and falling in with the notion that I actually labored under a delusion. My own heart needed softening, no doubt, and the means to that end were found in a sight of a sweet face flitting here and there in the garden that my window overlooked. It was the face of a lovely young girl tending her flowers beneath the window. I dare avow this, that the sight of her awakened within me all my powers, set me to thinking, and in the end was the cause of my liberation.

In seeing her at first I felt a breath of the cool air of freedom. I saw myself as I was, a foolish fellow with wits unused. So, with the passing days, as I saw her again and again, new hope came into my soul, and with deep purpose I planned and plotted for my liberty. There is, after all, no incentive to action so grand, so complete as the motive that a woman gives. If one can fall in love with a moving picture, then from my window I loved, though as yet I had not heard her speak. She came and went day after day, and I only watched her, thrilling with pleasure as she came into the garden, and with disappointment when she left it.

I began my studies in patience—affected an air of melancholy resignation, no longer loudly proclaimed my sanity, nor cursed those who came near me. The three wise doctors came as usual : wise-visaged as ever at first, then puzzled, then interested, questioning, and in the end affably conversing.

The questions, as before, related to my past life, as to who I was, and whence I came; but these I parried, pretending that I could not recall my identity, and being especially careful that I did not claim to have been dropped by the sea upon the island. I would press my hand upon my temples, put on an air of thoughtfulness, and express myself as longing to recover a something that I felt was missing.

One day the trio came together. The door was un-barred by an attendant—the black, ill-looking fellow to whom I had, on many occasions, manifested a desperate aversion. They entered, and with one accord began to talk. They felt my pulse, and went over the old round of queries. " Did I still persist in the absurd notion that I had come to the island from across the sea?" they said.

I smiled, as if at the absurdity of the notion, as a man might recovering from the delusion that he had dropped from the sky from some other planet.

"That is all over," I answered, "but yet I am quite unable to account for my presence here."

" Very good," said they, " you are recovering. It will now be only a question of time."

Thus, consulting together, they agreed that my disease, as they were pleased to call it, was likely to be of no long continuance. A name they had for it, of course—a good long name, but this I have forgotten—and there was much said about diet, and some suggestions as to exercise. To all I listened with much placidity, greatly long-ing to have my fling at their follies, but impressed with the hopelessness of so doing.

The oldest and wisest looking of the three, whose opinions I plainly saw guided the rest, now hinted that according to the method—as I understood him—habitu-ally pursued in cases like mine, the time had come for some stimulating recreation and society. My heart gave a great bound as I heard this ; but I took care to express myself very guardedly, saying that the confinement had become intolerably irksome to me, and that I felt an intense longing to be free from under restraint. "Though, gentlemen," I went on, hating myself as I spoke for my hypocrisy, "I feel the need of medical care. I am greatly impressed with the conviction that by following your directions implicitly I shall recover the use of all my faculties, some of which I now clearly understand are impaired."

The doctors, and especially the wise old one, were delighted. "This is a very peculiar case," said they, and whipping out note-books they jotted down the whole matter. All shook hands with me, a thing that had not happened before, when they left, promising that in a day or two everything should be duly arranged.

After they had gone, a sober, serious, long-faced individual, whom I had seen perambulating up and down the corridors at intervals during my sojourn, came to my door, accompanied by the black-looking keeper. This person introduced himself to me in a gentlemanly way, saying that his name was Nudwink, and that he was the chaplain of the institution.

I bowed, and offered him the only chair, a light steel concern, with back and arms, a very good imitation of canework, whilst I myself sat upon the bed.

"I am rejoiced to learn, sir," said Mr. Nudwink with a smile, "that you are in a fair way toward recovery."

I replied that my joy was also great, but that I was well aware that I still needed advice.

"And now as to your spiritual welfare," said the chaplain, after we had conversed upon the subject of my health for some little time, "I trust that the time has arrived when I may speak freely."

I assured him that he need be under no restraint, and yet, I do not know why, I began to feel just a little bored, for when he mentioned my spiritual welfare, the man's manner became instantly sanctimonious, exactly as our parsons act at home. Furthermore I felt a little loath to enter upon a conversation respecting sacred subjects, as I was not a member of any church, and was also averse to have any one pry into what I, perhaps too modestly, regarded as a private matter between myself and my conscience. I did not think it prudent to repel Mr. Nudwink, who, taking my assent for granted, proceeded:

" Have you known what it is to trust in Mathematics ? "

Very naturally I stared at this peculiar question.

" Pardon me," I said, " I must have misunderstood you."

" Have you ever been led to a consideration of the truth—the truth of overruling Numbers ? "

" Numbers ? "

" Yes, yes," he answered, impatiently.

" No," said I, doubtfully, " I cannot say that I have exactly; perhaps it is because I do not altogether understand."

" My question was a plain one, young man," said the chaplain, frigidly, " the wayfaring man need not err."

" Oh," said I, brightening, " you mean religion. If you mean that, I must say that I am not a member of any church."

" Did you not have a religious training, my friend ? "

" Oh, yes, I go to church pretty regularly."

" What church were you in the habit of attending previous to being brought to this institution ? "

" Well, I went to the—" I hesitated, having learned wisdom and being unwilling to commit myself to anything that might savor of a disordered imagination. It was on the tip of my tongue to declare point blank that I occasionally dropped in at the Methodist church, but I was not sure how this statement might be received, so I hesitated.

"Perhaps it was the Established church?" he suggested.

"Sometimes," I said, guardedly.

"Then you must have heard the truth in its purity."

"I suppose I did," I replied, being as non-committal as possible.

"And there you heard of Mathematics?"

What did he mean? I felt myself turning very red in the face. I certainly had heard of Mathematics; but then it had so happened that I had never heard of it in the Established, or in fact any other church. I felt a reluctance to avow this, and so, shamefaced, I contented myself with the statement that I had heard of Mathematics.

"And Numbers?" he interrupted.

"Yes, I have heard of Numbers."

"And the Nine Digits, you have been taught of them?"

"Oh, yes," I replied, truthfully enough, but not at all comprehending the relevancy of the chaplain's remarks.

"Then the groundwork at least has been laid," said he, with a smile that to me was very awful. "Perhaps at the knees of a pious mother?"

I replied that my mother was certainly very pious.

"Then doubtless you owe it to her, your acquaintance with these sacred things?"

I said nothing.

"Your mother taught you, I presume?" he continued.

"No," said I, forgetting myself and my prudence, "she didn't. When I was a little shaver I had a governess; after that I went to a day-school—"

"Do you mean seriously to tell me that your mother, being a pious woman, never herself instructed you in the knowledge of Mathematics?"

" Never."

" That is incomprehensible to me," he said, very solemnly.

" My mother had a large family—" I began, apologetically.

" But still, a mother's duty, surely—"

" We were all turned over to the governess, and afterwards when we got older went to day-school."

" And she never herself instructed you? I am surprised."

He certainly appeared to be so, as also probably did I.

" I was taught at school," I said, thinking it necessary to say something.

" Sunday-school, I presume you mean."

" No, day-school. I had my first lessons there. I was taught, to be sure, by the governess, but I really learned very little from her."

" Did not your mother attend church? "

" Oh, yes."

" Let me put a few questions to you," he said, airily, crossing his legs complacently.

" Certainly."

" In the first place, to acquaint myself with the exact state of your heart, I shall ask you : Who is Mathematics? "

" Who? "

" Yes, yes, who? "

" You don't mean who? " said I, astonished beyond measure.

" Yes, I do, of course I do ; why not? "

" You don't mean who, you mean what."

The chaplain gave himself an impatient shake.

" Let me ask you another question : Who is Numbers? "

" Numbers? "

"Yes, yes."

"One, two, three, four," I began.

He stopped me abruptly.

"That is not what I mean. You say that you have heard of Numbers: who is he?"

"Who?" I asked, more puzzled than ever.

"Yes, who?" he answered, rather crossly.

"You mean what are numbers, don't you?"

He stared. I met his look frankly, trying to divest myself of all appearance of impertinence, or what was more difficult, of folly, and making a desperate endeavor to infuse into my manner an inquiring docility. He kept on staring till it embarrassed me.

"Perhaps I do not exactly understand," I stammered.

"It is quite evident that you do not," he answered, "but it is not your fault, of course; and yet I was given to understand that your mind had recovered its tone—"

I started, glad of this information.

"Do not be hasty," said Mr. Nudwink, also starting, perhaps with trepidation, for he cast a quick, uneasy look towards the door. "Do nothing and say nothing rash. No doubt these vagaries will also disappear speedily, but, poor man, you ought to be fortified—"

"With a demi-lune?" said I jocosely, and thinking what I said was, under the circumstances, a very fair joke.

Mr. Nudwink scowled.

"I do not gather anything relevant to our subject from your remarks," he said.

"I dislike to explain a joke," I said, "but if you can spare half an hour, I shall be most happy to make this one plain."

He scowled more than ever, and went on, disregarding what I had proposed: "Fortified with that trust in Mathematics, which will enable you to be serene under all adversities."

I began to think that the chaplain must himself be one of the patients.

" Do you read your Arithmetic regularly? " he asked, this time in a perfunctory way, quite as if he regarded me as utterly given over to an evil power.

" At home, do you mean? "

" No, here."

" I can't say that I have," I faltered.

" You have a copy, have you not ? "

" Copy?—of what? "

" Of your Arithmetic, of course ; to what else could I refer? Young man, do not trifle. Surely you cannot fail to comprehend so simple a question." Mr. Nudwink looked very fierce for a chaplain, and fortunately I was able to mollify him. It occurred to me that I had seen a little book on a shelf over my bed when I was first admitted to the cell. Perhaps that was the work on mathematics to which he referred. I now recalled the fact that I had kicked it under the bed one day in a moment of irritation.

" I guess I know what you mean," I said.   " I'll look for it."

With that I got down instantly on hands and knees, and searched under the bed. My long experience at home with the female named ·Bridget—alas! I had never imagined that the tears would fill my eyes at the thought of her—enabled me to know by instinct that the book was in the remotest corner, and, as my slippers used in days of yore, would be found covered with dust. I dragged myself out at last with the volume in my possession.   I got up and slapped the lids together with a bang.   The dust filled the air.

"Phew!" exclaimed Mr. Nudwink, while I made a desperate effort to free my own person, as well as the little book, from the dust and wretched little odds and ends of ravellings, and hairs, and feathers that are so persistent in their embraces when one has crawled under a bed. Except that my chamber person was named Tom instead of Bridget, there was really little difference in the way the room was looked after. But this is a digression.

"Phew!" repeated the chaplain, as I slapped the book again. "You are raising an intolerable dust, and besides "—he lowered his voice—" it is irreverent."

"Is this the book?" I said, holding it out. He took it.

"Have you not read it?" he asked, with a very sour face.

"Read it! No, I haven't. Why should I read it?"

"Why, young man, do you ask that question seriously?"

"I do, of course. It seems to be nothing but the four ground rules."

The chaplain stood up, full of wrath.

"Wretched young man," he said, "be warned in time. Your conduct indicates either the most lax training, or a moral obliquity for which I am totally at a loss to account. I trust it may not be the latter."

I made some effort to convince him that it was not moral obliquity that had restrained me from the perusal of the volume; but Mr. Nudwink was not to be appeased by any protestations of mine.

"Take it and read it," he said, solemnly, "and may its principles sink into your heart and be productive of great good."

CHAPTER IV.

THE GIRL OF THE GARDEN.

NO doubt Mr. Nudwink reported adversely to my sanity; but happily for me he was not the sole expert in such matters, and in due time, it is to be presumed after consulting together, the three doctors came and informed me that my case had been considered, and that it had been determined to afford me a certain amount of relaxation and amusement. "In fact," said they, "this evening the Governor gives a little entertainment to those of the patients who are convalescing, and you have been, at our desire, included among those invited."

I expressed my sense of gratitude, and they all three felt my pulse, and gave me many cautions as to my behavior; telling me that they held themselves responsible for my good conduct. Of course I assured them that I should not misbehave, and as a stroke of policy, remarked that I should always regard the taste of liberty as of their procuring.

It is unnecessary to state with what intense longing I looked forward to the evening. They brought me my dinner at the usual time, but I could eat nothing. At nightfall the lamps were lighted here and there. The shadows deepened into night, and as time passed I became more and more anxious. At last two of the attendants came and unlocked my door.

"Come," said one, laconically.

This man was not the surly, black-faced fellow towards whom I had conceived so great an aversion. He was exceedingly mild and gentle, and though not given to the use of many words, had a knack of imparting much information with the few he employed.

I followed him along the corridor, delighted at the chance of even that much freedom. We descended the great iron stairs, and on the lower floor I found myself among a number of others, whose subdued manner and general air of being under subjection instantly convinced me were convalescents like myself. They were all young men with one exception, and he could hardly have passed fifty years, though his hair, which fell over his shoulders, was white as snow, as was also his flowing beard.

The attendant politely bowed, and waving his hand towards me ejaculated : " Mr. Cliff."

Several of the patients smiled and greeted me in a friendly way, and I was speedily informed as to their names. The elderly gentleman was perhaps the most civil of them all; and in the interval that ensued before the attendant came to conduct us to the place of entertainment, he became very communicative, telling me that his name was Bullinger, and confiding in a whisper that in his case a strange mistake had been made.

" The fact is, Mr. Cliff," said he, shaking his head, with a pitying smile, " I have never had anything the matter with me at all. My friends won't believe it, because they are so stupid; but I have made a great discovery." I began at once to take an interest in him, and yet fearing that it might be regarded as presuming, I refrained from asking the nature of his discovery. He talked on, amplifying upon the ignorance and incapacity of his relatives, and the ingratitude of the world, and was so exceedingly affable and entertaining that I found myself taking a sincere interest in his affairs. My attention having the effect to render him confidential, he proceeded to relate certain particulars respecting his treatment. I felt irresistibly drawn towards him, and was debating in my mind whether it would not be well to confide in him when, lowering his voice, he asked if I had no desire to know of what his discovery consisted.

I begged him to tell me.

"You will not divulge my secret?" he asked.

I assured him that he might safely trust me.

"If it should be known that I have mentioned the matter," said Mr. Bullinger, "it would be considered evidence that I was not yet well enough to be trusted. You can see for yourself," he added, "how perfectly sane I am; and I suppose to you my prudence in not mentioning the discovery to others ought to be sufficient evidence of a sound mind."

"Certainly," I replied, convinced from his manner that the old gentleman had really been made a victim of. Then in a fit of confidence I added, "I too am accused unjustly of a delusion."

"Ah," said he, rather vacantly.

"But tell me of your discovery," I said.

His vacant expression left him in an instant.

"It is a grand discovery," he said, rubbing his thin hands joyously, "but one that as yet the age frowns upon. I am a very diligent observer of nature, and I have discovered— it has in fact been revealed to me—that spiders have souls."

Perhaps my face, always tell-tale, revealed my disappointment at this revelation. He seemed to notice that I exhibited no elation.

"Are you, too, incredulous?" he asked, mournfully.

3

"I know as wonderful things," I answered, evasively.

"Do you? Are you too a student of nature?"

"To some extent."

"Ah! then you can sympathize. You are one of the few who understand and appreciate. You are one who knows the abounding mystery of nature."

"What would you think of one," I said, experimenting, "who knew of a vast country to which this Inquirendo Island was but a tiny place? who had indeed himself come from this strange land beyond the sea, where there were many wonderful things wholly strange to the Inquirendians? who came hither in something that floated over the sea till it came to this shore—"

I was going on, giving in the form of an anecdote my own adventures, when Mr. Bullinger broke out laughing.

"You are a most genial gentleman," he said, "most companionable and entertaining in trying to beguile me into temporary forgetfulness of my own misfortunes; and you exhibit a most surpassing talent. You would succeed admirably as a romancer, for the imaginings of your mind are truly astounding. Why, my dear sir, if you had searched the universe from end to end you could not have conceived of a more incredible thought. I presume that it was your object to delineate by a few expressive word-strokes the worst vagaries of which the mind could, by any possibility, be capable. Permit me to add that what you have said is a fitting prelude to your own revelation. You have, in romantic fashion, pictured the ravings of a madman. Now, sir, I long to hear from your lips the secret of nature that is yours."

He paused, smiling, and looked at me inquiringly.

What was I to say? No doubt something was expected. Perhaps I appeared confused. He hastened to reassure me.

"Say on, Mr. Cliff," said he, most urbanely, "whatever your secret may be, it is quite safe with me."

"And I have your word that you will not divulge—"

"Divulge! never. I am a man of the highest honor."

"Then listen."

I laid my hand on his arm, and whispered in his ear · "I have discovered that sand fleas can be developed into cows and oxen by feeding them on—"

"On what? on what?"

Mr. Bullinger turned his large eyes upon mine and almost trembled with expectancy.

At this instant a large door at one end of the apartment in which we stood swung open, disclosing amid a glare of light from a hundred brilliant gas-jets a beautiful salon, in which moved forward, as if to greet us, a number of ladies and gentlemen. In obedience to a signal from our conductor, or attendant, or keeper, whichever he might be styled, we all turned towards the open door, and to our promised festivities. As we advanced, a volume of entrancing music burst forth, filling all the space, and thrilling me with a sense of indescribable and satisfying harmony. In the midst of the bewildering cadences of the music, my friend, who adhered all the while closely to my side, took occasion to whisper earnestly in my ear: "On what? on what, Mr. Cliff?—for the sake of all the digits, on what?"

I was too much annoyed at the interruption to my enjoyment of the melody to pay special attention to the peculiar oath. "Hush!" I said, with some impatience, "listen!"

"Tell me on what you feed the fleas," he persisted. "Tell me that and I shall be content."

" Pure oxygen," I said, snappishly, uttering at random the first idea that occurred to me.

Mr. Bullinger kept his word, like a man of honor, as he had claimed to be. He relapsed instantly into a placid and well-satisfied silence, first murmuring : " Thanks, many thanks. You shall see that I deserve your confidence."

The extensive corridor in which we had been waiting was, though lighted by a number of bracket lights, dull and sombre compared to the bewildering glare that burst, like the delightful music, upon our senses as the great doors swung outward.

In obedience to the signal, I moved forward with the rest, Mr. Bullinger keeping close to my side, somewhat to my annoyance. We passed on, through the wide doorway, and a vision of beauty burst upon my sight. Forgot were all the others in their gaudy apparel ; forgot the bewildering sights and sounds in the one glory that greeted me. Standing a little apart from the rest, her lovely white hands clasped in front of her and with a wistful expression upon her beautiful face, upturned as if to respond to the look I bent upon her, was the girl of the garden, the maiden whom, day by day, from the solitary window, I had watched among the flowers, not thinking that so soon, and upon such equal terms, I should be permitted to enter her presence. In my turn I was formally presented, and our hands met in one glad thrill of joy.

Who, recalling that entrancing hour when first they saw the divinity of their lives—the girl who first inspired them with the emotion of love—will not sympathize with me in exhibiting a little exhilaration of spirits in describing the charming being upon whom now my eyes rested. Even if you have been married dozens of years you can afford to forget that little trouble about the spring bonnet and listen.   Perhaps you are still a bachelor, through no fault of your own ; or worse still—some might cynically say better —a divorce court may have intervened; but yet there must have been times when fond memory has pictured the maid as she first appeared to you.   So, consider this one of those times, and foregoing your cynicism, let me tell you how sweet Margery Mayland looked that night.   It needs no flight of imagination to enable me to depict her, for I see her, hovering sprite-like, all clad in fleecy white, between the pen and the paper even now.   A form of beauty, not too tall, and yet of that comely and correct stature that is at once dignified and intensely womanly; shapely, with the shape of well rounded arms, bare to the shoulders, and a supple, swaying figure.   Beautiful, with beauty of abundant brown hair, falling in the island fashion in a rippling wave about her shoulders; with the beauty of sparkling blue eyes, whose long lashes rested for a moment as I looked upon her peach-bloom cheeks, whereon the color came and went like the pink aurora, changing and glowing, flushing or paling, as the thought or fancy changed, even as the Arctic blazonry pales and flushes on the cheek of the fair Northern sky.

I know if you had seen this maid that evening you would pardon any attempt at poetry of description, even if futile to arouse the old emotions in your stoic senses.

We—the half dozen or so convalescents—were speedily presented, one after another, to the assembled guests. There were altogether about half a score, and of these several were ladies; but with only two have we, in this narration, concern.   The young girl's mother was presented, a mild, gentle, blue-eyed lady, with long white hair wound about her head, and a soft, low voice.

The Governor of the institution, husband of this lady
and father of Margery, was tall, dignified, and elegant.
A man of commanding presence and of rather austere
bearing, he moved about as a gentleman among his guests,
talking now to one and again to another and affable to
all. The three doctors were also there, smiling and courteous, but I could see watchful also, as were the half
dozen attendants, among whom, to my disgust, I recognized the black-browed turnkey who had been my abomi-
nation from the first. None, however, were obtrusive, and
while the music went on, in fitful, fanciful cadences, I contrived to bring about an interview apart from the rest
with Margery. To do this required some little tact, for
my companion of the outer corridor, Mr. Bullinger, was
pertinacious and strove to affix himself to me, doubtless
with a view to further information respecting the evolution of the oxen.

I think that from the first moment our eyes met there
was a subtle attraction between Margery and me. At
all events, in the course of an hour we were together in a
recess of the large apartment and talking like old friends
while the others were waltzing to the strains of the band.
A curtain of fine but heavy fabric was swung over the
embrasure—a curtain embroidered with golden figures
on a green ground, looped up with heavy gold cord, and
pinned with fire-gilt rampant lions. The floor was of
iron of most peculiar texture, inlaid in squares and figures
of varied hues, with an artistic blending of shape and color.
Tapestries hung from the walls, and pictures of strange,
uncouth design were pendant here and there. The arched
roof was of alternate beams and panels, the beams bev-
elled and of lustreless gilt, the panels deep blue, studded
with golden stars.

CHAPTER V.

SO strange, so extraordinary indeed, were all the details of that place, and so peculiar the various incidents of the dancing, the music, the supper, and the devices by which amusement was provided, that in a description of these things alone there might be sufficient interest; but I am not ashamed to confess that in the enjoyment of the delicious society of Margery I was to a great extent oblivious of all else. I could not avoid perceiving that the manners of all present were cultured, and differed in no essential respect, save in trifling points of precedence and etiquette, from those of the best society to which I had been accustomed at home. Perhaps not exactly of all present. I shall have to except one individual, whose uncouth and unmannerly ways were, before the festivity was over, a source of considerable annoyance. But this will more fully appear afterwards. Let me now relate something of the conversation that I had with Margery.

We waltzed together, swinging round the vast apartment to the time of the fifes and cornets of the band. Oh, that waltz! how charming it was, and yet more charming still was the time I passed in the curtained alcove.

Margery appeared a little shy at first, and this was no doubt very natural, as she must have regarded me as one of whom it would be well to beware, so far as any sud-

39

den intimacy went Being the daughter of the Governor
of the asylum she was in a measure conversant with the
peculiarities of the convalescents, and probably past experience had told her that there was little or no danger
in any intercourse with those favored with invitations.

Still I perceived some little evidence of shyness, and
being piqued thereby, strove to impress her with the
fact—to me undoubted—that my faculties were unimpaired.
I said something to this effect.

"You are quite well now, are you?" she asked, de-
murely.

I looked at her full in the face. She blushed slightly
and I began to laugh.

"Why do you laugh?" said Margery.

"Oh, I was going to tell you something ; but on reflection I conclude it would be better not."

"You had better tell me," she said, very sweetly ; "you
may trust me, even if I am the Governor's daughter."

"Well, I will trust you," said I, impulsively.

"Thank you."

"Though I know what you will think—"

"I will tell you what I think, Mr. Cliff. I can promise
that."

"I was going to tell you that there really never has
been anything the matter with me."

A shade came at once over Margery's face.

"I knew that I had better not say that," I said.

"Why?" she answered, looking down.

"Because you would not believe me."

"I did not say so, Mr. Cliff," she answered, soberly.

"But I know what you think. You need not tell me,
for I know."

"Then you need not ask me, and I am relieved from m,
promise."

She looked up again and laughed.

"I suppose almost all who come here say the same
thing," I said, "do they not?"

"Sometimes, not always."

"Do you ever believe them?"

"I have never believed any one—before."

"Ah, then," I said, joyously, "you do, after all, believe
me?"

She was silent.

"There is Mr. Bullinger," I said, as that person paced
along in front of the alcove, looking in with an impatient
expression, "would you believe him if he told you that?"

"No indeed;—but still, he would be likely to say so.
They all do."

So saying, Margery sighed.

"All but me," I said softly, "I do not so pretend. I
know that I have been ill and that I yet require care; but
I am also very sure now that it will not be for long."

Instantly into the girl's face there came an expression
of delight. She raised her sweet blue eyes directly to my
own. She blushed vividly as she said:

"How glad I am, Mr. Cliff, to hear you speak so. Papa
tells me that the doctors all say it is a sure sign of recovery. I am so glad for your sake."

"Do they say that it is a sign of recovery when one real-
izes his illness and the necessity of a cure?"

"Yes."

"Then I must be getting well," I responded, affecting
great joy, "for I do realize that."

"So Dr. Setbon says," said Margery.

"Dr. Setbon? Which is he?"

"The oldest of the three doctors who have the care of the patients—the one with long white hair."

"So he has been speaking to you of me, has he?"

"Not to me exactly. I heard him talking to papa."

"And the other doctors—do they say the same?"

"Oh, yes."

"And your father?"

"Papa is guided by the doctors' advice. You know that he has really no power to say that any one is well. He has to recommend."

"Recommend that they be discharged?"

"Yes, he recommends those he thinks ought to be discharged, when the doctors agree, to the judge."

"And do you think he will recommend me?"

"Oh, I am sure he will. The doctors all say that you have gotten over—what they called the delusion. You won't mind my calling it that now, will you?"

"Of course not," I said, lying shamelessly. "I understand myself that it was delusion."

"I am sure it will not be long now before you will be entirely free," she continued, "and I am so glad for your sake. Every one says so—at least they all do who have any power; papa and the doctors."

"You speak as if there were others who did not favor my release, Miss Mayland. Who are they?"

"I do not know that I ought to speak of them."

"I shall regard the confidence as sacred," I murmured softly. "Tell me, please, I should be on my guard." My manner was so persuasive and my voice so beseeching that Margery yielded.

"Yes, there are two who are opposed to your release. I will tell you this frankly and trust to you. One is Mr. Gallwood—"

" Gallwood ! " I exclaimed, vehemently, " that black-looking turnkey ! "

Margery blushed and looked pained.

" He is certainly dark complexioned," she said, mildly, "but, Mr. Cliff, he is not a turnkey. He is the assistant superintendent—and besides," she added, after a short pause, " he is papa's cousin."

" Your father's cousin ! That is a surprise. Then he must be yours also."

"Oh, no, he is not mine. Cousinship, you know, only goes one remove." She blushed again very deeply.

" That is true," I responded, " I had forgotten that ; but why should he be unwilling that I should be free ? "

" I cannot tell ; but he persists in declaring that you are not yet recovered."

" Who else is there, Miss Mayland ? You spoke of another."

" It is the chaplain."

" Mr. Nudwink ? "

" Yes."

" And what cause has he to be unfriendly ? " I asked in amazement.

" I think it is on religious grounds," she responded, with some hesitation.

" Religious grounds ! " I said, in more amazement still, " what does he know of my religious convictions ? "

" Hasn't he spoken on the subject of religion to you ? "

" Not one word," I replied, solemnly.

" That is certainly very strange. I heard papa and Dr. Setbon talking with the chaplain, and I am sure Mr. Nudwink's opposition is all on account of what he called your irreligion."

" What did he say ? "

" He said that your views of religion were so absurd as
to indicate an unsettled mind."

" How extraordinary ! " I exclaimed, " how very extraordinary, when not a single word has passed between us on
the subject—but—stop !—I do remember that he spoke of
my attending church, and said something that I thought
very impertinent about the instruction my mother gave
me ; but he dropped that, and began talking about arithmetic till I confess I thought he was by far the crazier of
the two."

Margery laughed.

" You made him angry, Mr. Cliff ; you did, indeed.   It
was unwise ; but he is à good man if he is persistent and
peculiar.   Promise me when he comes again to talk to
you that you will listen."

"Of course I shall listen.   I did listen, and I was very
polite to him notwithstanding all his nonsense."

" He says that it was you who talked nonsense."

" He is an old fossil," I said, indignantly.

" I don't mind telling you that I am of the same opinion ; but Mr. Nudwink is very good ; mamma thinks so
much of him.   She says he is so spiritually minded."

" It is your mother who is spiritually minded," I responded, gallantly.

"Yes, mamma is very lovely," said Margery.

" Is Mr. Nudwink married ? " I asked.

" No, indeed; but why do you ask that question; does
it appear to you that he is the sort of gentleman that a
lady could love ? "

I shuddered.

" I should say not, most decidedly ; but speaking of
marriage, may I ask a question ? "

I looked at her searchingly, and her eyes fell before mine as she inclined her head.

"Are you engaged?" I whispered.

She shook her head with a little coquettish movement. "No, I am not engaged; and what is more," she added, looking up with sudden vivacity, "I do not propose to be."

This reply was a discouragement. Not that I had any definite purpose then formed respecting Margery, but her tone was so determined that I interpreted it to mean a fixed opposition to matrimony.

"That will be some man's great loss, I fear."

"Indeed it will," she responded energetically, and then recollecting herself, added hastily, "Oh, what am I saying? That was all foolishness—I only meant that I am yet too young. I am only seventeen, Mr. Cliff, and that is too young to be thinking of such a thing."

"Decidedly so," I answered, "if such a thing be the wrong man."

"Who told you it was the wrong man?" Again she raised her eyes to mine.

"I guessed it."

"Are you in the habit of making such guesses?"

"Did I guess right?"

"Perhaps," she answered in a low tone.

"Tell me," I said persuasively, "tell me about it. If you are in any trouble, Miss Margery, tell me about it please, perhaps I can help you."

Margery toyed with the deep fringe of her fleecy dress, her eyes cast down.

"Ought I?" she murmured.

I was about to renew my persuasions when Mr. Bullinger, whom I had observed, not without apprehension, pass and repass the alcove with staring eyes, suddenly stopped in his walk and advanced a step within.

I rose to my feet instantly, a trifle vexed to be thus interrupted.

"What do you wish, Mr. Bullinger?" I said, perhaps a little hastily

"The oxen, the oxen," he answered, his voice trembling and his eyes bloodshot and gleaming. "I must know more. You must spare me the time to explain your method. I have waited till I can stand it no longer."

"Another time, Mr. Bullinger, I shall be most happy."

"No, now, now." He stamped his foot angrily.

"That is impossible," I said, firmly.

"Tell me," he cried, in a voice husky with passion, "tell me or I shall reveal the whole thing. I shall divulge the fact of your insanity—your hopeless insanity."

"You are forgetting yourself, Mr. Bullinger," I answered, sharply, "you forget that you are in the presence of a lady."

"So you refuse, do you?"

"Most certainly I do, and I request you to withdraw at once."

He became at once livid with passion. Words burst forth from his lips in a torrent that caused him to gulp and gurgle. Stammering and choking, his words thumped out, like wine from an upturned decanter.

I pitied the man, and yet fearing, for Margery's sake, lest some violence should be attempted, I made haste to place myself between her and the madman.

This action irritated him to an extraordinary degree. Shrieking out, "Tell me your method—if you don't, I'll have it out of your throat," he advanced toward me.

Mr. Bullinger was not a very large man, and I had no

fear whatever of the result of a personal encounter; yet I
felt an extreme pity for him. Poor fellow, he could not
help his delusion. I turned my head—"What shall I do,
Miss Margery?" I asked. "Do nothing," she replied,
" I am used to these things." So speaking, she drew aside
the drapery that hung over the alcove, and touched a gilt
button in the iron wall.

Two or three sharp clangs as of little gong bells were
heard at a distance. Mr. Bullinger appeared to hear them
also, and they rendered him frantic. He fairly foamed at
the mouth as he rushed forward towards me, his fists
doubled up menacingly. He threw himself upon me
white with passion, striking out aimlessly right and left.

CHAPTER VI.

THE CONVALESCENT COURT.

MARGERY'S presence of mind did not desert her; she rose at once and stood in silence. There was a sound of hurrying feet, making their way among the dancers; for the dance still went on, and as Mr. Bullinger, white with fury, assaulted me, two of the keepers, followed by the black-browed Mr. Gallwood, entered the alcove.

Two or three of Mr. Bullinger's frenzied blows I had parried; but he was wary and agile, and moreover very mad, and the third time he struck out his sharp knuckles made themselves felt upon my lower lip. For an instant, realizing that he had hurt me, I forgot my caution, and mad in my turn, I beat down his guard, and launching out, came home upon the man's eye and sent him sprawling on the floor.

At this very instant in rushed the attendants, and Gallwood, despite my protestations, seized me by the arm.

"Let go," I exclaimed passionately, struggling to free myself. But he only clung the closer, and one of the others, while Bullinger was led away, came and held me.

I looked around in despair for Margery, but she had left the alcove.

"What is the meaning of this outrage?" I asked defiantly.

Gallwood sneered.

"Outrage, indeed," he answered sullenly. "This comes

from letting you out too soon. We'll have you back again, my fine fellow. I see you are violent yet—oh, you need a little taking down, and you are likely to get it. Now march."

Of what avail would any further struggles be? Margery had apparently deserted me. Well aware that any resistance would be futile, I submitted with an ill grace, and was conducted ignominiously back to my solitary room. The music sounded ominous and harsh and discordant; it seemed to speak of treachery and desolation, and for a time when I found myself alone it was only to brood despairingly over my forlorn condition. As Gallwood shut and bolted the iron door, he leered at me through the grating.

" It won't do, you know, to try your games on me," he remarked savagely. " I've been watching you, and I know what you're trying to do. Let me tell you you can't come it."

Perhaps unwisely, I retorted with some imprecation, letting the scoundrel know that I had no fears of him.

He went away with his usual odious grin upon his face, and I stood for a moment glaring after him, and feeling that if only once I was free how rejoiced I should feel to stand face to face with the man.

Though Margery had left me with such apparent unkindness in the alcove, yet, as I afterwards discovered, it had been to seek her father on my behalf. The Governor, a stern man and conscientious in the discharge of his duty, had been unwilling at the time to interfere, knowing that Gallwood was himself attending to the matter. So it had happened that I was dragged away in company with the unfortunate Bullinger, and like him regarded as one whom it would be unsafe to trust.

4

Although Margery's persuasions had not prevailed with
her father that night, she had renewed her efforts in the
morning, and by this time had enlisted her mother also in
the endeavor.

Governor Mayland then sent for Gallwood, and the two
had a private conference. To this finally Dr. Setbon had
been summoned, and it was at last determined, much to
Gallwood's chagrin, that a special examination should be
accorded to me.

I had been gazing out upon the little garden where first
I had seen Margery, and was terribly depressed in spirits,
when there was a rattling at my door and the three doctors
entered. This time, primed by Gallwood, they were scep-
tical enough, and it required all my self-command to relate
without acrimony the incidents of the previous evening. In
the end, to my great joy, I succeeded in impressing the doctors if not with an assured conviction of my sanity, at least
with doubts. They were all honest men, and did not fail to
understand, in some degree, the position in which I had
been placed by Bullinger's importunities. They left me
with assurances that I might trust to them for justice. This
comforted me beyond measure. So I waited all that day and
part of the next in the hope that every moment would bring
me release. At the usual time my meals were brought; but
I could hardly bear to leave the window, where I watched
expectant of the lovely form of Margery. Once the vil-
lanous Gallwood came to my door, and looking in, scowled
at me hatefully. Again the tall, angular form of Mr. Nudwink appeared in the corridor; but he strode past my cell
without even looking in, and with an expression that
seemed to me one of great ill-nature upon his uncomely
face.

About noon the next day Dr. Setbon, accompanied by one of the attendants, appeared.

" Come with us, Mr. Cliff," said the doctor, kindly.

I obeyed, of course, with much alacrity, and descending to the lower floor, we were ushered into the Governor's private room.

I had been presented to my Margery's father at the ball, and then he had been all affability and good humor. Now, however, he was on duty, and I found him strict, sober, sedate, and unapproachable.

" Take a chair, Mr. Cliff," he said, in a voice of military precision.

I obeyed promptly.

" Mr. Cliff," he continued, " your case is one that seems to be a peculiar one, and to demand a most thorough investigation. At the ball, night before last, to which you were admitted, by the advice of the physicians, as a convalescent, you suffered yourself to be betrayed into excitement; you showed irritation, and you ended by committing an assault upon another of the convalescents, one Bullinger."

" It was he that assaulted me," I said ; " I was forced to defend myself. Your daughter, Miss Margery, can tell you that I am speaking the truth."

Mr. Mayland waved his hand.

" Allow me to conclude my remarks, Mr. Cliff. Do not permit yourself to become excited. You will be allowed ample opportunity to present your case. As I before stated, you committed an assault upon Mr. Bullinger. As to whether you or he was the aggressor that remains to be determined. It is a serious thing and one that our law does not tolerate, the keeping of an innocent or sane man under restraint : but it is even more serious to let loose

upon society one who might prove dangerous to its peace.
It is true that you have been duly pronounced convalescent, and as such entitled to a certain limited amount
of freedom, consistent with your own safety, and with the
safety of those about you. At the ball you were on trial,
and it is now a disputed question as to whether on that
occasion, in your encounter with Mr. Bullinger, you did or
did not give evidence of a want of control over yourself
sufficient to deprive you of your convalescent privileges.
It is my duty to decide this matter. If you choose you
may employ counsel, and this course I strongly advise.
If, however, you decide to conduct your own case, I wish
to warn you that, not only will the previous facts be considered, but your actions, bearing, and words during the
examination will also be considered, and have great
weight in the decision."

While the Governor was speaking, a door at one end of
the room opened and Gallwood and Nudwink entered.

" What is your decision, Mr. Cliff ? " said the Governor.
" Shall counsel be assigned to you or not ? "

I cast one glance at those two men, both standing by
the door, stiff and sombre.

" If it involves any special question of law," I replied,
guardedly, " I shall have to ask the aid of counsel."

The faces of the two men clouded directly.

" Only matters of fact are to be considered," said the
Governor.

" Then," I responded, " I shall conduct my own case."

Mr. Gallwood's expression changed instantly. a peculiar
light shone in his savage eye, and Mr. Nudwink also appeared to be well satisfied with my answer.

" Very well," said the Governor, serenely : then turning
round in his chair he addressed Mr. Gallwood :

" Are you ready to proceed ? "

" We are," responded Gallwood.

" The convalescent court is now open," continued the Governor, in a louder tone.

At these words a young man in uniform stepped forward, and tapping three times on the floor with a staff of steel, cried, " Oyez ! oyez ! oyez ! the convalescent court stands open."

The door by which Gallwood and Nudwink had previously entered now again swung wide, and the two associate doctors entered, followed by Mrs. Mayland and her daughter Margery. Margery's eyes were cast down, and they all took the seats assigned to them without a word.

" The defence will now open," said the Governor, " and in accordance with the law, and the will of the crown, I here exhibit my writ under seal."

A document was produced by an official, and held up for inspection.

" Mr. Cliff," continued the Governor, " it is now your privilege either to relate what occurred yourself, or to call such witnesses as you may desire to have heard respecting the occurrence of night before last."

In response to this intimation I told my story ; making it as short as possible, and being particular to evince no hostility to Mr. Bullinger. When I had finished I had the satisfaction to perceive that the Governor appeared satisfied, and Gallwood and Nudwink were scowling. With some trepidation I then requested Margery to testify. She told her story quietly, without questioning, and fully corroborated all that I had said. After this the doctors in turn testified, at my request, stating that they had made certain examinations touching my mental condition, and

that, in their opinion, I was and had been for some time
in a convalescent state, and that, assuming the facts to be
as stated by myself and Margery, nothing that happened
had caused them to alter their views.

When the third doctor had finished testifying there was
a short interval of silence, and then I was asked by the
Governor if I closed my case.

I signified that there was nothing further to be offered
on my behalf, and then Gallwood came forward and told
his story of the encounter. What he said was fair enough.
In fact so fair that I was in the highest degree astonished
to hear him. When he had finished he called the doctors
one after another, but, to my great astonishment, he asked
them only one question : " Had they conversed with me
at any time upon religious subjects ? "

To this query they all responded, " No."

" The Reverend Mr. Nudwink," said Gallwood.

With a self-satisfied smirk the chaplain came forward,
and sitting down leisurely in the witness chair, crossed his
legs, and folded his thin arms.

" You have attended Mr. Cliff constantly since his admission to the asylum, have you not ? "

The chaplain bowed.

" Have you had opportunities for frequent conversation
with him in respect to his religious belief ? "

" I have."

" In your capacity as his spiritual adviser, have you at
any time become informed as to his views of religious subjects ? "

" Until he was pronounced convalescent," responded
Nudwink, " I of course refrained from unduly exciting him,
although, as with all the other unfortunates committed to

my spiritual charge, I caused him to be provided with a copy of the Arithmetic."

I started. "There was that infernal arithmetic again," I thought. Perhaps Gallwood perceived my slight emotion. He seemed to brighten perceptibly, and went on with his questions :

"Since he was declared convalescent have you had any conversation with him, and if so, what was the nature of such conversation ? "

"The day that he was pronounced convalescent I visited him, and I regret to state that not only was he perverse and flippant in the extreme, and even derisive in his treatment of sacred things, but he seemed to be absolutely insensible to all good influences ; and not only that, but he manifested the most utter ignorance upon religious subjects, as well as profound indifference to them.'

"Did you question him as to his religious faith ? "

"No, I found that to be quite futile."

"On what account ? "

"Solely on account of his utter insensibility."

"To what did you attribute that ? "

"I was at a loss to know. At first it appeared to me to be either complete depravity, or the grossest levity ; but after thinking the matter over more deliberately, I have become convinced, with all due deference to the previously expressed opinions of Dr. Setbon and his learned associates, that his want of comprehension and disregard of religion was, and I may say is, due to some peculiar mania. I can account for his manifest peculiarities on no other ground."

"Give some instances of these peculiarities, Mr. Nudwink, as they came under your observation."

"In the course of this conversation which I have mentioned, I took occasion to ask Mr. Cliff if he had ever been instructed by his mother in respect to Mathematics. His answer astonished me. He gave me the information that all he had learned of that great theme had been taught him by a governess or at a day-school. This he said, although having previously admitted that his mother was a pious woman, and an attendant, as I understood him, of the Established church. There was some more conversation of a similar character, and his remarks were of so peculiar a nature that I determined to probe the thing to the bottom, and to that end I propounded a series of questions. His replies to these queries convinced me that his mind was either given over to corrupt influences or was still darkened. I trust for the sake of his soul it may be only the latter."

As he said this, Mr. Nudwink eyed me grimly.

"You had better state your questions and Mr. Cliff's replies," said Gallwood, cheerfully, seeing that apparently his cause was prospering in Nudwink's hands.

"I asked him," continued the witness, "'Who was Mathematics?' and he replied, with the most irreverent manner, 'You don't mean who, you mean what.' Astounded beyond measure, I then asked him, 'Who was Numbers?' He replied in exactly the same way as before—"

"By calling Numbers, what?" said Gallwood.

"Yes."

"Abominable!" ejaculated Gallwood; "that is, it would have been, had poor Mr. Cliff been responsible."

"Of course I have great charity," said Nudwink, complacently.

"Certainly, we understand that; but your duty to so ciety is paramount. Now was there anything further took place—any further remarks of Mr. Cliff of a similar tenor indicating, in your opinion, unsoundness?"

"Yes; some of his remarks were wholly irrelevant. I utterly failed to understand their drift. Among other things which he said was something respecting a joke, and he invited me to come some time when I could spare half an hour, when, as he said, he would explain it. Then I asked him if he read his Arithmetic. To this he responded that he had not, and in fact that precious book had been tossed under the bed, from which he extricated it covered with dust."

"Did you question him concerning his knowledge of it?"

"I did."

"Did he appear to be acquainted with its contents?"

"Not only unacquainted, but absolutely indifferent, and boastful of his want of knowledge; and yet—and this was the most singular circumstance—while actually deriding the Holy Arithmetic he referred to the Four Ground Rules as if he did, after all, possess a certain degree of information. I confess that I was shocked beyond measure; but as I before remarked, I am now convinced that in respect to these subjects Mr. Cliff is still insane."

CHAPTER VII.

GALLWOOD'S ENMITY IS MANIFESTED.

" THAT will do, Mr. Nudwink," said Gallwood. "Now, Mr. Cliff," he continued, with a patronizing smile, " I shall, if you please, propound certain questions to you."

I felt very nervous, for this was a course that I had not expected. I was acquainted in a general way with the rules of evidence of our own courts, and had even taken some little interest in the controversy respecting our criminal code of procedure.

I was aware that under our New York law, I had the privilege of refusing to testify, on the ground that what I might say would have a tendency to criminate myself ; but I had found the customs of Inquirendo so widely at variance with those of the State of New York, that, bearing in mind the Governor's declaration that my method of defence would go far towards forming his opinion, I quickly decided that I had best not offer this plea.

I did debate with myself for an instant the advantages of a strict course of lying ; but this I at once discarded, not so much that it was wicked, as that it was not feasible. In lying, I did not feel myself at all a match for the unscrupulous Gallwood.

It was evident to me that the line of questioning to which I was about to be subjected was not at all in the nature of a cross-examination. But whose witness was I,

my own or Mr. Gallwood's? While I was trying to deter
mine what my course should be, Gallwood, all urbanity,
proceeded :

"What is your full name?"

"John Cliff," I answered promptly.

"Your father's name?"

"William Cliff."

"His business?"

"Stock broker," I responded unthinkingly, and then remembering that I was wholly in the dark as to the existence of any such profession in Inquirendo, I blushed
and probably looked guilty.

"What do you mean by the term broker?" said Gallwood. I thought a moment, very vigorously. Clearly
here was a case where wits were better than lies.

"One who breaks," I answered, well satisfied.

"Does he break cattle, or sheep?"

"Sheep; that is, lambs—mostly lambs."

I said this knowing that breaking lambs on Wall Street
was in fact my father's vocation, and also persuaded that
my reply was in strict accordance with the ways of business in the island as well as in New York.

My readiness of reply seemed to disconcert my prosecutor slightly ; but he was not easily abashed, and went on
directly : "Where do you live?"

"Just now," I answered, "my residence appears to be
in the asylum."

"No levity, Mr. Cliff," interposed the Governor, and
then I was aware that I had made a mistake.

"Answer the question," said Gallwood.

What could I say to this? Could I declare that I
lived, when in the city, on the south-west corner of Park
Place and Sixty-oddth Street? Manifestly not ; nor could

I proclaim my home to be at Far Rockaway, where we had taken a furnished house for the summer. I might, it is true, have mentioned some locality on the island, but for one or two reasons : in the first place, if I did mention a locality the probabilities were quite strong, and favored the conclusion, that I would be remanded to my cell while some one,—most likely Gallwood himself,—would go to that identical spot and make inquiries ; in the second place, I knew of no locality to mention.

It had been suggested to me that I came from the east end, but at this time my notions of the geography of Inquirendo were extremely vague, and if I had stated that my home was at the east end I was not sure what the effect might be. All these forms of reply being, it appeared to me, inadmissible, I boldly resolved to avow my ignorance, and frankly lie.

In the United States, as I have had frequent occasion to observe, there is nothing so convincing and so plausible as a frank lie. I found it much the same in Inquirendo.

" Answer my question," repeated Gallwood.

Then with an appearance of the utmost frankness and candor, I avowed my total inability to tell in what part of the island my home was situated. I explained that in most respects I felt myself to be thoroughly recovered, but that I was aware of a lack of memory, the defect of which I was unable to overcome.

This answer had an effect upon the Governor that I saw was displeasing in the extreme to Gallwood. Mr. Mayland nodded in a way that appeared to indicate satisfaction with my reply, and Dr. Setbon smiled complacently. He was evidently on my side, and looking towards the corner where Margery sat beside her mother, I noticed that she was also sweetly smiling. This greatly encouraged me, and I felt nerved for anything further that the odious Gallwood might have in store.

"You have listened to the testimony of Mr. Nudwink, have you not?" asked Gallwood.

He spoke angrily, and his brow was blacker than ever. I knew that even if I had foiled him on that special point, the man would be pertinacious. What was the cause of his antipathy to me I did not then know, but that he hated me I was convinced.

"I have heard what Mr. Nudwink said," I answered calmly.

"Who is Mathematics?—or, rather, let me put the question in a different shape : give me your idea—if you have one—of Mathematics."

Who was Mathematics? Here was that same question that the absurd Nudwink had poked at me. It was quite evident that a trap had been laid for me. If I should retort as I had on the previous occasion would not that be detrimental to my interest? I pondered a moment. Give him my idea of mathematics, of course I could do that. That appeared easy. As to *who* mathematics was I could not pretend to say : but I could certainly define the abstract idea.

"Mathematics is the science of the relations of quantity," I said. Mr. Gallwood scowled furiously. Mr. Mayland smiled and so did Margery, while Mr. Nudwink moved uneasily in his chair and seemed to be much incensed. All this appeared to me to be a very large effect from so simple a cause as my plain answer.

"What is the Arithmetic?" continued Gallwood, abruptly.

"The science of numbers," I answered, promptly.

This reply seemed to astonish Gallwood greatly. He lowered on me savagely with his black, brutal eyes. in which glittered unmistakable hatred.

"One question more," he hissed, leaning forward and holding up his forefinger menacingly; "how many digits are there?"

"Nine," I answered.

"What is your idea of a cipher?"

"Nothing, naught."

"What do the Four Ground Rules treat of?"

"Addition, sub—"

"I did not ask you to name them; I asked you of what they treated?" he snapped.

"Of the processes—the fundamental processes of Arithmetic."

"Of *the* Arithmetic?"

"Yes."

"What is the first called?"

"Addition."

"The others, in their order?"

"Subtraction, multiplication, and division."

Mr. Gallwood, for some cause unknown to me, was now perfectly furious. His face was actually livid with passion; but controlling himself, he continued with a bitter sneer: "So, Mr. Cliff, in your conversation with our worthy chaplain you saw fit to deliberately deceive and prevaricate. Well, I shall question you no more. The Archten himself can, we are told, quote Arithmetic, and I presume that is the case with you."

Having so delivered himself Gallwood sat down abruptly, and turning to Nudwink, the two entered at once into conversation, which, though conducted in a very low tone, was accompanied by much vigor of expression and gesticulation.

" Have you any further questions to put, Mr. Gallwood ? " asked the Governor.

" None, sir," responded Gallwood, sulkily.

" Do you desire to call any further witnesses ? "

" No, sir, none ; we rest."

"And you, Mr. Cliff," continued Mr. Mayland, politely, " are there others whom you desire to question ? "

" No, sir," I answered, politely, " none."

" Then I shall myself ask a few : have you no recollection at all as to your home ? "

I adhered to my previous statement.

" You say that your father's name is William Cliff ? "

" It is."

" Mr. Gallwood."

" Sir."

" Have you ever known of a family of that name upon the island ? "

" Never, sir."

" Do you believe there is a family of that name ? "

" I do not."

" Mr. Nudwink."

The chaplain responded. He was asked the same questions, and his answers were of a like character to those of Gallwood. The three doctors in turn were questioned, and they all admitted that the name was unfamiliar.

" If you know of any one, Mr. Cliff," said the Governor, " who can testify respecting your family, you may have time to call them." I explained that I was unable to do this ; but that I was still confident as to my own name and that of my father.

"Now as to your knowledge of Mathematics. How is it that, while here in court you have, without hesitation, and with a manifest comprehension of the subject, replied to the inquiries that were made, when, according to the testimony of Mr. Nudwink, you showed yourself on a former occasion either so indifferent or so ignorant?"

I had certainly hoped that with the ending of Gallwood's attempt to disconcert me, all reference to the subject of Mathematics had been over; but here it was again. The very word itself had become hateful to me. I could not help associating it with the sanctimonious and, as I believed, hypocritical chaplain, and also with the yet more distasteful Gallwood. For a moment I cudgelled my brains in silence. It would not do, I thought, to say that I had not understood Nudwink, for I feared a renewal of the inquiry as to the exactness of my views, which were indeed very vague. I deemed it best, therefore, to boldly avow a want of confidence in the man. The reference that had been made to my joking aided me in this, serving to render my story probable. "I was only having a little fun," I answered meekly.

"Fun," said the Governor, "on such a subject, and with the chaplain, who only had your good at heart! Do you regard such conduct as seemly?"

"Perhaps not."

"Decidedly not," said the Governor, with much emphasis.

I ventured to say that I thought Mr. Nudwink was a very peculiar man.

"He is a most devoted man to his duties among the inmates of the asylum," said the Governor, severely, "and in addition preaches most acceptably to a large congregation in the adjoining village."

To this I made no response.

"He is a most exemplary Mathematician, Mr. Cliff," the Governor proceeded to say, "and you would do well in the future to profit by his admonitions."

I inclined my head submissively.

"Is there anything further in the way of testimony?" said the Governor, casting his eye around the room.

Mr. Gallwood rose and stood erect in the midst of a deep silence. My friend—for so I must now call him—Dr. Setbon, gave me a little nudge.

"Stand up, Mr. Cliff," he said.

So I also rose.

"There seems to be nothing further," said the Governor, when he had gazed about for a short interval. "Now, Mr. Gallwood, if you so desire, you may proceed with your argument in the case; the court allows twenty minutes."

My friend the doctor gave me a little tug from behind and I resumed my chair.

Gallwood availed himself of his privilege of speech to the fullest extent, and managed to crowd more vituperation and venom into that space of time, as well as more lies, than I could have believed possible. I shall not report his argument—if argument I were justified in calling it. He took the ground that my defective memory, in addition to the irrelevancy of my replies to Mr. Nudwink's pertinent inquiries, and my reckless behavior to the chaplain, constituted valid evidence that I was totally unfit for convalescent privileges. There was one allusion that he made which I did not understand at the time, and this, as it was quite short, I take the liberty of quoting from memory:

"Not only unfit," said Gallwood, passionately, "but so

5

far removed from fitness that, despite the kindly hearts
of our good doctors and the strong religious charity
of our estimable chaplain, I am almost persuaded to declare him to be hopeless. Full well I know the awful
significance of those two brief words—well styled the
dead language—which, if pronounced by the court, are
terrible as fate. Full well I understand my own responsibilities as prosecutor; yet mindful of my obligations, I
dare aver, in my paramount duty to the entire community, that not only is Mr. Cliff not convalescent, but
he is also in my opinion ' *non compos.*' "

So, amid a breathless silence, and an attention that I
myself regarded as greater than the gravity of the occasion demanded, Mr. Gallwood sat down.

I observed that Margery and her mother were both
crying bitterly ; that Dr. Setbon was furtively wiping his
eyes, and that even the Governor seemed to be affected.

Recovering himself promptly, Mr. Mayland asked me
if I desired to make an appeal in my own behalf. I rose,
and in a very short and temperate speech, I expressed
my willingness to leave the matter to the judgment of the
court.

When I had concluded there was another pause, and
then the Governor, in the same tone in which he had
pronounced the court open, declared it closed.

The tip-staff was instantly upon his feet, bawling :
" Oyez ! oyez ! oyez ! the convalescent court stands closed."
All rose to their feet. Mrs. Mayland and Margery went
out noiselessly by the door through which they came.
They were followed by Nudwink and Gallwood, the latter
casting back at me one baleful glance. Then I was
conducted into an ante-room, and waited there, I confess

in some suspense, in company with the three doctors and an attendant, for perhaps half an hour.

There was then a bustling, and the tip-staff came out and summoned us to re-enter the court room.

Mr. Mayland was seated at his desk, in the same attitude of magisterial dignity as before ; but his countenance being perfectly impassible, nothing indicated what his decision might be. As we sat down, the further door was thrown open, and the others entered. Margery and her mother both held their heads down, and it seemed that the girl was weeping.

This I thought rather strange ; but my attention was diverted by the constable, who, with his " Oyez ! oyez ! oyez ! " opened the court as before.

The Governor now looked at me a moment fixedly, and then proceeded, in a low calm voice, to pronounce his opinion.

CHAPTER VIII.

ON THE COURSE OF DISCIPLINE.

"THE circumstances in your case, Mr. Cliff," said the Governor, "are very peculiar. It is seldom that so many intricate questions are involved in a matter of convalescence, as in yours. Questions of fact have arisen in three specific details; namely: the question as to your accountability for the attack upon Mr. Bullinger; the question of the defective memory; and the further question of aberration as indicated by your unaccountable conduct in reference to religious subjects. The law is plain. It is that although a patient may be pronounced convalescent by the physicians, and thereby admitted to certain privileges, yet this action is subject to reversal on a proper presentation of the case, and for good cause shown.

"You have, I will say at the outset, Mr. Cliff, shown a fertility of resource, and a very considerable degree of information upon various subjects, and in respect to your own conduct of the case, no fault whatever is to be found. You are probably not versed in the law, but it is my duty to see that you do not suffer from any lack of legal knowledge. I will therefore briefly state that, in his capacity as assistant superintendent of the asylum, it has devolved upon Mr. Gallwood, entirely within the scope of his powers, to present you to the court as one to whom it is unsafe to intrust the privileges of convalescence. He

68

has, in the course of the proceedings, fully demonstrated his wisdom and fulfilled his duties well, and having arraigned you on the three several questions of fact before enumerated his responsibility ceased.   This responsibility is, as the law very properly provides, of a very serious nature.   The responsibility of our three physicians, Dr. Setbon and his associates, is limited to fine, and in serious cases, to loss of position; and is also limited to three days after recommendation of convalescent liberties. Within three days an act was done by you—the attack upon your fellow patient—which, had it resulted in death or serious injury to him, would have rendered the physicians amenable to the law in such case made and provided. Fortunately there was no serious injury done; but in his province of assistant superintendent it then became imperative that Mr. Gallwood should take action.   Had he acquiesced in your view of the case,—that Bullinger was the sole offender,—he might have become, in case any future act of yours should result in serious bodily harm to any one, personally liable to the full extent of the statute, which, as you may perhaps not be aware, provides an adequate pecuniary compensation to the sufferer, or in case death should result, to his heirs; and also, in that event, imprisonment.   It must therefore be plain to you, Mr. Cliff, that in prosecuting you to the extreme limit, Mr. Gallwood does not in any degree exceed his rights, and would even be derelict in his duty to society had he done otherwise.

  " In the act of the arraignment, however, Mr. Gallwood's responsibility ceases, and under the law it again devolves upon Dr. Setbon and his associates, and also upon the court, to this extent, that if, by accepting your pleas in whole or in part, you were to be restored to your conva-

lescent liberty, and any untoward event should occur, we
would be each severally liable, as before noted, in pecuniary damages, and also subject—at the crown's discretion—
to loss of position.

"It now lies within the prerogative of the court to adju-
dicate in one of four ways : First, you may be either remanded absolutely to the asylum, and your assignment
as a convalescent declared invalid ; or, second, you may
be declared to have sustained your position in every
respect with full convalescent liberties unimpaired ; or,
third, it is within the court's power to place you on the
course of discipline, whereby your liberty as a convalescent would be much curtailed ; or,—and I hesitate before
naming that dread alternative ; but as an adjudication is
asked on that special matter I must do so,—in the fourth
and last case I can pronounce the awful sentence,—subject, it is true, to revision by the Sun Court,—of *non compos.*" The Governor paused, and appeared greatly moved
by something, the nature of which I hardly comprehended.
In the silence that ensued Margery's voice was heard passionately sobbing. Of course I knew that it was a very
dreadful thing to be pronounced a lunatic : but why
should the Governor be so perturbed ? and why should
Margery feel moved by such strong emotion ? I confess
that I was puzzled ; but so many things had happened to
disconcert me that I regarded this as only one of many,
and not more formidable than what had preceded. I
sat stolid, concerned, it is true, and impatient, but not, I
think, manifesting any great distress.

The Governor proceeded : "Having indicated the several courses that are open to the court I now pass to
the questions of fact. In the encounter with Mr. Bullinger, were you blameworthy ? I answer, No." My heart

gave a joyous bound. "In respect to your defective memory, your own testimony is the controlling testimony. You have admitted with much candor your own incapacity, and, in so doing, have established the point conclusively in my mind that no danger is to be apprehended from that source alone, and on that count also you are absolved from blame. To come to the third point, is it or is it not a fact, that your levity towards our estimable chaplain was of such a character as to justify this court in regarding it as serious ? To the mind of the court this point seems to be involved in very great obscurity. Your own explanation is either truthful—in which case it was levity almost unpardonable—or it was ingenious, and by your very ingenuity you thereby demonstrated your own defects.

"No point is better established in our system of jurisprudence than this : that cunning is always an attribute of impaired mental faculties. It is true that on other points you sustained yourself admirably, and the court gives you due credit for the excellent temper you have shown during the examination ; still, all this may have been assumed, and I take this occasion to state that had you shown more feeling at the allusions to a possible decree of *non compos* it would have been more becoming. However, we are not all constituted alike, and this may have been only a matter of phlegmatic temperament.

"It is not, under our law, in a trial of this character, the province of the prosecution to touch upon the original charges which lead to incarceration ; but in its judgment the court has the right to take that into consideration in rendering a decision. Bearing all the facts in mind, the court determines that the first charge, an unprovoked attack upon Mr. Bullinger, is not sustained, and therefore pronounces you of that charge not guilty. Of the second

charge, defective memory, guilty, but the court attaches
no blame to you thereby, and regards it as but a physical
impairment, which time may, and probably will, remedy.
Of the third charge, undue levity, the court pronounces
you guilty."

The Governor's voice was intensely solemn as he pronounced this ominous word, and again Margery broke
forth into sobs. I was by this time somewhat moved myself, but I sat expectant of what was to follow. After a
brief interval Mr. Mayland proceeded : " The court now
in its discretion, aware of the high degree of responsibility attaching to its action, decrees as follows : that you be
placed upon the course of discipline from this day for one
year, unless sooner discharged."

As the Governor pronounced these words he bowed his
head gravely; there was a simultaneous sigh from the
three doctors. I looked towards Gallwood and Nudwink ;
both were scowling, while the faces of Mrs. Mayland and
Margery brightened into smiles. Both the smiles and the
scowls were alike reassuring. I was in dense ignorance
as to what the course of discipline consisted; but that
Margery should smile and Gallwood scowl thereat was
sufficient evidence that it was not especially dreadful.
The whole matter was explained to me in the ante-room
by my good friend Dr. Setbon, who shook my hand
warmly, congratulating me upon the favorable impression
I had made. Margery and her mother also came and
spoke to me.

There was a tear in Mrs. Mayland's eye as she took my
hand. " While you are filled with joy at your wonderful
preservation do not forget to whom you owe all this," she
said.

"The Governor?" I asked, "do you mean him ?"

"Oh, no, I refer to a higher than the Governor, in whose hands are all human ordinances, and from whom proceed all human judgments."

"Oh, yes," I answered humbly, being indeed fervently thankful to that higher power.

"I grieve to think," continued the old lady, "that you should have treated the counsels of the chaplain in an unbecoming way—"

"Mr. Cliff explained that it was only an aversion to Mr. Nudwink, mamma," said Margery, stealing a glance at me out of her lovely eyes.

"Still he ought to have remembered the sacred character of the man and of his mission. Promise me, Mr. Cliff," Mrs. Mayland added, with much fervor, "promise me that you will read your Arithmetic hereafter with due diligence."

"I shall certainly do so," I answered, "as you and Miss Margery request it."

"We do request it," said Margery, sweetly.

"And pray," added Mrs. Mayland, "pray to Mathematics, and may the Greatest Common Divisor sustain and comfort you. Now I shall say good-by. When it is all settled in respect to the course of discipline no doubt it will be permitted that you shall visit us."

Mrs. Mayland gave me her hand, Margery smiled charmingly, and they both withdrew, leaving me alone with Dr. Setbon.

The excellent doctor rubbed his hands gleefully.

"I am charmed, Mr. Cliff; charmed with the way in which you conducted yourself during the examination. My professional reputation was at stake, and I was, I confess, for awhile exceedingly anxious, but you sustained yourself through the trying ordeal with the greatest coolness. Now as to the future—"

"There are one or two things that I should like to have explained," I said, feeling that I could trust the doctor in some measure.

"Name them, Mr. Cliff, I shall be delighted to afford you any assistance in my power."

"You are aware that I have admitted my defective memory, doctor?"

"With uncommon candor, my dear sir, with most uncommon candor."

"You remember the course the examination took respecting my so-called levity with the chaplain?"

"Perfectly, sir, perfectly."

"You recall that I laid it to a little pleasantry on my part on account of a personal dislike I had for Mr. Nudwink?"

"I don't wonder at it, not in the least. He is a man for whom I have myself the very strongest aversion."

"It seemed to me that I had no other course open to me than to explain my apparently unaccountable conduct as a joke."

"And was it not a joke?" asked the doctor, opening his eyes very wide.

"No, doctor, I was not joking ; that is, except in one instance. I dislike to prevaricate, but to have told the exact truth at court I feared would have been prejudicial to my interests."

"Then what was the true explanation? I am quite at a loss to conceive of any other."

"The explanation is a simple one."

"What is it?"

"I may trust you, doctor, may I not?"

"Thoroughly, sir."

"Then I shall have to admit that my defective memory extended to all those points referred to by Mr. Nudwink."

"You do not mean to tell me," exclaimed the doctor in amazement, "that you have lost all memory of religious truth?"

What was I to say in reply to this? The questions of religion and arithmetic had become so inextricably involved in my mind that I felt myself quite incapable of disentangling them. Still, the doctor must be answered. I had declared to myself that I would trust him, and he had given me the assurance that he was to be trusted.

"To be frank, doctor," I said, "I fear I must say that, if not all, I have at least lost the memory of much. As to what constitutes religious truth I seem to have now only a dim perception."

"Remarkable, most remarkable."

"I realize my own deficiency in this as in those other respects of which you are aware, and I deem it my duty to be thoroughly candid."

"You are quite right, Mr. Cliff, quite right. However, this puts quite a new phase upon the matter. Yours, sir, is a most remarkable case; the most remarkable that has ever come under my observation."

He paused and rubbed his brow reflectively. "Singular, very singular," he continued, "that a mind as bright as yours in so many respects should yet fail utterly on these points. We physicians are of course continually dealing with lapses of memory of almost all degrees, but your case stands by itself. However, one great point gained is this, that you know your own weakness to its fullest extent, and will therefore be prepared to coöperate with me

in such efforts as I shall think best to make during the
ensuing year, while you are on the course of discipline."

"Will you kindly explain what is meant by this course of
discipline, doctor?"

"There are really several grades of the course of discipline," he replied, "and it is mainly my duty to assign to
each patient thereon his proper grade; each has its special
hardships and special exemptions. In your case, as I am
informed by the Governor that you are possessed of ample
means, the burden will not be as heavy as it otherwise
would."

"In what way?" I asked.

"You will have to be continually under supervision, of
course. That is requisite more or less in every grade of
the course; but I shall arrange it so that you can travel,
if you so desire it, with your attendant."

"Travel!" said I, delightedly. "I should like that."

"And perhaps on your journey over the island, it may
happen that your eye may light upon some familiar scene
that will revive the dormant smouldering cinders of memory."

"That is possible," I answered, overjoyed at the prospect before me of a certain degree of freedom.

"I shall arrange at once for a suitable attendant,"
continued Dr. Setbon. "Let me see; who is there I can
get? You need a man of more than ordinary intelligence,
who would be able to inform you on all points."

"Yes, doctor," said I, hypocritically. "I am well aware
that on these points where memory fails I must be taught
as a child."

"Right, sir; you have hit it exactly," exclaimed the doctor, taking my hand with enthusiasm. "You inspire me
with more and more confidence, and in your case I am

going to depart somewhat from my ordinary custom. I shall assign as your companion a young man—a nephew of my own—whom you will find an agreeable associate, and who will be more likely than any one I know to impart the knowledge you desire quickly and ably. With him as your instructor I feel convinced that before the year rolls round you will have become completely restored to yourself."

Dr. Setbon then left me, having called in one of the attendants. In about an hour he returned, and with him he brought his nephew, whom he introduced simply as Oliver.

CHAPTER IX.

SOME NECESSARY STATISTICS.

HAVING learned by some sad and some rather humorous experiences, I diligently set myself to the task of acquiring information respecting the singular land in which my lot was now cast. I called to mind the old adage that "a shut mouth makes a wise head," and in my intercourse with those in whose company I was thrown I contrived after a time to extract a considerable amount of information without directly asking for it. Then, too, the Governor's library was at my disposal, and of the works therein I availed myself freely. There was of course a great deal that was wholly incomprehensible, for the majority of the subjects treated of were of a mystical character; and of the remainder the greater part were dissertations in which the crudest notions of the properties of numbers were combined with moral speculations, and essays of a recondite and didactic character. There was one book, however, that afforded me some insight into the origin of the peculiar islanders. The style of this work was of an elevated and poetic type, but the printing was blind, the paper, though heavy, was of a poor quality, and the language at times, on account of the remarkable spelling, almost incomprehensible. I shall not venture to quote—although my memory of its contents is excellent—from this singular production; but shall endeavor to recount such of its statements as may serve

to give some general idea in respect to the history of
the island. Like the narratives of the beginnings of
all other lands, the early history of Inquirendo Island is
evidently either myth or garbled statement, part fact and
part conjecture.

It is gravely stated that in the beginning Mathematics
created all things ; that nine days were occupied in this
work, and that on the ninth day nine individuals—three
males and three females, and three others—who are described as workers, were sent from Heaven, or Oversea, as
it is indifferently called, and from whom all the dwellers
in the island were descended.

From certain matters of internal evidence, and a process of deduction based upon the character of the writing
and the description that was given of these nine original
Adams and Eves, I arrived at the conclusion that they
had been inhabitants of the British Isles, and flourished,
as the historians say, about the close of the sixteenth century. The three men are described in the first chapter of
the narrative as being very distinct in their characteristics : one, who was called the Angel, was of a high and
noble disposition ; another, called Caledon, was similar to
the first, but, as I gathered, more warlike, and also more
industrious, but far less able ; while the third, named
Erin, was of a truculent and at the same time submissive
disposition, and who appeared to be more allied to the
workers than to the others, and particularly to Angel.

This latter personage seems to have possessed qualities
that lifted him far above his companions, and it is to him
that the civilization of the island was attributed. Indeed
so extraordinary does he appear in the narrative that I
was at first tempted to regard him as purely mythical.
He was credited with the invention of every one of the

appliances by which this people mitigated the severity of life. To him was due the discovery of the ores of iron, gold, silver, and copper, and to him the processes by which these ores were utilized.

From him this peculiar people received all they had of religion, as to which I shall be more explicit further on.

Then also he devised the system of computation, by which all accounts were kept, and by which all reckoning was done. From several sources, including information procured from time to time in conversations, I became acquainted with certain facts pertaining to the knowledge which the islanders had of the exact sciences. Their year was divided into three hundred and sixty-five days, and, by a system of intercalations, the want of accord between the apparent and the real was remedied. The notation by which they expressed quantities was of the most extraordinary description, and which, so far as I have been able to discover, bears no analogy to that of any other known system that has ever existed upon the face of the earth. It was all based, as I discovered only after much diligence, upon the remarkable assumption that nine was the extreme limit to which the human mind was capable of expanding. Of course they discovered that multiples did exist; but their only notion of large aggregations of things was by combinations of nines and other lesser numbers, arranged in accordance with empirical formula. For instance, to designate 365 they used this expression: 985 + 5,* which puzzled me at first exceedingly. In my researches I discovered that so long as computations were confined to the nine digits, their methods and ours were identical; but, as will more fully appear hereafter, ten

---

* $(9 \times 8 \times 5 + 5 = 365.)$

was to them an unknown quantity: 10 was to them 9 +
1; 11, 9 + 2; 81 in their method was written 99; 82, 99
+ 1, and so on. All this appears to us exceedingly complex and cumbersome; but I could not see but that all
ordinary operations were performed with exactness and
despatch by the islanders.

Every year consisted of thirty-six weeks of nine days
each, the ninth day corresponding to our Sunday. By
this arrangement four days were of necessity left over:
but this was remedied by adding one additional week every
two years and subtracting one every sixth year; but as
this, in the course of time, would cause the year to fall
short, every thirty-sixth year there was no subtraction.
This with the dropping of a day every forty-fourth year,
when the new moon coincided with the opposition of
Mars, brought the civil and solar year in almost exact
accord; fully as much as by the Gregorian calendar.

Since my return I have been able to compare the methods of the Inquirendians with those of other civilizations,
and I find some strange similarities between them and the
Egyptians, and also the Aztecs. But upon all this I shall
not enlarge. I might have had more to say in respect
to these coincidences, but the Lentor Library has been
closed so long, and apparently so purposelessly, that I
have been unable to examine certain very valuable works
there, and especially the "Codex," a fac simile of that in
the Bodlein Library. The system of nines prevailed in
every relation upon the island. The political arrangements were dependent upon nine and its multiples.
There were nine departments, and the Council of Elders,
by which appellation I refer to their legislative body, was
composed of eighty-one delegates, nine from each department. The judiciary consisted of what were called the

6

star courts, presided over by a justice, appointed by the
elders in the several departments, and which had jurisdiction in minor cases.   Next to these were the moon courts,
one in each department, having original jurisdiction in
criminal cases only, and appellate jurisdiction in civil matters.   The judges were appointed by the council and held
office for life.   Above all these courts, and having original and appellate jurisdiction in criminal cases, was the
Sun Court, whose sittings were held at the capital or chief
city in the centre of the island, where also the elders met.
There were three judges of the sun court, elected by the
council and holding office for life.   In all these courts
there was a system of jury trials, in which, as with us,
matters of fact were submitted to the jurors.   There was
also what was designated the supreme jury, consisting of
nine men chosen by the elders for their high character,
whose province it was solely to try those who, for any
cause, should be impeached by the elders.   The officials
subject to impeachment were the judges of the different
courts and the executive.   The code of this singular people was in nothing more extraordinary than in the powers,
privileges, and responsibilities of the chief magistrate.

He was chosen by the popular vote ; his term of office
was three years, and during the time of his occupancy of
the executive chair, he was to all intents and purposes an
absolute despot.   He could, if it so pleased him, usurp the
functions of any courts or any judge, and by his arbitrary
word alone mete out any punishment that did not extend
to death.   The police or army of the island, as well as all
the subordinate officers, particularly those of finance,
the special officers, such as governors of mines, mints,
prisons, and the asylum, were all directly under his sway.
It was his prerogative to issue writs over his own signa-

ture to the several moon courts—or for that matter to the other courts—whereby any one who appeared to be acting in a manner inimical to the peace of the realm could be summarily treated, being either taken before the executive in person, or to such other as he might designate. It was thus that I myself was dealt with. The writ of *Habeas Corpus* was unknown ; but a far more potent power was retained by the people, and which, if the history that I have quoted is to be relied upon, had always proved suffi cient to preserve their liberties : it was the powerful weapon of impeachment, held by the council of elders, who, being directly responsible to the people by whom they were elected, had the most extreme interest in preventing the least approach to an abuse of the arbitrary power confided to the chief magistrate. The punishment which the supreme jury was authorized to inflict was death—if innocent, acquittal ; if guilty, death. This tremendous power had been sufficient, so it was asserted, to prevent any despotism and to restrain the successive despots.

During my residence on the island I visited in succession every part, and made myself acquainted with the working of the system of government, and also with the social constitution in every respect. As nearly as I could approximate, the island was one hundred and sixty miles long from east to west, and about ninety miles wide in the widest part. The population I estimated to be about one hundred and sixty thousand, of whom about forty-five thousand were gathered in the several towns, and a little less than ten thousand in the capital, from which the asylum to which I had been first conducted was distant not many miles. Communication was kept up by means of roads, some of which were macadamized after a rough fashion and kept in order by the government, and the remainder of which, called department roads, were ill made and dusty or muddy, and kept in such repair as they were by the funds of the several departments.

The iron mine in the sixth department was under the charge of an officer directly responsible to the chief magistrate. There was also an officer in control of the copper mine in the fourth department. The silver workings were in the seventh and the gold in the ninth department : but these were not productive, and the chief coins of the country in use were of silver and copper. My possession of fourteen five-dollar gold pieces and some silver was a very great advantage, for although I was compelled to have my gold recoined, the amount of it that I possessed was sufficient to give me in the money of the island a very considerable property.

I was careful to make an estimate of my fortune, and comparing it with our own standard I arrived at the conclusion that I was worth in Inquirendo the equivalent of seventy or eighty thousand dollars, enough to render me independent of all labor.

Stock companies were unknown; but partnerships were common. There were only a few ways by which capital could be invested. The land itself was subject to purchase and sale ; but there were large tracts kept by the government as common land upon which at a fixed rate cattle and sheep could be pastured. Money could therefore be invested in lands and houses, in cattle or sheep, and also in business in the towns. But the investment most favored by the people of means, who wished to spare themselves all trouble, was in the " funds " or bonds of the government. This was the way in which I disposed of my own fortune, and although only two per cent. was realized, I found that my income was quite sufficient for all my needs.

The most interesting of all the government works that I was enabled to visit was the great iron " Fabrican " as it was called, situated on the outskirts of the town in the sixth department, adjoining the iron mine, and in close proximity to the anthracite coal deposit, which I omitted to state above was also under official supervision. This " Fabrican " was an immense structure, or rather collection of structures, covering altogether as much as six acres. Its walls were of stone and very massive, the bond being a cement composed mainly of puzzolana, although iron bolts and braces were used, especially at the corners. The roof was peaked, and of iron, as were also the interior partitions. Far more interesting, however, than the building itself was the process of manufacture carried on within. As to this it will be impossible to make more than a brief mention. It is proposed to make an early visit to the island, and certain scientific gentlemen have agreed to accompany me thither, from whom a more full and interesting report may be expected.

My own scientific education is, I confess, limited ; but I happened to inherit half a dozen shares of the stock of a gas company in New York, and so became interested in all matters pertaining to gas ; for the excellent reason that the original half dozen shares, by a judicious process of watering, has since become a liberal fortune. They call it now " consolidated ; " perhaps a better name would be " expanded."

This, however, is digressing. I felt called upon to allude to gas, inasmuch as in the " Fabrican " the ores of iron—a very inferior carbonate—were converted by a series of processes into any desired manufactured article by the aid of oxygen, carbonic oxide, and hydrogen in regulated proportions, and, what was more remarkable still, the articles so manufactured were absolutely non-corrodible, not only as to their surfaces, but throughout their structure.

I have now in my possession samples of this iron which I shall be pleased to show at any time ; although, as I stated above, a full report upon the whole subject may be expected very soon.

CHAPTER X.

THE GREATEST COMMON DIVISOR.

IN the preceding chapter I summarized the information that I gathered from time to time respecting the Inquirendians and their manners and customs. In obtaining all this I was under the necessity of observing great caution ; for from the first Oliver assumed that I was well informed upon all ordinary subjects. If I was compelled to be reticent as to a great many things, in one point my tongue was allowed full swing. I was at liberty to ask any question I saw fit as to religion, and indeed my friend Oliver, being of a serious turn of mind, was exceedingly diligent, in season and out of season, in striving to impress me with what he was pleased to call the truth.

All our arrangements having been made, Oliver and I set out upon our tour of exploration of the island. I had the joy of being permitted to pass an evening in the society of Margery before we departed, and—Oliver having been discreet enough to engage the attention of Mrs. Mayland—I found myself so enraptured by her beauty and loveliness that I could not avoid making some reference to the passion that consumed me.

" I have never known what love was, Miss Margery," I said, as we sat apart from the rest at an open window of the Governor's villa.

She looked up shyly, her face suffused with blushes.

" Never until I saw you." Then I continued, telling her

how hopeless life would be if I could not look forward to
the day when she would be my own. Seeing that in spite
of my ardent words she remained silent, I pressed her for
a reply.

"Can you not bid me hope?" I said.

She had cast down her eyes after that first eager, burn
ing look. She now raised them again to mine.

"You do not know what you ask, Mr. Cliff," she answered, in a tone of the deepest dejection.

"Why, oh, why?"

She shook her head sadly.

"Tell me," I continued, "only tell me what it is that
stands between us. Is it this ban that is upon me? Is
it because I am not yet wholly free?"

"No, oh, no."

"Say only that I may hope," I cried, "say only that,
and I shall be satisfied."

Still no reply. Margery was painfully embarrassed.

"I love you," I exclaimed, "I love you, my darling,
devotedly. Can you not say that the time may come
when I may—"

Suddenly Margery started. I looked hastily in the direction of her glance. There stood, with a grim smile upon
his scornful mouth and a sinister look in his black eyes,
the hated Gallwood.

He approached slowly.

"Is it not too cool by the open window, Margery, my
dear?" he said, in his low rasping voice.

As if under the spell of a fascination which she could
not resist, Margery moved away from the window, and
from me.

I rose to my feet angrily, and had I dared, would have
spoken my mind freely to the man, bidding him begone.

But luckily I remembered my own condition, and knew in time how futile it would be to provoke a contest of any sort.

Gallwood was wonderfully polite to me, and to Margery deferential in the extreme, notwithstanding the slight tinge of exaction in his arbitrary tone. What right had he, I asked myself, to even suggest to the girl that she should leave my side? I glanced toward her, and one look of encouragement, however slight, and hopeless as I felt, would have caused me to throw off all restraint. Alas, no look was there; but on the contrary a listless, forlorn expression, almost despairing. Oliver had now risen, and Mrs. Mayland came forward.

"Must you go so soon?" she said, with a smile.

"We start to-morrow early," replied Oliver. "So I think Mr. Cliff and I had better say good-night."

Of course I could do nothing but acquiesce. I strove in vain for a glance from Margery. As I took her hand for one instant in mine I felt that it was cold as ice, and with the touch a shudder passed over her, and her lips were white and her voice tremulous as she said "good-by."

Oliver was in high spirits as we left the asylum on our journey. Our light steel buggy was drawn by a spirited team of steers, who bore us swiftly away from those gloomy precincts. On the crest of a hill I turned and cast back one wistful glance, not at the bleak iron walls which had been to me a prison, but at the lovely villa where dwelt my Margery.

Oliver talked continually, pointing out the different spots of interest as we spun past them, and explaining in some detail the plan which he had marked out for our journey.

It is not needful that the thread of the narrative should be broken to relate our various adventures. Suffice it that on the first night we found ourselves in the capital city, having traversed the greater part of two of the departments. We drove directly to an inn, on the main street of the town.

"To-morrow," said Oliver, as I was about to retire for the night, "to-morrow will be Numbers' day, and we shall then begin in earnest that instruction in sacred things which it is my province and duty to impart."

As we had ridden along over the roads on our way to the capital, Oliver had taken occasion to impart considerable information, some of which I have in fact incorporated into the prosy chapter that preceded this. Little by little the astounding character of the religion of this wonderful people was made known to me. Astonished as I was by the revelation of the nature of what I heard, I was yet exceedingly careful to manifest no undue surprise. I heard with amazement the most profound that the Arithmetic was the revealed word of Mathematics, and that in the four ground rules was to be found the way of life, in which the fool need not err. I said nothing when Oliver told me that he had himself once been a unit, but was now an integer, having been cancelled by the written solution. I kept silent when he informed me that he was thinking of becoming a minister of the Established church, whose doctrines were based upon division, resolved into its component parts of dividend, divisor, and quotient; and I was careful not to interrupt when he told me that there was not only much worldliness but considerable heresy on the island, and that erroneous and strange doctrines were being preached.

"Hold fast to the truth, Mr. Cliff," said Oliver, earnestly, "as you shall hear it expounded, and do not suffer your-self to be led astray by any fallacy, however alluring."

I was awakened the morning after my arrival at the cap-ital by the chime of bells. We had arrived so late the previous night that I had only been able to get a casual glimpse of the town. I now went to the window and looked out. Below in the street the tide of life was already begin-ning to surge to and fro. I dressed myself, and then Oliver came to my door, (our rooms adjoined,) and we went down to breakfast.

At an hour corresponding to our half-past ten the chimes again began.

"To-day," said Oliver, "we shall devote the morning to the services of the Established church, and this even-ing, if agreeable, we shall go to the Church of the Holy Decimal."

I had arrived at a point now when I was astonished at nothing; so I responded, "All right," in a tone of satis-faction, and we set out on our way to the Cathedral.

"The Cathedral of the Greatest Common Divisor," Oli-ver explained, "is considered by far the most beautiful building on the island. The ceremonies that you will see to-day are of the most convincing character, and you will understand better by your own observation the sacred realities which they typify, than by any remarks of mine."

"What do these ceremonies consist of?" I asked.

"The rite of cancellation will be administered by the apostle, and after this, and the services of high notations, there will be a sermon by the reverend Paul Patmos. It is this sermon to which I desire to call your especial atten-tion, for it is always the custom to deliver a discourse to the newly cancelled integers, which you will doubtless find replete with just the information befitting your condition."

By this time we had arrived at the door of the vast
cathedral. It was indeed a superb building.

A tall iron tower rose in the centre, from which the
chiming bells pealed forth. The walls of the edifice were
of solid stone, beautifully laid in courses and adorned
with sculptured figures of stone and iron, all of surpassing beauty. Here and there, too, at the angles were iron
turrets, partly gilded, and ornamented with intricate
arabesques. The style of the architecture differed from
any that I had ever seen, though I have since found that
it was not uncommon in the island. Square in shape, the
size of the cathedral was immense. It must have occupied, with its adjoining structures—wherein, as Oliver explained, dwelt the apostle and the ministers of the diocese,
—upwards of ten or twelve acres.

Within, the sight was one of entrancing beauty. As the
exterior of the building was square in form, so the interior
was circular, and the roof, supported by elegantly chased
and enamelled columns, was arranged in segments and
angles in such a manner that the slightest sound from the
central platform, whereon all the ceremonies were conducted, was reflected to the audience, who sat, tier above
tier, in rows of seats in a great circle.

When we entered, the larger part of the audience was
already seated, and it was not long before, at the sharp
clang of a silver bell, the doors of the cathedral were
closed, and a dead silence fell upon the multitude. Then
in a low plaintive cadence strains of subdued music rose
upon the air, and at the same instant, as by magic, the circular platform or dais in the centre was filled by a multitude of children, all clad in blue garments, and from whose
arms were suspended fleecy white draperies. As they sang
or chanted, keeping time to the music that rose and fell,

these children swayed their arms to and fro with an har
monious motion.

I could distinguish no words, but the air seemed to be
a familiar one that I had often listened to at home.

The hymn ended, the children disappeared, and their
places were supplied by a number of individuals who appeared to be clergymen, although their vestments were of
a pattern hardly befitting my own ideas of that sacred calling. They were all in fact arrayed in azure, as the children had been, but without the fleecy white wings. A
long and peculiar ceremonial now ensued, in which reading
alternated with music, and wherein at intervals the children appeared and disappeared and reappeared, flitting in
and out among the azure-clad elders. There was little
that I could understand of the reading, except that it was
from the Arithmetic, the drawling tone of the reader preventing any sure comprehension.

At last there was a sudden hush, and from the midst of
those who were officiating, stepped to the circumference
of the circular dais an aged and venerable prelate, who
moved round till he had made the entire circle of the platform, crying as he went in a loud voice: "Ciphers about
to be enrolled as integers by the rites of the church will
now come forward."

There was a movement amidst the audience, and down
the convergent aisles, here and there, young and old were
seen making their way.

The blue and white children reappeared, chanting,
"Cancellation! oh, glorious cancellation!" to which the
prelate who had first spoken responded, "Who are to
be thereby made fit for Oversea."

Various other sentences were sung and recited, sometimes in unison and again alternately, the people joining.

Meanwhile, the candidates for cancellation had come forward and were arranged on a row of seats immediately in front of the platform. When they were all seated, the music ceased, the children vanished, and the clergy in silence and with a ghostly, gliding motion, filed around and seated themselves, facing outward, at the foot of a sort of rostrum in the exact centre. Upon this rostrum now mounted the venerable prelate, who appeared to be the chief of the ceremonial, and who was indeed (as I was afterward told by Oliver) the apostle, or chief bishop, of the Established church.

Here the apostle stood erect at his full height, but turning round continually with his head thrown back and face upward, till I thought it must surely have made him dizzy. All the time he kept up a monotonous mumbling, the purport of which I could not understand. At length he called aloud the single word " Numbers ! " There was intense silence for an interval, and then he cried again, yet louder, thrice : " Numbers ! Numbers ! Numbers ! " As he concluded, down from the summit of the dome above him, held by golden cords at the corners, appeared a square concern that I saw instantly was made of wood. It was the first wood that I had seen on the island, and more intently observing it, I perceived that it was evidently a raft, an ordinary raft, made up of detached parts of a vessel of a very old-time pattern. It swung down lower and lower, till it was suspended directly over the prelate's head. He reached out his hand and touched it, saying as he did so in a loud voice, "Oh, blessed raft, to whom we owe our lives eternally. Be blessed forever."

When these words had been uttered the raft, swaying from side to side, was drawn up again by the golden cords into the dome. As it disappeared all the multitude

bowed their heads, and the apostle lifted up his arms, holding them extended wide, his eyes cast upward. Then
gradually his arms fell to his side, and as he turned his
face earthward, three young priests issued forth from
beneath the dais, bearing on their shoulders an immense
silver bowl. They circled round the platform while the
apostle, descending, came and walked beside them. At
intervals the apostle reached out his hand, dipped it into
the contents of the silver vessel, and, reciting certain
words monotonously, sprinkled the candidates with the
fluid contents. It was a dense black liquid that the bowl
contained; but it was not till afterwards that I was informed by Oliver that it was ink—the ink washed from
the sacred notations inscribed by the candidates as a prelude to cancellation.

It was the sacred written solution of the Arithmetic.

When thrice again the circuit had been made the
three young priests descended into the dim recess beneath
the chancel, and the apostle continued his solemn pacing
alone; chanting—now in unison with the children and
the cancelled ones—a low melodious refrain, weird and
wonderful.

The journey ended, the apostle seated himself upon
the cushioned steps of the dais, and the music and the
chanting ceased. There was an interval of solemn silence. All heads were bowed, and I heard now and then
the sound of low sobbing from the benches below where
the new-made integers knelt. Oliver at my side had also
sunk upon his knees, and his eyes, cast reverently upward, were filled with tears. His attitude of devotion,
his clasped hands and streaming eyes, were positive evidences of the most devout and intense religious feeling.

All that multitude were engaged in prayer, in which—

so potent is the example of true emotion—I unconsciously joined, praying to the God in whom I had been
taught to believe for help in all my adversity.

The silent prayer ended, one of the younger priests
arose, and circling the platform announced that the Reverend Paul Patmos would preach.

" My discourse, it is true," said the Reverend Mr. Patmos, " is addressed to you, beloved integers, who have just
been cancelled, and thereby become the inheritors of a new
nature : no longer naughts or units, the old things have
passed away, and you have entered upon a new life.
With your cancellation vows you have put off forever the
old leaven of abstraction, and are henceforth concrete
and heirs of Oversea.   For what saith the Arithmetic?
' A concrete number is applied to a particular thing ; but
an abstract is not applied.'   What could possibly be
plainer or more convincing than this?   By a particular
thing (or person, as the marginal reading is), we plainly
discern one who is particular in his daily walk and conversation.

" There has been much diversity of opinion among
mathematicians as to the sense in which the word ' applied ' should be taken, and some, not sufficiently ap-
prehending the spirit of Division, have insisted that the
word was really apples, and in support of this argument
the story, plainly a myth, of a certain Adam, is gravely
brought forward.

" You have, as problems, been duly instructed.   You
have learned that Mathematics is found in the Dividend,
Divisor, and Quotient, and that outside of the Arithmetic was nothing to be learned of any abiding value.   In
the act of being plunged into the written solution and receiving on your brow the mysterious and sacred sign of

division, you have become integers, and as such, heirs of
the promise.

"Brethren, do not forget your high calling. Be instant
in expressing yourselves, not alone by notation, but also
by numeration. There be those who will seek to delude
you from the plain path; but be not deceived, neither
notation availeth anything nor numeration, but to be an
integer.

"To express numbers, as the Arithmetic plainly read-
eth, three methods are given: by words, which, as the
context justifies us, meaneth aloud, that our fellow men
may know how firm we are in the faith; by letters—also
called the Roman method—whereby we write down our
desires, and place them in the hands of our pastors;
and by figures, where we indicate, or our pastors indicate
for us, our desires in what is commonly called chalktalk on
a blackboard. All these methods are admissible, and are
acceptable to Numbers and to Mathematics. In this capital city I need hardly call your attention to the manifest
wording of the Arithmetic, which speaks of the seven
capital letters, and is an assured revelation that the so-
called Roman method is more acceptable here than
either of the other two.

"I need not warn you, brethren and integers, of the devices by which the Arch Ten seeks to destroy you. Do
not suffer yourselves to be deluded. Some will seek to
persuade you that to express numbers by letters is wrong,
because it is called the Roman method. To all such turn
a deaf ear. Truth is mighty and will prevail.

"Let me earnestly counsel you to beware of false
prophets. Give diligent heed to what your pastors incul-
cate, so that when you are divided at last there may be no
remainder. Remember what the Arithmetic saith: 'The

7

dividing of both divisor and dividend by the same number does not change the value of the quotient.' And again in another place, 'The multiplying of both divisor and dividend by the same number doth not change the value of the quotient.' And mark the fate of the wicked! Again the Arithmetic saith : 'Cut off the ciphers from the right of the divisor,' and a part of the same passage, 'Annex the figures cut off to the remainder, if there be one.' How solemn these words, and how their import should sink into the heart. It admonishes us to keep our loins girded."

CHAPTER XI.

MR. PATMOS here concluded his sermon, and stepped down from the rostrum. At a signal from the apostle all the multitude, priests, integers, singers, and the whole assembly, rose to their feet, and the music swelled out into a delicious strain.

At the conclusion of the anthem, which was now chanted, the congregation again bent their heads for a short time in silence and then slowly dispersed. Oliver and I made our way down the aisle into the street, and on our way back to the inn we were both very thoughtful. What a strange spectacle it was of which I had been a witness. The gorgeous ceremonial and the devoutness of that vast multitude were contrasted in my mind forcibly with the frivolity and absurdity of the rites of the church. The sermon, to which I had listened most attentively, had been delivered in a perfunctory, almost indifferent way, in a droning voice, and with hardly any gestures or inflection. What Mr. Patmos delivered had been read from a roll held in his hand, from which occasionally he lifted his eyes, and when he turned a leaf of the manuscript he sometimes took the opportunity to gesticulate in a feeble, inanimate way. Feeble and inanimate as he had been, I could not fail to observe that there were many there, besides the integers to whom his remarks had been especially addressed, who were deeply affected. My friend Oliver was profoundly so.

As we walked on in silence I took note of the appearance of the throng that issued forth from the portals of the cathedral. While within the walls the greater portion of these, especially the elders, were grave and subdued; but once outside they began laughing and chatting in the most frivolous and worldly way imaginable. They were without exception well dressed, and their manners were those of cultivated people.

Some of their conversation I could not avoid overhearing.

" Oh, Mira, did you notice that odious bonnet? "

" Whose? " responded the one addressed, a girl in her teens, as was also her companion.

" Why, Kate Puff's, to be sure."

" Yes, I noticed it; wasn't it abominable ? "

" And how rudely she behaved during the service—"

" I wasn't paying attention to her. It was as much as I could do to keep my face straight, seeing that Louisa Bolster being cancelled—"

" Louisa Bolster ! you don't mean to tell me that she was cancelled ! "

" She was, I saw her with my own eyes."

" You don't tell me ! "

" Isn't it too absurd ? "

" I should say so. The way that girl carries on is perfectly shocking."

" But how did you like Mr. Patmos? Isn't he fine-looking ? "

" La ! no, do you ? "

" By the way, to change the subject, when did you see Fred last ? "

The other girl blushed, and laughed, and tossed her

head. She made some response, but as they turned down a side street, I did not hear it.

Two stout, elderly gentlemen were directly behind us. At first they talked in low tones, but as they went on they became animated, and I caught something of what was said.

"What was the quotation at the last call?"

Some reply was made that I did not catch.

"It's going to be a bull market all next week," the first speaker continued, "mark my words."

"That depends upon the news from the East," said the other. "I tell you, prices are up now higher than they ought to be—"

"Perhaps so; but they're bound to go higher."

So they talked, elbowing their way past us. As they went by I recognized the two pompous, burly, well-fed, elderly men who sat in the pew in front of us in the cathedral, and who had been especially diligent in making those responses in which the congregation joined.

Oliver and I sat down in the little parlor of the inn, but for some time nothing was said. Oliver had his Arithmetic, and employed himself in perusing its contents. At last, holding the book open in his lap, he looked up at me.

"Did you not find the services very impressive this morning, Mr. Cliff?" he asked.

"Very," I answered.

"Mr. Patmos' discourse was a very able one," continued Oliver, "and one calculated to do great good."

"It was certainly very instructive."

"Yes, and what is more to the purpose, so doctrinal. Mr. Patmos is a most excellent man, and more than that, a good churchman."

" There were some few things that I did not exactly understand—"

" Ask any questions you like, Mr. Cliff. I shall be most happy to explain; though it did appear to me that the entire scheme of division was most ably elucidated in Mr. Patmos' excellent address to the integers."

" What was that thing that was let down from the roof ? "

Oliver looked at me with a horrified expression.

" Is it possible that is unknown to you ? "

I nodded.

" Strange, strange," murmured Oliver; " that was the Holy Raft."

" What is that ? "

Oliver hesitated.

" I hardly know how to explain," he answered, " so as to convey the sublime truth of which that is the sign and token to your unenlightened mind. It is the emblem of our division, whereby we are saved from Undersea. Thereby Numbers in a mysterious way rescued our fathers, and thereby rescued also us. They who are only ciphers become by the means of the Holy Raft and the written solution saved forever."

" Saved from what ? "

" From Undersea."

" Where is Undersea, and what is it ? "

" It is a place of endless drowning : a place of eternal torment, of groans and gasps, and frantic cries, and strangling and despair. A place where the Arch Ten holds sway over all who neglect the ordinances of the church and deny the truths of the Arithmetic; a place where Mathematics is not; but where despair reigns."

" Then to be saved one must believe—" I began.

" Believe on the Holy Raft," Oliver answered, solemnly. " Be a partaker in the ordinances, and be made an integer by the written solution."

" And is that the only way ? "

" The only way," he repeated.

" And if I do not, or cannot believe ? "

" Then you are eternally drowned. The Arithmetic is conclusive on that point. Here in this volume I turn to passage after passage, all having the same fearful import. The one quoted by Mr. Patmos in his sermon this morning is apt and to the point : ' Cut off the ciphers—' so it reads. What could be more conclusive ? Those who do not become grafted into the church by cancellation are ' cut off forever,' so the Arithmetic saith, ' from the right of the Divisor.' Thenceforth for them is nothing after ocean but Undersea."

" After ocean ? "

" In other words, after death."

" Oh, then ocean and death are equivalent terms."

" Certainly ; were you not at least familiar with that fact ? "

" It did not occur to me," I answered, a little embarrassed at Oliver's surprised tone.

He sighed deeply, as he said, " It is my sincere hope that what you have heard to-day may be the beginning of a new life to you, Mr. Cliff, so that at the last you may dwell forever in Oversea. Ah! here comes dinner : roast lamb and mint sauce. Draw up your chair, Mr. Cliff, we can converse upon these subjects again at our leisure."

After we had finished our pudding I ventured thoughtlessly to say that I should like a good cigar.

" A what ? " asked Oliver.

" A cigar. I haven't had a smoke in an age. I am not

a slave to the weed, but I confess now and then I like a good havanna."

Oliver stared.

"I wholly fail to understand you, Mr. Cliff. What is it you mean by a cigar or an havanna?"

At once I recollected myself. In my fraternizing with Oliver I had almost persuaded myself that old times had come again. The church services that morning, the snatches of conversation to which I had been a listener, and the geniality of my friend had been all so like home scenes, in the general tone of human sympathy pervading them, that I had been beguiled into forgetfulness. I blushed, and for a moment hesitated.

Oliver noted my embarrassment, but like the kindly fellow that he was, he put the matter aside.

"Don't fall to dreaming, Mr. Cliff," he said; "of all things don't allow yourself to do that. Now this afternoon you can have your choice; you can either remain here comfortably at home—take a nap if you choose—or, if you prefer it, there are services that you can attend—"

"Church services?"

Oliver smiled.

"Hardly that. We of the Established church are not willing to go quite that length. Say rather services of the other denominations. Our own we regard as the only real true church, though I am free to admit that in their way most of the others have their uses."

"Then there are other bodies of—"

"Sects; oh, yes, I am sorry to say that sectarianism is rife at the present day—painfully so."

"How many of these sects are there?"

"There are quite a number professing doctrines widely at variance with the truth. One—which, by the way, I

am perhaps not altogether justified in calling a sect—i
the Church of the Decimals. They are a part, so to
speak, of our own church, though out of the Establishment."

"And the others—what is their belief?"

"Oh, as to their belief," responded Oliver, airily, "what
they profess and what they practice are two very different
things."

"Then these others are not good people," I ventured
to remark.

Oliver shook his head.

"I am not prepared to say that there are not many
without the pale of the church who are actuated by good
motives. Some I know are estimable citizens; but yet
they are not partakers of the ordinances."

"Do they not believe as you believe?"

"In a measure I must answer yes; at least they profess
to."

"Do they believe in Mathematics?"

"Oh, yes, of course."

"And in Numbers?"

"They nearly all profess to do so; how sincerely I
cannot myself say."

"Do they believe in the raft?"

"That is, in the main, the profession that they make."

"Then in what respects do these sects differ from the
church?"

"They differ radically in many essentials—"

"For instance?"

"In the first place, take the Multipliers—"

"The Multipliers?"

"Yes; those who adhere to the doctrines of one Calvin

Multiple, who assert that Mathematics consist solely of
the Multiplier, Multiplicand, and Product—"

" That is absurd," I said involuntarily.

" Of course it is absurd ; but I am extremely glad to
see that you appear to grasp the subject so quickly.
Then that does really strike you as absurd ? "

" To be sure it does," I answered. honestly enough.

" There is great hope for you, Mr. Cliff.   I feel confident that in your case the right course is being taken."

" Are there other sects beside this one ? "

" Oh, yes ; the next in point of influence, and superior
to that which I have named in the sum of attendants, is
the Subtractors, who adhere to the pernicious notion that
the Subtrahend, Minuend, and Difference constitute Mathematics."

" How ridiculous ! " I observed, naturally feeling profoundly what I said.

" How glad I am that it presents itself to you in that
light," said Oliver, earnestly.   " It shows conclusively that
the morning's work has not been in vain.   Beside those
named there are others, inferior in influence, who promul-
gate their doctrines : the Adders, the Numerators, and the
Denominators.   Then there are others still, calling themselves the Reformed Adders, the Reformed Numerators,
and so on."

" But still you say that all these sects believe in certain
things in common with the church.   Please explain
wherein the exact difference lies."

" For one thing, they all—I may say all—refuse due
submission to the church ; impiously denying the validity of the authority of the apostle, and of the priests
and pastors, and sacrilegiously scouting the truth in

respect to the mysterious change whereby in the written solution ciphers are changed to integers."

"You speak of ciphers being changed to integers. I noticed a number of babies on the front row during that ceremony this morning."

"Oh, yes, the church receives infants."

" And do they too become integers by cancellation ? "

" Not by cancellation, but by the written solution."

" And is the effect the same ? "

" Precisely, in effect it is. When these infants arrive at mature years they renew their vows by cancellation."

" Do the other sects admit infants ? "

" Some do, and some do not ; but let me assure you, Mr. Cliff, that all these other sects have very widely departed from the truth. They have, or some of them have, a form by which they profess to believe a cipher can be converted into an integer by what they call a mental solution."

" Then they use no ink ? " I asked.

Oliver became very grave.

" It is not called ink, it is the written solution," he replied.

" I think I should like to go to one of these churches this afternoon," I said, after a pause, " if it is agreeable to you."

I saw that Oliver felt a little annoyed, but he was very polite, and expressed himself as being perfectly willing to accompany me.

" There is the Multipliers' place of expression on the corner of Main Street, just above here," said he. " They call it the Church of the Least Common Multiple. I do not know how true it is, never having heard him, but they say that Mr. Straitlase is a fine pulpit orator."

CHAPTER XII.

CHURCH OF THE LEAST COMMON MULTIPLE.

THE edifice that was usually known as the church of the "Least Common Multiple" was a structure of a very different character from the magnificent cathedral. It was, without and within, strikingly plain—indeed, barn-like in want of ornament.

We entered and were shown to seats with much politeness. These seats were arranged in rows facing in one direction, and the appearance of the interior did not differ greatly from one of our plainer churches in New York; that is, so far as the general characteristics went.

In the place usually allotted to the reading desk was a long platform, upon which were already seated when we arrived three persons in the ordinary attire of the islanders.

The audience collected slowly, and was not nearly so large, in proportion to the size of the building, as the one which had witnessed the ceremonial of the morning. There were many more women than men, and they all appeared to be persons of less wealth than the worshippers in the cathedral.

I call them worshippers; but the name in Inquirendo was expressers, or those who express opinions. The word express is also used by the islanders in the sense of to pray.

The service began by a hymn, started by one of the

gentlemen on the platform, who came forward, and, waving his hand, a simple little hurdy-gurdy in a loft overhead struck up a tune. The gentleman began to sing, keeping time with his hand and fore arm, which he kept working like the handle to a pump. One by one the congregation joined in, till, by the time they had arrived at the third verse, there was a great noise.

When the hymn was over the precentor sat down, and another of the trio stepped to the front. He raised his hands, and all in the pews bent their heads while a prayer was offered : a prayer so simple, so touching, so pathetic, so beautiful, that despite the terrible eccentricity of the language, I felt moved by it to the heart, and while the pastor poured out his petition to his unknown God, I felt my heart yearn as it never had before towards the Heavenly Father who knoweth the infirmities of his children, and remembereth we are all but dust. My eyes unconsciously filled with tears as the minister prayed for those in affliction or adversity, and I could not forbear, in view of my own forlorn condition, lifting up my own thoughts, not ashamed that they were in company with such strange speech.

The prayer closed with an appeal to Numbers for guidance and protection. " And may the product be with you all. Goosetracks."

There was another hymn, and then the Reverend Mr. Straitlase came forward.

" My text will be found on the seventh page of the Arithmetic, sixteenth line," said the Reverend Mr. Straitlase. " It includes in reality the whole of that line, but I shall confine my remarks chiefly to the two words ' mental solution.'

" The word solution in the original, as all commentators

agree, signifies to dissolve in its primary and to solve in
its secondary sense; so that it is a dissolving and a solv-
ing at one and the same time. The language of this passage is figurative, as is indeed the major part of the
Arithmetic, and if we would read the sacred volume aright,
we must very carefully avoid the evils of a too close ad-
herence to literalism. This is the rock upon which the
Established church and the Decimals have stumbled.

"How unworthy of Mathematics does it appear to us
who believe in the truth as it is in Numbers; how unworthy, I say, that a written solution should be deemed
essential to fit a cipher to become an integer. No, my
friends; it is not essential that we should be cancelled by
any written solution. The mental will suffice.

"You naturally ask the grounds of these conclusions. It
is not alone that as Multipliers we profess a certain rule;
but we ought to be able to refute the sophistries of those
who may seek to draw us aside from the straight path.

"Let me go back in history to the time of that illus-
trious reformer, Calvin Multiple. He came upon the
arena of the island at a time when all were given up to
the service of Decimals. He it was who burst our bonds,
and by pointing out the manifest fact that it was the product alone that should be our guide, he dealt a vigorous
blow for truth that even his enemies acknowledge.

"The product alone, did I say? no, it is the product enlightened by the Arithmetic.

"The teachings of the Arithmetic are plain; no one need
err therein; but until the time of Multiple they were
kept hidden from the people. The Arithmetic was not
suffered to be read, and in consequence men's minds
were kept in bondage. He caused the first copies to be
inscribed, and to-day it is the proud boast of the people

of Inquirendo that each family is provided with at least one.

"Before his time no other solution than the written was used in the process of cancellation. To-day a large majority use only the mental. Truth is mighty and will prevail. It is because it is truth that the mental solution has prevailed.

"It has been made a subject of objection to this doctrine that by taking sufficient time any one could cancel himself by a written solution, but that only a few were capable of performing the mental solution. I need only say in conclusion, beloved, that the ways of Mathematics are not as our ways, and that if it be foreordained that only a few should be cancelled the wisest and most befitting thing that we can do is to see that we are numbered among the few.   Goosetracks ! "

While I was diligently employed in listening for the grounds of the reverend gentleman's opinions, which I certainly understood he had promised to furnish, he brought his discourse to a close, as I thought, somewhat abruptly.

There was more singing, but as the music was insufferably poor, and as I was annoyed at what I regarded as a logical failure, I was not sorry when the service ended.

On the way back to the inn I expressed myself quite forcibly as to the want of logic in the discourse. Oliver, who had in fact dozed through the services, and who, having missed his comfortable nap at the inn, was now yawning, brightened up perceptibly at my remarks.

"Your perceptions are excellent, Mr. Cliff, most excellent. Really, I hardly gave you credit for such discernment. Of course, what was said was in the highest degree illogical."

" There didn't seem to be either head or tail to what he said. It was only a string of dogmatic assertion."

" Very true," responded Oliver. " To a churchman the cold platitudes of the Multipliers are entirely unsatisfying. The doctrines they teach are quite erroneous, but of all others that of the mental solution is the most absurd and unmathematical."

" They all seemed to be very devout and attentive," I observed.

" Oh, no doubt they are," said Oliver. " Do not think me uncharitable. I do not say that the Multipliers are not a very respectable body of citizens."

" What do they mean by goosetracks ? "

" Goosetracks?—h'm—well,—that means—in fact, it is—I don't know that I can explain exactly."

" I heard it also in the cathedral."

" Oh, yes—to be sure,—it is a form of assent, so to speak."

" Of assent? "

" Yes, literally it signifies—" Oliver scratched his head and looked puzzled. " The fact is, Mr. Cliff, that is quite an immaterial point. My mathematical studies were, as I think I told you, interrupted a great deal, but the idea to be conveyed is about this : that is our opinion. It is a term employed to convey the idea of strong emphasis."

That evening, although I was very tired, having attended church twice already—a proceeding to which I was wholly unaccustomed—Oliver had no difficulty in persuading me to go with him again.

This time we went to the church of Saint Complex Fraction of the Decimal denomination, or, as Oliver called it, the Arithmetical church. It was situated at a distance from our hotel, and although we found it large and elegant, it was in the midst of the very poorest quarter of the town. The length of our walk gave Oliver an excellent opportunity to impart information.

"The Decimals," he said, "are the oldest of all our denominations. They are, in fact, the original church established by our forefathers by direct command of Numbers. Together with the establishment they constitute the valid church of Numbers upon the island. They hold with us the same essential truths, and are imbued with the same spirit. In their expression you will find a strong similarity. The bond of sympathy is very powerful."

"You say there are no differences in your beliefs? "

"Very slight differences."

"Then why not unite ? "

"There is a very powerful body—with which I confess myself in hearty accord—who are looking expressively to a closer union with the mother church. In the opinion of many of our prelates the time is not far distant when we shall go over to the Decimals. Many are now uniting themselves singly ; but that I do not approve of, it weakens our own body. When the time is ripe the church as an organization will take action."

"How did it happen that you ever separated? "

"The separation occurred on no point of doctrine. We always have been, as we are to-day, in full and complete sympathy. It was in the main a political measure, brought about by the perversity of one of our crowns, one Henry Huit, who had a quarrel with the chief apostle. According to the best accounts—you can read up on that when we return, Mr. Mayland has a fine library—he had some trouble with his wife. I don't know exactly about what ; but the result was as I have said. He formed a new body, which has since been known as the Established

8

church. In essentials it differed in no particular from
the old church, though on account of the prejudices of
some of the sects—"

"Were there already other sects?" I interrupted.

"Oh, yes; the spirit of dissent was rampant at that
time; but very little is really known of that remote epoch.
Speaking of the sects a thought occurs to me, Mr. Cliff;
curious I never thought of it before—"

"What is that?"

"You say your father's name was W. Cliff?"

"Yes."

"I wonder, I do really wonder if that could be possible?"

"What could be possible?"

"One of the originators of these sects had a similar
name to yours. He was called Iccliff or Yccliff. W. Iccliff, I think it was. Do you think it likely that you belong to that family?"

"Very possible," I answered, not wishing to commit myself further than this.

Oliver slapped his hands together.

"I do verily believe it may prove to be so," he said, en-
thusiastically. "At all events, we shall probe the matter
to the bottom."

"You were telling me about the formation of the Established church," I said, anxious not to pursue this subject.

"Yes, our establishment, as it is at present constituted,
was brought about by this Henry Huit, and, as I stated,
there was an unfortunate pandering to the views of some
of the dissenters. The result was that in our expression
book, based for the most part upon the Arithmetic, were
incorporated many things that the mature judgment of
the church at the present day does not approve. How-

ever, I am happy to say that the Fast church is largely in the ascendant."

" The Fast church ? "

" That is the term designating those who favor a closer union, in fact an absolute one, with the Decimals."

" What are the others called ? "

Oliver laughed. " Oh, we call them slow; but there is only an insignificant minority left, which, after all, is of no vital importance."

" Between these two divisions, the fast and slow, what are the real points of difference? I ask because these questions interest me greatly."

" I assure you, Mr. Cliff, nothing affords me more pleasure than to give you all the information in my power. It is my duty in the first place, and beside that, your anxiety shows that your complete recovery is not remote. As to the slow church party I can only say this, that their opposition is frivolous and unbecoming. They make ridiculous objections to certain of our most cherished tenets, and have even gone to the extreme length of getting up a new expression book, from which they pretend to have extracted what they wickedly call the Romanizing germs : of course we churchmen know that this is preposterous, that the book is saturated through and through with Roman methods."

" Why do you call them Romans ? "

" Because the church—and by that term I mean all, both Decimals and Fast—uses the Roman method of notation exclusively."

" Do both branches, fast and slow, have the same ceremonies ? "

" By no means, and there is another point of the similar

ity. The Slows approximate in their mode of worship to
the Multipliers, and even use the mental solution."

"Please explain the Roman method."

"I would, Mr. Cliff, cheerfully," replied Oliver, "but
you can see for yourself. Here we are at the church."

CHAPTER XIII.

I REFUSE TO PARTAKE OF PARSNIPS

LOOKING up, I saw a stately portal, of an order of architecture somewhat similar to that of the great cathedral. Over it hung a vast pointed arch, decorated and adorned by a profusion of the most fantastic vagaries of hammered iron. On either side were great stone buttresses, and towering overhead were two immense spires reaching up towards the clouds. There were turrets and pinnacles also, and in every available spot images, graven in stone or cast in iron; some were beautiful, some grotesque, and some commonplace enough.

I had but a moment to view all these things, for Oliver passed directly on into the great doorway. With us went in a large concourse, almost all of the poorest class, but all with bent head and devout demeanor.

Oliver's manner was subdued and sober. Within the porch, on one side, was a niche, containing a sculptured group, and held on the shoulders of two iron cherubs was a silver flagon. To this Oliver went directly as I saw also others go. He dipped his finger in the flagon, and with the contents smeared his forehead lightly with a long stroke and beneath and above one dot, thus : ÷

Nothing that I now saw was in any degree surprising; but this, until I thought the matter over, was a little mysterious. I convinced myself, however, very speedily that this was the sign of division with which my friend had be-

117

daubed his forehead. Strains of music swelled forth as
the inner doors, swinging noiselessly, admitted us into the
church. It was in many respects the counterpart of the
cathedral, but there were points of dissimilarity that were
marked. For instance, back of the audience were large
recesses, all of a highly ornamental character, emblazoned
with gilt and gorgeous coloring. Here too were multi-
tudes of images, clothed in a profusion of robes in various
colors, but chiefly purple and scarlet. Over the entrance
to each alcove, and again, over the heads of the images,
were reproductions in iron of the great raft which was
swung in the cathedral. These were sometimes plain but
more often richly gilded, and in some instances embossed
with singular profusion. We sat down, and then while
the music filled the vast space, I looked towards the central platform. The arrangement here differed from that
in the cathedral, inasmuch as in the centre was no rostrum, but elevated ten or twelve feet upon four gilded
columns was an exact copy of the wooden raft. At first
so remarkable was the likeness, I was not sure that this
too was not of wood; but I was afterwards assured by
Oliver that it was of iron.

One of the strangest of the peculiarities to which I was
now attracted was the multiplicity of lights, not, as in the
cathedral, swung from the roof or on brackets, but standing on gilded candlesticks in front of and around the
various images. At the base of those gilded columns in
the centre were also statues, larger and more ornate
than those in the alcoves, and also more richly clad, and
before these the lights were almost innumerable. About
half a dozen young men and boys, apparelled in scarlet
raiment, fluttered about, in a meaningless manner, back

and forth, round and round, going through a remarkable series of evolutions, wholly incomprehensible to me.

The music, which had been low and soft and plaintive, now swelled out into a tide of harmony, and a rich pageant appeared as by magic; children, dressed as the others, came singing up from beneath the circular platform. These were followed by a numerous retinue, some with arms folded upon their breasts, others holding aloft gilded poles, on top of which were various carvings, imitation rafts and images, and others still bearing flagons on their heads, that smoked, sending up long slender spirals of incense, whose entrancing perfume was wafted towards us—which was, in fact, sorely needed, for the natural odor was intolerable.

They all now began singing or chanting a loud refrain, the words of which it was impossible to understand.

The chanting stopped, and one of the red-robed priests, holding a book in his right hand, circled round the dais, calling out at intervals :—

"Great Raft ! "

When he did so almost all the people shouted back something, reading out of the books which they too had. Oliver had one of these books, and by looking over his shoulder I was enabled to follow the responses.

"Great Raft ! " said the priest.

" Most excellent and extraordinary ! " responded the multitude with one accord.

" Remarkable pontoon ! " cried the priest.

" Floating bridge ! " answered the people.

" That helped us in our trouble ! "

" That will help us now."

" That helped our fathers ! "

" And will rescue us from eternal ocean ! "

" Great Raft ! "

" Wonderful ! "

" Mysterious thing ! "

" That we cannot comprehend ! "

So back and forward between the priest and the people these and similar epithets were bandied. While the
priest talked he circled round, and when his lungs became
fatigued another started up and circled in his turn in a
weary round.

It would be almost impossible, and certainly as fatiguing
to the reader as to myself, to recount the marvellous per-
formances that I was a witness to. The reading over,
there ensued a most extraordinary spectacle, wherein mingled priests, and boys, and candles, and rafts, and censers,
slowly revolving, like the images in a kaleidoscope, round
and round, while chants mingled with the voices repeat-
ing words at intervals.

I noticed that no one of all the throng was more attentive than Oliver, and that he made all the responses quite
as familiarly as any one else. On our way home I asked
him how it was that he, professing to belong to the Divisors, was so fervent in his observance of another and dissimilar ritual.

" The ritual is a little different, Mr. Cliff," replied
Oliver, " but there the difference practically ends."

On arriving at the inn Oliver showed me what he
called the " Rule " of the two churches, or, as I should
have called it, the creed. It was the same in the expression books of both the Divisors and the Decimals.
As I afterwards memorized it I am able to give it in
full :—

" I am of the opinion (or, ' I guess,' the priests being
privileged to allow the use of either form of expression)

that Mathematics made the island. I believe (or I guess
that I believe) that all there is to Mathematics is contained in Division, and consists of the Dividend, Divisor,
and Quotient. I believe (or I guess) that ocean has beyond it Oversea, and that Undersea is beneath it. I believe that Numbers will save me from Undersea, and that
by the raft I shall be conducted to Oversea. I believe
in the nine digits, and in the Four Ground Rules."

Oliver said much more to me that night than I have
been able to remember. In fact I was so sleepy that I
was hardly able to pay attention. When at last I retired
sleep came almost instantly, but my dreams were full of
strange sights, and weird and painful fancies, wherein,
jumbled together like phantoms, were Numerators and
Numbers, quotients and dividends, multiples and decimals, jogging each other and gibbering noisily all the long
night.

"How do you feel this morning, Mr. Cliff?" Oliver
asked, politely, at the breakfast-table.

"To be honest," I answered, "I feel like a mixed number."

I intended this only as a silly joke, not being—as the
kind reader has perhaps taken the pains to find out for
himself — very wise. This phrase happened, singularly
enough, to indicate that peculiar state of mind which with
us is sometimes alluded to as "the anxious seat." Of
course, being unaware of this, I was not a little astonished
when Oliver promptly grasped my hand and fervently
congratulated me.

I thought it best to dissemble, and to let Oliver do the
talking, a privilege of which he availed himself to the
utmost. His theology, or what he called his mathematics,
was not especially entertaining, for I had experienced a

surfeit of that the previous day; but when he began to allude to a continuance of our journey I listened with attention.

" I find," said Oliver, " that there are several families of the name of Ycliff at the east end, and therefore I suggest that we make our way thither by easy stages."

Of course I acquiesced ; not that my hopes were very strong that in any of these people I should discover relatives of my own, but impressed with the idea that the faster we got on the sooner our journey would be over, and the sooner I should be permitted to return to my beloved Margery.

I do not think that in the proper place any statement was made in respect to my purchase of a complete outfit of Inquirendian costume.   It is well that the reader should know that by the kindness of Dr. Setbon all this had been attended to, and that by him also my gold had been invested.   We therefore attracted no especial attention as we drove on across the country.   We traversed the sixth and the greater part of the seventh department without any special incident happening.

Oliver was very hopeful that in the Ycliffs I should find my kindred, and on Thursday morning, as we drove down a long slope, lined on both sides of the highway with extensive plantations, he kept asking if there was anything familiar in what I saw ; and when I felt myself compelled to answer that so far there was nothing, Oliver was evidently disappointed.

" I was in hopes," he said, " that when we crossed the hills you would recall something of the scene.   I feel convinced that your home is really at the east, and that when you are seen by your friends they will recognize you."

We drove into the chief town of the department about

noon, but there had been no such recognition. The inhabitants appeared to regard us with complete indifference, unless, as was sometimes the case, we wished to purchase something, when all we met became on the instant wondrously civil. I cannot say that their charges were extravagant, but I feel convinced that we usually paid too much.

I was very much gratified by observing that the prevailing sad colors of the ordinary Inquirendian citizen's costume was varied at the east end now and then, and at the tavern where we put up for dinner one of the hostlers had on a checked suit, not altogether dissimilar from the one that I had on that unfortunate morning when I was cast ashore upon the island.

" I am led to think that you are from the east," Oliver remarked, as we sat down to the table, "from the fact of the strong probability that your name is really Ycliff, and from the further fact that the inhabitants of the ninth department dress in a peculiar style."

I told Oliver that I had noticed the hostler.

"Yes," he answered, " my own attention was drawn to him. The eastern people are not usually fond of going far from home. I took an opportunity to question this man. He says he is acquainted with two families named Ycliff, and one is engaged in sheep raising. I think you testified that this was your father's business? "

I managed to make some confused reply.

" At all events," continued Oliver, " we can do no better than to push on towards the east. I feel the greatest confidence that if you once find yourself among familiar scenes that old memories will reawaken." Then dinner was brought in and Oliver addressed himself to carving the steak.

There was a dish of parsnips upon the table, which I passed to him.

"No; no parsnips to-day, Mr. Cliff," said he.

"I thought you were fond of parsnips," I said, surprised.

"So I am, exceedingly fond of them, but this is Thursday, and the church rules are stringent in respect to parsnips on Thursday."

"Oh! I was not aware of that," I said.

"Were you not? Did I not explain that to you?"

And Oliver continued, as he helped himself to the steak, and a plentiful supply of every other vegetable, to explain the motive of the church in proscribing parsnips.

"It is a mortification of the flesh," he said, "and is in the highest degree conducive to the mathematical life. While we are refraining, we are afforded an excellent opportunity for meditation and expression. The mind is rendered clear, and we are purged thereby from all gross and carnal desires."

"Is this a common custom," I asked, "among all the denominations?"

"By no means; it is the exclusive privilege of the Decimals, by which term I, of course, as you now understand, include the Fast of the Established church."

"And the Slows do not consider this essential?"

"The majority, I grieve to say, ignore this solemn obligation altogether."

Out of deference to my friend's principles I did not myself partake of parsnips. As a mixed number, I thought it prudent to abstain, and besides, I never was very fond of that vegetable.

CHAPTER XIV.

GALLWOOD'S PROMISED WIFE.

AFTER dinner, while we waited for the steers to finish their corn, we sat in the parlor of the inn. Upon the centre table were a number of papers and some pamphlet literature of an ephemeral character. To while away the time, I looked over some of these. The *Eighth Department Chronicle* was a stupid affair, filled with a mass of local nonsense and with absurd advertisements. The *Capital Register* was a little better, but I turned away from these and picked up a slender magazine, the title of which had some attraction for me. It was called the *Knowledgable.* I turned over the pages listlessly, and my eyes lighted upon the following lines:

THE POET PRIEST.

I.

There are times when the heart
 Of a poet is full,
And his thoughts would fain strike
 Though the weapon be dull;
And innate ideas
 Flash, like glittering swords,
Forth fierce from their scabbards
 Of thought into words.

II.

Oh! speed the glad time
 When the soul shall be free
From the bondage of sect,
 And shall hearken to me;

125

When thought shall be prophet
And poet be priest,
And the shackle opinion
From truth be released.

III.

There are pitiful things
In this island to-day;
Our mission it is
To drive doubt all away.
Things *are* what they seem,
And black never is white;
For creeds are but rhymes
For the rhythm of right.

"Who are these Knowledgables?" I asked.

Oliver was reading a red-covered pamphlet. He put it down as he replied:

"They are nothing but infidels, Mr. Cliff; if you will be advised by me, you will not even peruse their literature. It is pernicious in the extreme. They profess that they are guided by reason, and that morality is the sole end of man. That publication is edited by one Festus Idler, who is at the head of an institution called the Association for Mental Advancement. He is all the more dangerous, inasmuch as he professes to be doing a good work among the poor of the capital. I am told that he has a free school which is somewhat largely attended, where, in addition to secular knowledge, he imparts so-called instruction to the young in his peculiar views."

"A school of morality?"

"That is what he proclaims it to be. Yet it is not, I apprehend, needful to call your attention to the self-evident fact that no mere morality can be of any avail that is not rooted and grounded in the Arithmetic. The only truth

that this island knows, is that which has there been re
vealed—the truth as it is in Numbers."

So saying Oliver resumed his reading.

I put down the *Knowledgable*, and picked up a more
bulky magazine.

"That is the *Diatribe*," said Oliver, looking up. " In
that you will find nothing especially offensive, although the
tone of some of its articles of late has not been quite in
accord with the teachings of the church. It is, however,
purely literary in its character, and you will find nothing
between its covers particularly offensive. I must warn
you, Mr. Cliff, that as a mixed number, it behooves you
to be especially on your guard."

I turned over the pages of the *Diatribe*. Its contents
consisted of the usual miscellany ; but there was one little
poem that I read with interest. It was entitled

PERHAPS.

More of the island do they see
    Whose feet the highest summits press,
And more of death—that dreadful sea
    For whose deep wrong seems no redress.

Vain, o'er the dark horizon, vain
    For the white angel's wings I scan ;
They come, they go, they come again;
    But in them is there hope for man ?

But they who from deep caverns gaze,
    Or who on highest summits are,
Behold the glory he displays
    Who gave the eye to see the star.

Perhaps our Undersea begins
    Here; through eternity to run,
For those who suffer for the sins
    In some far purer island done.

I view the ocean—stormy, still—
　　It seems so sure; it seems so vast,
I only trust th' Almighty will
　　Some happy home shall give at last.

Where I shall find my Oversea
　　When the tense cord of living snaps
I do not know; but life must be;
　　For justice there is no perhaps.

No truth, whatever be its name,
　　To Mathematics is offence;
For love demands no mightier claim,
　　No holier creed than innocence.

We hear opinion's vain perhaps,
　　And think it faith to call unwise
Who hear the heart's low thunder claps
　　Of some grand cadence—truth's device.

Oh, truth, thy growth is slow of speed.
　　First must thy roots strike deeply down,
Thou hast the life within the seed,
　　The tree, alas! has not yet grown.

Prophet is he whose earnest brain
　　An upturned cup yet holdeth still,
Waiting in trust the holy rain,
　　That blackest clouds shall soonest fill;

Or one whose thoughts, like falling rain,
　　Pour forth from overflowing cup;
Who could not, if he would, restrain
　　What the glad sunlight gathered up.

And if upon his bosom writ
　　Some bow of hope mankind may mark,
Or on the tears wrung out of it,
　　What matter if himself be dark.

When I looked up from the perusal of these lines, which in portions had certainly impressed me as being very admirable. I found Oliver's eyes fixed upon mine.

" I see you have been reading Mr. Janus' poem," said
he, with a smile.

" It is called ' Perhaps,' " I answered. " I had not noticed the author's name."

" It is by Janus. That poem has excited considerable
attention."

" On what account ? "

" Chiefly, I presume, for the originality of the thought.
It is, of course, unarithmetical ; but being novel, there
have been found many who consider it a fair piece of
writing."

" It did not occur to me as being so very original," I answered. " The lines are very pretty, no doubt, but I
should not say that the ideas were new."

" They have been considered so."

" In what respect are they so original ? "

" It is universally admitted that Oversea is situated beyond the ocean, and that Undersea is beneath it ; but in
his poem Mr. Janus seems to imply that it may be situated above us. Of course, as a good churchman I cannot but regard this as rank heresy. We know very well
that there is nothing above us ; that is apparent to the
senses—nothing but the lights of the sky. Of course,
some concession is due to poetic license ; but there ought
to be a limit somewhere. I am exceedingly chary in perusing these secular publications. There is one verse
which is peculiarly objectionable."

" Which is that ? "

" Wherein he speaks of no truth being an offence to
Mathematics."

" Well, is not Mathematics all truth ? "

" Of course it is; but not in the sense in which Mr.
Janus writes. What could be more contrary to the spirit

9

of the Arithmetic than the statement that no better creed
was needed than innocence ? "

" That struck me as the most beautiful of all the
verses—"

" Beautiful ! oh, I am willing to grant that it is all beautiful.   No doubt the merit of the verses is considerable,
though I should say not sufficient to evoke the comment
they have.   But that is not the point ; it is this : all truth
is of Mathematics, that is granted ; but how contrary to
the Arithmetic that a cipher, innocent or guilty, should
have any value.   No, a cipher must first be washed in the
written solution ; must first become an integer to be saved
from ocean.   No cipher can float."

" Yet it seems to me that the thought expressed in that
verse is one that is deserving of attention."

" Mere words, Mr. Cliff," said Oliver, with much earnestness, " mere words.   We are expressly told that we must
rely upon the truth as it is in Numbers.   No doctrine is
more pregnant with fallacy than that the unenlightened
cipher can hope to be saved."

" But how is he to be enlightened ?   I ask for information, having a very strong desire to learn these things that
are to me yet so obscure—"

" Your yearning is commendable, Mr. Cliff."

" And I begin to feel," I continued, thinking with good
reason that this would be an incentive to Oliver, " some
glimmering that I have somewhere heard something similar before."

Oliver, as I had expected, brightened up at this.

" I am truly glad to hear you speak thus.   It gives me
much hope.   You ask how a cipher is to be enlightened.
I reply, by the change into an integer.   A cipher must
first be enlightened by the Arithmetic.   It is only by

Numbers that a cipher can be saved from ocean. Trust in the raft, Mr. Cliff. Have faith in its mysterious and awful power. You are now mixed, no doubt, and that · is encouraging. Mixture is a sure sign of ultimate solution. That is proverbial. In all your enquiries, I beseech you to abjure that reasonable spirit which thinks itself sufficient of itself. The church, through her accredited and responsible priests, is the only interpreter of the Arithmetic. Discard, as beneath your consideration and unworthy of it, all that tends to distract your mind from a consideration of what is vital and essential."

"But has a cipher no value whatever in the Arithmetic ? "

" I am astonished that you should ask that question, Mr. Cliff," replied Oliver, gravely, "after what you have heard and witnessed. No indeed, no value can by any possibility be attached to a cipher who has not been changed in his whole nature."

"I admit that a cipher of itself has no value. I see that now distinctly, but—"

" Much has been done, Mr. Cliff, much," Oliver interrupted, heartily. " When that is once admitted all the rest is easy. How simple the rest ! only trust, only believe."

"And yet," said I, "on reasonable grounds, that seem to me to be purely Arithmetical, which includes being reasonable—"

" Of course," said Oliver, sententiously.

"On those grounds." I continued, " the value of a cipher would depend upon its distance from the decimal point, would it not ? "

Oliver, who had been sitting leisurely with his red-

covered book open upon his knees, turned towards me
with a start.

. "Then you do indeed see that?" he exclaimed, earnestly.

"Why, of course, that is self-evident."

Oliver got up, and coming over to me grasped my hand
warmly.

"You have arrived at the truth," he said. "Wonderful,"
he continued, half to himself, "wonderful. The ways of
Mathematics are passing strange. Then you do thoroughly realize that."

" I do."

"And in the realization has not a chord been awakened
of some forgotten memory?"

"I confess," I responded, truthfully enough, "that all
this appears to have been instilled into me in earlier
years."

"Then be assured," said Oliver, "that the time of your
probation will now be short. If you see clearly that you,
as a cipher, depend upon your distance from the decimal
point, the time is not far distant when you will have passed
your mixed condition, and will resolve to connect yourself with the church, knowing that therein lies your only
hope of escape from the sea."

"Well," I said, "I shall think over all that you have so
kindly told me, and when I feel impelled to actually join
the church I shall mention it."

"Do so, do so," said Oliver; "but now we had better
be on our way. The steers are ready. Now that your
memory appears to have been in some degree re-awakened
I am more than ever anxious that you should visit those
families in the east."

It does not appear to me that any detailed description

of our further journeyings, either in the ninth or eastern department, or through the interior of the island, would be either profitable or entertaining. I believe that we traversed almost every nook and corner of the east end in search of my relatives, and interviewed any number of Ycliffs, who one and all promptly disowned me. All this was very irksome, and finally became so unbearable that I implored Oliver to let the matter rest.

"What great harm is done," I remonstrated, "even if I do fail to provide myself with a local habitation? Let us be on our way westward again."

Oliver sighed deeply and seemed much depressed.

"I had great hopes," he answered, "that here at the east something would have occurred to evoke the latent memory of your home; but it appears that this was not to be."

Again he sighed.

"Is it so important?" I asked.

"Yes, it is in the highest degree important. It was my uncle Dr. Setbon's most ardent wish that this should happen, for thereby no doubt you would have cleared yourself from the course of discipline, and probably on our return have been restored to perfect freedom."

"And is that absolutely essential?" I asked, feeling myself turning pale.

"No, I do not say absolutely," replied Oliver. "The strong presumptive evidence that your present mixed condition gives of mental soundness, may, and I trust in Mathematics doubtless will, have a very great influence. Should you elect to become an integer and come out before the island as a Mathematician it would have still greater weight; but—" Oliver hesitated, "I need not tell

you that for one cause or another you have made enemies—"

"Yes," I broke in impetuously, "that damned infernal
Gallwood, and that snivelling hypocrite Nudwink. They
are both precious scamps."

"Well, Mr. Cliff, perhaps you are not far astray in your
estimate of Mr. Nudwink. He professes to be a good
churchman, and yet uses only the mental solution. On
that ground alone I should be inclined to coincide with
you. In your reference to Gallwood you used two epithets
that are very peculiar. May I ask what the words damned
and infernal mean?"

I now felt myself blushing, as before I had felt myself
paling. I had spoken hotly and in wrath. Still the
words had been uttered and they must be explained.

"I had a bad habit once of swearing," I said, "and to
break myself of it I invented some meaningless phrases.
I find it answers the same purpose as a vent for emotion,
and hurts no one."

This explanation satisfied Oliver completely, so much
so that he complimented me on the ingenuity I displayed
when I made the matter clear that damned was a harmless word for drowned, and that infernal was a gentle
term for Undersea. I was able to interpret myself in
this manner by hanging around the stables on several
occasions when the steers were being harnessed, and
thereby overhearing the hostlers.

The first time this occurred I remember how astonished
I was. It was at the chief town of the eighth department,
and there had been some delay in bringing our conveyance. I found the chief of the stable, and made inquiry
for our steeds, if I may be permitted so to designate the
steers ; 'tis but a slight change of orthography.

It seemed that a stable-boy or hostler had been remiss, and on him the other vented himself with much foul language, which was returned, quite as well as a Yankee boy of twenty might have done, with lip.

"Why in Undersea and drowning didn't you have those steers ready when I told you?" demanded the boss.

The boy was sulkily getting out the vehicle.

"Mathematics drown you, why don't you answer?"

The other got very red in the face and muttered some reply.

"You Mathematics drowned Undersea cipher," roared the enraged livery man, "if I catch you forgetting again I'll discharge you."

"Go to Undersea," retorted the boy, "I ain't going to be bullied by you."

Then they had it hot and heavy. It was an excellent lesson for me, and one that was of avail to me in furnishing Oliver with an explanation of my meaningless jargon.

"The fact is," I continued, "I do not feel very mathematical when I think of that Gallwood."

"Yet it would be better if you did nothing further to provoke his anger," said Oliver.

"Then let him beware how he interferes with me. The way he interrupted that evening at the Governor's when Miss Margery and I were talking I regard as rude and ungentlemanly in the extreme."

"Yes, I know he can be abrupt in his manner," said Oliver, soberly, "but perhaps you gave him some little cause to feel irritated—"

"I! What cause have I ever given him? For some reason utterly unknown to me he seems to have taken a dislike—"

"Is it possible, Mr. Cliff, that you cannot surmise the reason?"

"Indeed I cannot."

"Have you not manifested some slight interest in Miss Margery, Mr. Cliff? Of course I understand nothing serious—"

"Nothing serious," I exclaimed, passionately. "Oliver, I will tell you, because I believe you are a true friend; but I would die for that girl—"

Oliver started. We were riding along at a slow trot up a long incline. Perhaps the oxen were tired (we had come a considerable distance), for when Oliver started, he unconsciously tugged at the lines, and we came to a dead halt in the road, and sat there looking into each other's eyes.

"Yes," I continued, "I love her as I do my very life."

"You astonish me," said Oliver, "beyond measure."

"I loved her the first time I saw her."

"That was at the convalescent ball—"

"No, I had seen her before that,—I had seen her in the garden—"

"From your window?"

"Yes."

"Have you spoken?"

"To her?"

"Yes."

"No, not yet."

"Then, Mr. Cliff," said Oliver, with a sigh of relief, "let me warn you never to do so."

"Why not?" I asked, with some dignity. "If I love her why should I not speak to her?"

"Because by so doing you will gain the deadly enmity of Gallwood forever. She is his promised wife."

CHAPTER XV.

TWO months had passed since Oliver and I left the asylum, when, having traversed the island from end to end, we again returned to it. It was an intensely hot day in August, and I was feeling terribly depressed, not only on account of the blow that I had received in learning of Margery's engagement, but from another and totally different cause.

Two days before, in passing through the third department, it had happened that I became a reluctant witness to a strange and remarkable spectacle, and one so entirely at variance with our own customs that it may perhaps be worth while to digress a little in order to give some account of what I saw. Thoughtlessly I asked my friend what was the meaning of a certain large concourse of people wending their way in the direction of the ocean that lay not far from the highway. Oliver responded by telling me that it was a funeral, and at the same time suggested that we might wait and witness the ceremonies.

My desire for information had been much lessened since I had been told that my beloved Margery was forever lost to me; but a spectacle of a gloomy nature was in consonance with my depressed feeling, and I acquiesced at once in the suggestion. It was a strange procession

137

in whose wake we followed. First came an immense cata-
falque drawn by thirty or more oxen, all moving at a slow
and stately walk; on either side of these and of the cata-
falque itself were youths and maidens, clad in white from
head to foot, wrapped in one immense garment that, covering their heads, trailed on the ground behind them.
They were all singing a weird and solemn dirge, in which
the whole of the cortege joined in a sort of chorus at intervals. On the vast palanquin, each one covered with
sheets of different dyes, were long narrow iron boxes that
I was aware from the manifest weight must be of iron,
and I was also aware that they were coffins. Behind
this peculiar hearse came a great multitude, partly on foot
and partly in the various conveyances peculiar to the
country; but all were sombre, and while some wept
others joined their voices in the sad refrain.

Besides the young singers there were others in the
midst of the procession who were clad in white. These
were the mourners. As we drew up on the crest of a
height overlooking the sea the cortege filed past, and
then I saw, seated among a number of others all clad in
white, the cadaverous visage of my ancient enemy, the
Reverend Mr. Nudwink. He saw me by the side of
Oliver; for one moment he fixed upon me a frigid, stony
look, but offering no sign of recognition, he passed
slowly on.

I now looked about me for signs of a graveyard, but
I could see none. Oliver motioned to me to follow him,
and in silence I did so. In silence the mourners filed
ahead with the clergymen, Nudwink prominent among
them. In silence the singers took their places, and the
multitude ranged themselves in a semi-circle round what
I at first supposed was the opening to a vault. There

were so many in front of me at first that it was with difficulty that I could see ; but it happened that Oliver had
been at the Mathematical Seminary with one of those who
officiated, and this young clergyman procured us standing
room near the spot where the funeral ceremonies were to
take place.

This clergyman was quite a young man, of a slender
build and pale countenance ; but in the short interval we
had to converse I found him exceedingly affable, not to
say jocular. He wore glasses, and had a slight cough,
and was in all other respects similar to the usual young
man in orders at home, except that his surplice was a
little more like a sheet, and was made of some heavy
woollen fabric.

Oliver introduced me, and Mr. Ezra Smalls (that was
his name) chattered with us placidly, divesting himself for
the time of the solemnity habitual to such an occasion.

"We're going to have a shower," said Oliver.

"Yes," replied Mr. Smalls, looking up, "I hope we
shall, for, through some inadvertence, the sexton has
omitted to bring the usual supply of water."

While I was wondering what this could mean, the
hearse had been disembarrassed of its load, and the iron
boxes or coffins were piled in tiers on either side of what
had appeared to be the gateway or door to a vault. A
few moments after Mr. Smalls was summoned to join the
other clergymen, and we were left alone. We could see,
however, all that was passing, and it is needless to say
that I was intensely interested.

The singing began again ; a chant, the words of which,
being so near, I was able to follow. It was singularly
beautiful. I can recall only a few lines, and even these
indistinctly. After the chant there was an expression

from Mr. Smalls, and then the Reverend Mr. Nudwink
delivered a discourse. It was not long. "His text,"
Mr. Nudwink stated, "was taken from the First Ground
'Rule, and was as follows: 'Only like numbers can be
added.'"

In the course of his remarks, which I make no effort to
report in full, Mr. Nudwink explained the difference that
existed between the various classes of men respecting natural characteristics. "First," he said, "are the naughts,
sunk in sin ; next, are the units, who are not naturally de-
praved, but are not on that account in a less perilous
condition ; next, the problems or mixed numbers, and last,
the integers. You know, my friends, that Arithmetical
scholars have differed greatly upon the great question of
the salvation of the cipher. All admit that he must become a whole number, but the point of difference is the
means by which this shall be accomplished. Some have
maintained that notation alone was sufficient, and others
that numeration would suffice. But the Arithmetic is
clear and precise. There is no uncertain sound about
this declaration that comes upon the ear like the sound of
many waters : 'A prime number has no divisor,' and
again, a 'composite number has other divisors,' thus
clearly proving that without the true divisor there was no
hope that there would be a quotient. Others have maintained the opinion that notation was of little moment, but
that love, charity, good-will, and so on, was all-sufficient.
Now I turn to the Arithmetic to see what these things
mean, and I read texts that appear to support all of these
seemingly contradictory views. I say appear to do so, for
we who believe and have been cancelled rejoice only in
Numbers and in the solution. I do not say only the written, but also the mental solution ; the main thing is to be

an integer. Trust to the saving power of the raft. We
assemble here to-day to commit to the ocean whence they
came the souls of twelve—" Some one by Mr. Nudwink's
side gave him a nudge, and whispered. He stopped for
a moment, stooped down, and listened. " Yes, fifteen, I
was in error," continued the clergyman, straightening up,
"beloved integers, I was in error; not that the exact
number matters—fifteen souls. Shall they all find an
abiding-place in Oversea ? It can be safely said of those
who relied upon the raft that they shall. Yes, beloved,
the raft can float their souls. ' How do I know that this is
true ? ' the prime number asks defiantly. I answer, ' By
notation.' No one has seen the raft float, but we have
the testimony of our fathers who passed through the flood
that it did float, and that Numbers was swallowed up
therefrom that our fathers might be saved. If our fathers
were thus saved so shall we be, and so shall the souls of
these now in the boxes be safe, and pass on to Oversea
through the waters. Be not deceived, beloved hearers,
there is no warrant in the Arithmetic for any other doctrine than this which I have taken for my text : 'Only
like numbers shall be added.' True, the Arithmetic
saith, ' A unit is one of a kind '—disposition being understood as it reads in the margin ; but of what avail is
mere kindness of disposition ? No, the cipher must become a problem presented for solution, must be cancelled
till there be no remainder, and this can only be done by
notation in Numbers, and numeration will then follow ;
but you must be first like Numbers."

Here the sermon ended. Mr. Nudwink got down
from the wagon which had served as an improvised pulpit. Four stout fellows now shouldered each a box, and
advanced towards the doors of iron. As the bearers ap-

proached others laid hold of these doors, and they, swinging, disclosed to my astonishment a wide opening that led
slantwise down the hill, fifty feet or more below to the sea.
This opening was not closed overhead, but was of solid
iron as to the bottom and sides, and perfectly smooth
throughout. Mr. Nudwink stood at the mouth of the
shaft, which was not unlike an immense coal shute. He
had a bottle in his hand, from which he sprinkled a few
drops on the iron box as it was held by the bearers for a
moment, while he pronounced in a loud voice the words,
" Water to water." Then he opened the Arithmetic and
read the following extracts :
" A factor of a Number is its Divisor."
" The Number above the line is called the Numerator."
" The Divisor and Quotient are factors of the Dividend."
When he had finished these quotations, Mr. Nudwink
again sprinkled his bottle over the box, saying again,
" Water to water," and at this the bearers heaved with all
their strength, and the heavy coffin went thundering down
the inclined plain till it reached the lower end, suspended
over the sea, into which it plunged with a great splash.
With the whole of the fifteen the same performance was
gone through, except that towards the close of the ob-
sequies it began to sprinkle, and the bottle was not
called into requisition. All the coffins were similar in
size and shape, and were massive in the extreme—all,
with one exception, which, though even more ponderous
than the rest, was shaped like a cylinder, and was, moreover, ornamented with various peculiar and singular devices.
As we drove away in the rain after the exercises were
over I asked Oliver to explain why it was that there was

this difference. In reply, he told me that the usual coffins were furnished at a fixed price from the "Fabrican," where they were kept in stock; but that if the deceased or his family desired a burial casket of a different pattern, and were able to pay for it, there existed no reason why their wants should not be gratified.

"The chief consideration with us all," said Oliver, "is that after life's journey shall be over our mortal remains shall be confided to the great deep."

"And is eternal life unattainable to those who are not consigned to the sea?" I asked.

Oliver looked at me in some astonishment.

"Of course not," he replied, "I thought you understood that. How else could the raft avail to conduct the integer to Oversea?"

"True," said I, "that was something I had not thought of before; but explain to me, if you please, why some prefer to have a different coffin."

"In the case of the person you saw buried to-day," answered Oliver, "he was a very eccentric man of large wealth. He had been, so I am told, ill for a long time, and amused himself with designing the peculiar round box which you saw. You know, of course, that the coffins are ordinarily arranged with hinges, so devised that no water can enter until the raft appears. These hinges this individual had made of silver. They were, I am told, of the most elaborate and expensive pattern, and there were, in addition, various appliances in the interior."

"Is it allowed to fill the coffin as any one's caprice may dictate?" I asked.

"Oh, yes; that is, if sufficient room be left for the body, and provided the external size be not too great for the sea-way or grave."

"What is the size of the sea-way?"

"Six feet each way."

"How many of these sea-ways are there?"

"There is one in each department; and besides that there is the criminals' sea-way in the fifth, and the non compos' sea-way in the fourth department."

"The non-compos'?" I asked, "pray what is that?"

"Can it be possible, Mr. Cliff, that you are not informed upon that point?" said Oliver, with a slight shudder. "Well, I will explain. Whenever a person, for any reason, such as habitual crime, chronic insanity, or any other cause, becomes unfit for society, and it has become certain that he never can be made fit, he being tried for his life before the Sun Court at the capital, then sentence of death is passed upon him, in order that society and the government may be relieved of the burden and danger of maintaining him."

While Oliver was speaking a light broke in upon my mind. I remembered the peculiar sensations that I had experienced when Mr. Mayland, in the court room, had alluded to a possible sentence of non compos in my own case. I now realized for the first time the danger in which I had been placed. My anxiety had in great measure departed, but I felt that I needed sympathy and consolation.

"Tell me, Oliver," I said, earnestly, "my lack of memory on certain points will not be a bar to my complete restoration to freedom, will it?"

Oliver shook his head, with some sadness.

"That I cannot tell," he answered, slowly; "you may rely upon me to make the most favorable report that is possible, but what the result may be I cannot possibly tell. It is a strong point, the very strongest possible point, that you have become a mixed number. That will have a very great influence ; but still there are circumstances which give great plausibility to Gallwood's claim that you are unfit for society—"

"You do not mean," I cried, turning pale, "you cannot mean that this infamous wretch would seek to have me pronounced—"

"Non compos?"

"Yes."

"It would not surprise me if that should be his object, Mr. Cliff; it would not, indeed, and therefore let me renew my caution to you in respect to the Governor's daughter."

I groaned aloud.

"I know it is hard," said Oliver, soothingly.

"Hard!" I exclaimed, with much bitterness, "it is deadly. I would willingly die to rescue that sweet girl from the clutches of such a scoundrel."

"You must not allow yourself to give way," said Oliver. "When we arrive at the asylum you will be subjected to another examination, and it is in the highest degree important that you should be able to pass it properly. If you can get upon the second stage of the course all may yet be well."

10

CHAPTER XVI.

I AM ENGAGED TO BE MARRIED.

DR. SETBON was at the asylum when we returned; but the Governor and his family were, I was told, at the cottage on the coast where they always went during the very hot weather. In the course of the next week the Governor returned, and I was subjected to a sort of examination. It was not very severe, however, for neither Gallwood nor Nudwink appeared to press the case against me. I fully understood that the best possible representations had been made in my favor by both Dr. Setbon and Oliver, and to my great joy, Mr. Mayland, having full authority, gave a speedy decision, placing me on the second stage of the course of discipline.

The privileges of this condition, as to which I had informed myself, were, for one who had for so long experienced the misfortune of surveillance, considerable. I was under certain disabilities; but, as these consisted only in being obliged to report at intervals of thirty-six days to the Governor, and to confine my wanderings solely to the limits of the third department, I did not regard them as excessively burdensome.

I was also told that in case I had any especial wish to visit any particular part of the island I could readily obtain the Governor's permission to do so by making a proper application. Of course my great desire now was to see Margery, but I had naturally some reluctance in pre-

146

ferring any request in this regard to Mr. Mayland. It fell
out, in a way much to my satisfaction, that Margery returned to the asylum for a brief visit, and to my unbounded satisfaction, I saw the girl whom I now regarded
as the one gleam of light in all the gloom of that desolate
place.

It seemed to me that she had grown lovelier than ever
in the two months that I had passed wandering away
from her. Her eyes lighted up, and a rosy blush overspread her smiling face as she held out her hand to me
with charming frankness. It was the day after her father
had rendered his decision in my favor when I met her
walking in the garden ; that same happy garden where, in
the days of my incarceration, I had first seen her.

She showed no coyness, but seemed, as I know she was,
glad to see me.

"Papa has been telling me about you," she said, "and
now that you can do so, I hope you will come and see us
at our summer house."

How my heart beat at that invitation, and then sank
immediately at the thought which flashed across my mind
of the vanity of all my hopes, and of the claim that the
infamous Gallwood had over this sweet creature.

I suppose Margery must have noticed some change in
my countenance, for she asked me at once with manifest
concern if I was not well.

I made an evasive answer, which, however, did not
satisfy her.

"Are you in any trouble, Mr. Cliff ? " she asked.

"Not more so than usual," I responded.

"But to-day I should think you would be feeling happy,
now that you are almost free."

"I should be happy," I answered, sadly, "very happy, if

it were not for having heard something lately that has
filled my heart with grief."

"What is it that you have heard, Mr. Cliff?" she
asked, with downcast eyes.

Should I tell her?—ought I?—dare I? I recalled the
warning of Oliver, and the fact that I was as yet not
wholly free. Would it be prudent to speak? While I
was debating these things, she raised her eyes furtively to
mine.

"Will you not tell me what it is that you have heard
that troubles you?"

With that sweetly voiced question, and in the light of
those lovely eyes, full of kindness and sympathy, I forgot
my prudence; I forgot—as wiser men than I have done
before—all but the fact of the presence of the woman I
loved.

"I heard that you were engaged to be married to—that
—to Mr. Gallwood."

Margery started, blushing hotly, and drew herself up
with an air of some indignation.

"Who told you that, Mr. Cliff?" she asked, impetuously.

"I heard it."

"And do you believe it?"

"What else could I do but believe it?"

"Distrust it," she answered. "After what I told you
once you should have distrusted such a story."

Then I remembered her remark that she was not only
not engaged but she never should be. In recalling this
I felt strangely renewed hope.

"I do remember that," I said, joyously. "Then it is not
true?"

"Of course it is not true. Do you think that I could
ever marry such a man?"

"I could hardly believe it, Miss Margery; but it has distressed me, nevertheless, more than you can think."

She blushed again vividly and her eyes were again cast down.

We were sitting on an iron bench in a secluded part of the garden. Over our heads and through a simple lattice all about us clambered a full-blooming vine of the morning glory. We were hidden away from all the world. A wild thrill of my long pent-up feelings suddenly burst forth. I could restrain myself no longer in the presence of the girl whom I so ardently loved.

"Margery, oh, my dearest Margery," I cried, turning towards her, "have you not seen how devotedly I love you? Do you not feel that it is I, and I alone, who claims your heart? Can I, dare I hope?"

I listened breathlessly for an answer. I leaned toward her. I looked into her downcast eyes, and then, moving nearer, put out my hand and took her own little one in mine. Thrill after thrill of exultant joy shot through me. She did not resist, but still, with downcast eyes and crimson cheeks, she suffered me to touch her.

"Shall it be as I wish, my own dear Margery?" I murmured, softly.

Her lips syllabled the low answer, dear to every lover's heart; the single sweet word, "Yes."

"Look at me, Margery," I exclaimed, passionately, pressing close to her side, and now holding her beautiful hands, one in each of mine, "look into my eyes."

She raised her long lashes, and the full light of the blue—a tiny speck astray from the heavens above us—flashed upon me. There was love in those sweet eyes; love, and peace, and gladness, and unutterable hope for us both.

"Darling, oh, my darling," I cried, and clasping my arms about her in one joyous embrace, I drew her rosebud lips, unresisting, to my own.

Oh, the sweetness of that hour. Long we sat there in the morning-gloried shade, thinking not of the flight of time, nor of aught, in fact, but our mutual happiness. Confessing her love for me with maiden shyness, Margery's head was reclined upon my breast. With my arm about her she felt no dread of the future, and I was buoyant with the strength of youth, and impressed with that power and confidence that is part of the blessing of life's morning.

Before we left the arbor Margery had told me everything. Gallwood had indeed sought her as his bride: but, even before she had seen me that evening at the ball, she had felt a strange repulsion towards her father's cousin. He had been persistent, and had won her father's confidence and esteem.

"But papa has not been in the least unkind," said Margery. "Oh, he is so good, so tender-hearted. Papa would not hurt a fly. He has urged me to try and like Roth, but I have always told him it could never be."

"Roth!" I said, "is that his name?"

"Yes, his name is Roth Gallwood," she answered.

"How glad I am, dearest Margery," I said, with my lips close to hers, "how glad I am that you were so determined."

"So am I glad," she responded; "more than ever now."

Saying this she looked blushingly into my eyes. Ah! that sweet time of love's delight; how sweet it was. We lingered long in the garden, roused only from our languid happiness by the deep stroke of the bell in the tower of the asylum striking one.

Margery started.

"Oh! I ought not to have lingered so long," she exclaimed; "papa will be wondering what has kept me."

"Shall you tell him, dearest?"

"Perhaps you had better tell him, John," she answered.

"Is he alone at home?"

"I think he will be after dinner. I am not sure."

"Who is there with him now?"

Margery's eyes sank. "Mr. Gallwood is with him now; he came last night."

"Oh, how I hate that man, Margery," I said, shuddering.

"But you must be very careful, John, not to show it. Remember, you are yet on the course of discipline. Perhaps it would be wiser, after all, that you should say nothing to papa until that is settled. Roth is very vindictive. There is no knowing what he may do."

"What can he do? I do not fear him."

We were now strolling through the garden; a thick screen of dahlias lined the path, hiding us from every eye. Margery leaned upon my arm, and looking up full in my face she responded, almost tearfully: "Oh, John, be careful; do not let your temper have the advantage over you. Gallwood is implacable. He will do all he can to hurt you."

"How can he hurt me?"

"He can; be sure he can, unless you are careful."

"Then for your sake, my darling, I shall be upon my guard."

We had now passed the hedge of dahlias. As we crossed the open space in that portion of the garden where I had first seen Margery among the roses and lilies, there was a sash raised in the iron turret above our heads.

Involuntarily we both looked up. There in the open window, looking down upon us with a sinister smile upon his dark countenance, sat Gallwood himself.

I felt poor Margery shudder as she leaned upon my arm. I whispered a word of reassurance to her, and then my eyes met the man's, I suppose somewhat defiantly.

"A pleasant walk, Miss Margery," said Gallwood, with affected politeness, bowing grimly as he spoke.

Margery raised her face.

"A pleasant walk," he repeated.

"Confound his impudence," I said, angrily.

"Say nothing; pray say nothing," said Margery, beseechingly. "You must not irritate him."

"Thank you, cousin," she said, aloud, "I have been showing Mr. Cliff the garden."

Mr. Gallwood made no reply. We walked on till we reached the gate leading to the Governor's house. "Shall I come this afternoon to see your father, Margery?" I asked at the gate.

"Oh, John," she responded, here yes filling with tears, "I feel so despondent I hardly know what to say. Roth will know. He will understand, and he will do all he can to prejudice papa. Oh, how unhappy I am." She covered her face with her hands and burst into an uncontrollable agony of tears.

I strove to console her, but all I could say was of no avail; she refused to be comforted.

"Go, John," she said at last through her sobs, "you had better go. Papa will be waiting for me. Yes, perhaps you had better come this afternoon. I don't know— do as you think best; but oh, dear John, be assured, whatever happens, of my dear love."

She burst out crying, more bitterly than ever, but would say no more. She gave me her hand, I held it one brief moment, and then she turned and ran into the house.

I returned to the asylum, where I was now comfortably provided with a pleasant apartment, my mind, it is needless to say, in a strange turmoil of conflicting emotions.

My interview with Mr. Mayland (for I had one that afternoon) passed off much better than I had reason to anticipate. I stated the case in respect to my love for Margery with all the skill and earnestness of which I was master. The Governor listened to me with politeness, but thinly disguised astonishment. He said nothing to interrupt me while I was speaking, but when I concluded, he asked me, not unkindly, whether I was aware of the fact that it was a very unusual proceeding for a person on the course of discipline to entertain seriously views in respect to matrimony. I answered with due deference that I presumed that this was the case. "Perhaps," I observed, taking credit to myself for the ingenuity of the answer, "perhaps it is also unusual for a young lady to accept as satisfactory the proposals of a gentleman under such circumstances."

"It is, indeed," responded the Governor; but though he evidently made an effort to preserve a demure expression, he could not forbear smiling, probably on account of the audacity of my suggestion.

"My daughter may have hinted to you, Mr. Cliff," continued the Governor, "that her mother and I have entertained other views."

"Yes, I have heard so," I answered, sorrowfully.

"It has been almost settled that Mr. Gallwood was to be our daughter's husband. He would be very grievously disappointed."

" I sincerely hope that you will so far grievously disappoint him as to permit your daughter to accept my addresses."

" There must be no engagement, Mr. Cliff."

My face fell.

" At least until you are wholly free.   I must, of course, consult with Margery and with Mrs. Mayland.   This. is a serious matter, and one that requires the deepest consideration."

" I may see her, may I not ? "

Mr. Mayland remained thoughtful for a moment.

" I do not feel myself at liberty to prohibit your seeing her altogether," he said at last, " but it will not be best that you should see her often.   In fact, there will be but little opportunity, inasmuch as we return to Lunatico cottage next Fourth-day; this being outside the limits of the third department will necessitate a discontinuance of all visits, for a time at least."   This information was not pleasing to me ; it was a misadventure upon which I had not reckoned ; but although my suit had not wholly prospered, yet, on thinking the whole matter over calmly, I could not but felicitate myself upon the courteous reception that had been accorded to my suit by Mr. Mayland. The next morning I saw Margery again in the garden.

No restriction was placed upon our meetings : but while we were together I could see that Margery was nervous and troubled.   It is needless to say that I did all that lay in my power to console her.   I pointed out to her the certainty that I should very shortly be a free man, and that then I could claim her hand without fear of refusal.

I felt very strong in the fact that my few five-dollar gold pieces were safely invested, and were now drawing a comfortable income in Inquirendian funds.   Money was a

power in the island as elsewhere.   Although at these in-
terviews no further mention was made directly of Gallwood,
yet I well knew that it was the haunting fear of his mach-
inations that caused Margery's trouble.   At last, I took
a sorrowful farewell of my darling.   We parted in the
arbor where our troth had been plighted.   She returned
to the villa, where the ox-team was in readiness to convey her to her father's country seat, while I remained
under the bower of morning-glories, from which, alas! the
bloom of the morning had now departed.   I sat there
brooding in deep thought, till, hearing a quick, impatient
step on the gravel walk, I looked up, and there, in the
doorway, with an evil light in his bold eyes, stood Roth
Gallwood.

CHAPTER XVII.

GALLWOOD'S LITTLE SUPPER.

IT was far more with wrath than fear that I trembled at
the sight of this man; and yet, had I not also good
cause to fear? Had I not made of him even a more
bitter enemy than ever? Did I not now stand between
him and the object of his unhallowed love? What mercy
could I expect at his hands? None, I told myself
promptly, none. Yet what especial harm could he do me?
I shuddered as I thought of Oliver's mysterious warning,
and thought also of my own ignorance of the law, and of
what Gallwood's official position might enable him to ac-
complish. But I took courage from the fact that he was
subordinate in authority to the Governor, who now, at least
for Margery's sake, would not be likely to wish me harm.

I returned the man's insolent and defiant glance with
one that had at least in it an equal determination. I rose
to my feet promptly.

"To what am I indebted for this—intrusion?" I asked,
with no pretence at civility.

"Ah, you show your teeth quickly," sneered Gallwood,
as he came in without ceremony, and seated himself in
the further corner of the arbor.

"Sit down, Mr. Cliff," he continued, with a cynical
smile, "sit down, and do not allow yourself to become excited."

I scowled.

" I shall not interrupt you long; pray be seated."

Still with the scowl upon my face I resumed my seat.

" Are you aware," pursued Gallwood, breaking off a spray of the convolvulus and twirling it nonchalantly in his fingers, " are you quite aware that in the absence of Governor Mayland from the department all his duties— and powers—have become mine ? "

I felt myself turning red.   I had not indeed thought of this.

Gallwood noticed my change of countenance.   His own brightened directly.

" I tell you this, Mr. Cliff, solely to put you on your guard. You may have thought, and perhaps still think, that I am unfriendly to you. You would err greatly if you continued to hold such views. I do assure you that I have your good at heart, and for that reason I have come to warn you. Your great trouble, I see plainly, is your ungovernable temper. Now I must beg of you to make a serious effort to restrain yourself. I need not say that you have my hearty congratulations upon attaining the second stage of the course of discipline ; but if you will calmly reflect you cannot fail to perceive that there is a wide gulf between your present situation and perfect freedom. My interest in you personally, Mr. Cliff, is very great, but in my official position my interest in any individual must of necessity, and from duty, be subordinated to the obligations I am under to society. Do you understand that ? "

I could not divest myself of the conviction that Gallwood was my bitter and determined enemy ; but his tone and manner and words were so polite and so courteous, that being a gentleman, I could not forbear to reply with equal civility.

"I understand that you have a double duty to perform," I answered.

"It lies in a great measure with you, Mr. Cliff," he continued, "whether that duty—at least respecting yourself—shall be made difficult and irksome, or whether you can relieve me of the greater part of my responsibility."

"Explain yourself," I said, uneasily.

"I will do so in few words: the second stage of the course of discipline permits you to wander at your own pleasure anywhere within the limits of the third department—"

"So I am informed—"

"Anywhere," Gallwood went on, disregarding my interruption, "provided you report every four weeks here at the asylum."

"Yes."

"There is a clause in the law respecting patients on the second stage of the course which authorizes the Governor, or in his absence, his deputy—"

"Yourself?"

"Myself—which in the present instance authorizes me to cause a strict watch to be placed upon the actions and movements of any one whose conduct is not, in my judgment, in all respects such as could be implicitly trusted—"

"And do you propose to have such a watch kept over me?" I exclaimed, with some heat.

"Tut, tut, Mr. Cliff," he responded, airily, waving the sprig in his hand with a little dramatic gesture. "Not quite so fast. You draw your inferences much too quickly. I had not referred to you—"

"No, but you meant to," I blurted out.

"Indeed no; you are much mistaken. I referred to

another, whose condition, I grieve to say, I deem somewhat precarious—"

"To another?" I stammered, confused.

"Yes, to another."

"To whom?"

"Ah, that I cannot tell you, Mr. Cliff, at least not until all our arrangements are perfected, and we come to a
distinct understanding."

"Do I know the person to whom you refer?"

"Oh, yes."

"Then why not tell me his name?"

"Listen, Mr. Cliff; I will tell you the exact situation,
and you can then judge better if it will be worth your
while to accept a proposition that I shall make to you."

"I shall listen, of course," I answered, by this time
much mollified.

"Your own position, Mr. Cliff, has, by the events of the
last few days, become changed for the better, very greatly.
I have only lately learned this fact—indeed, it was only to-
day that I was informed by my cousin, the Governor, that
this was the case."

"What was it he told you, Mr. Gallwood?" I inquired,
now all eagerness.

"The Governor told me of your proposals respecting
his daughter, and he told me, furthermore, that if you both
remained of the same mind at the close of the summer
that he should give his consent."

"He did?" I exclaimed, rapturously, "and you—"

Gallwood passed his hand across his brow with a
weary motion.

"Oh, I can only congratulate you both. I do so
heartily, Mr. Cliff, and I beg of you from this day to
cease regarding me in the light of an enemy. It is true

that at one time I sought the hand of my cousin's daughter in marriage; but I am not the man to press a suit that I find is distasteful. No matter how much my own heart is burdened I accept my position, if not with cheerfulness, at any rate, Mr. Cliff, with submission to the will of Mathematics—if there be such a thing," he added, with a lowering brow.

It is needless to say that I felt myself greatly relieved by what Gallwood had said. It was not only that from him had come the first intimation that Mr. Mayland was disposed to regard my suit with favor, but that such was the apparent sincerity of the man's manner that I could not but regard him as having spoken in serious earnest.

"What have you to say to my proposal?"

"What proposal?"

"Did you not understand? I did not, perhaps, finish my suggestion; it was this, that you should yourself be placed upon special duty with this other person of whom I spoke. He is on the second stage of the course, as you are; but, unlike you, I do not regard him as wholly trustworthy. He has the limits of the department; but I should like, if the matter can be so arranged, that you would accompany him in his rambles, being careful continually to note any undue eccentricities—"

"As an attendant, do you mean?" I asked, not at all liking the suggestion.

"Oh, no, not at all in that capacity; rather as a friend. You would bear to him very much the same relation that Oliver bore to you."

"That alters the case," I replied, promptly.

"You will find him a finished gentleman," continued

Gallwood. "One with whom you could associate on terms of perfect equality."

"Can you not tell me his name now?"

"Better wait until this evening, Mr. Cliff. We are to have a little supper at my rooms, and then you will meet him."

To this I assented.

"I am very glad that matters have taken this shape," I said. "Between us, Mr. Gallwood, there need be no further concealments. I can only say how pleased I am that there is to be no enmity—"

"Don't mention it, Mr. Cliff," Gallwood interrupted. "Pray don't. It is true that in one matter you have—" He smiled. "You understand?"

He seemed so pleasant, indeed jocose, that I could not forbear responding in a vein of similar pleasantry.

"You mean that I have prevailed where you have failed?" I said, with a laugh.

"Just so," he replied, good-humoredly.

"At all events," I said, more seriously, "I am very glad to find that you cherish no resentment."

"I assure you, none whatever," said Gallwood.

"I am very glad," I responded.

"Oh, well," he continued, "we all have our ups and downs. You know the proverb, 'What can't be cured must be endured.' I cherish no malice."

So we parted. I was much pleased at the very unexpected turn that my affairs had taken. It did indeed appear as if the clouds were lifting, and that I might now look forward to a union with Margery, untrammelled by any untoward event. It was in this joyous frame of mind that I made myself ready for Gallwood's entertainment. A servant had presented me with a politely worded note of invitation, and at the designated hour I repaired to the west wing, where the assistant superintendent's rooms were situated.

I found Dr. Setbon waiting at the door. He shook me warmly by the hand.

"You are looking exceedingly well, Mr. Cliff," he remarked, amiably. "Your trip with my nephew has put new life and vigor into you."

"Where is Oliver, doctor?" I asked, "I haven't seen him for several days."

"He has unfortunately been called away to the bedside of a dying friend," replied the doctor, his voice betraying the sympathy he felt.

I expressed my sorrow at the tidings.

"Poor fellow! poor fellow!" continued the doctor, "it will be a great blow to his family, and a great loss to the church."

"Was this friend you speak of in the church?" I asked, politely.

"Yes, he had only just left the seminary. He was in the class with Oliver, and was greatly esteemed by him. It was very sudden. To be cut off so in the very blush of his youth is indeed sad. I am sure I do not know what his poor mother will do without him. Mr. Smalls was her sole support."

"Mr. Smalls!" I exclaimed, astonished. "Not the Mr. Smalls that I met last week?"

"I do not know. Did you meet him?"

"Yes, I met him at the funeral."

"Oh! were you there? I did not know that."

"Yes, I was there."

"It was there that he was smitten," said the doctor, soberly.

" What was the trouble ? "

" Sea-sickness," responded the doctor, with a deep sigh.

" Sea-sickness ? " said I, amazed.

" You may well appear astonished. Mr. Smalls was ordinarily so careful."

I had, as the observant reader may have noticed, learned to restrain myself, but by dint of diligent and prudent inquiry I became informed that after the ceremonies were over, Mr. Smalls had thoughtlessly permitted himself to stroll along the beach underneath the rocks, with his expression book and his own holy thoughts. Unmindful of the flight of time, he had walked on and been overtaken by the tide.

Though not the exact language Dr. Setbon used, this was the purport of his remarks.

" Then he was drowned ! " I exclaimed, horrified.

The doctor turned, and fixed upon me a peculiar look.

" Drowned ! Oh, no, indeed ; Mr. Smalls trusted all his life to the raft that is abundantly able to save. Is it likely that ocean would have any power over him ? "

" Then why—" I began, but stopped, instantly biting my lip, and aware of the imprudence of showing ignorance.

" The truth is, he got wet through. Horrible, horrible."

The doctor shuddered.

" And caught cold ? " I suggested.

" Oh, no, the disease is not complicated in any way, but it is none the less mortal. It is a clear case of sea-sickness, for which there is no cure. He now lies at Lunatico, Mr. Mayland's house, which is situated not far from the spot where he was attacked, just across the line in the second department."

" Has he had proper medical attendance ? "

" The very best. I should myself have attended him
but that my duties here prevented. They sent at once to
the capital, and two of the most celebrated physicians
drove over at once. Dr. Wadewater Muir and Dr. Waltz
are both there, day and night."

" And you say there is no hope ? "

" There seems to be none whatever. No cure for the
sea-sickness has yet been discovered; that is, no real
specific."

" I believe I could effect a cure if I were allowed to
see him," I said, musingly.

" You ! " said Dr. Setbon with astonishment, " I was
not aware that you had ever made a study of medicine."

" No, I have not made it a study; but still I feel convinced that I could point out a remedy—"

" What is the remedy ? "

" It would be necessary for me to communicate that in
person."

" Is it a faith-cure ? "

" Well, yes," I responded, irresolutely, thinking that if I
could only convince poor Mr. Smalls that his ducking
was not necessarily fatal he would recover. " Yes, my
cure has, I confess, something of that nature about it."

Dr. Setbon smiled incredulously.

" That is wholly unscientific," he remarked, " and besides, Mr. Nudwink has essayed that already without
avail."

The dinner was really a charmingly gotten up affair, for
which Gallwood deserved the utmost credit. My former
aversion to this man had now so entirely disappeared that
I was able to meet him without an approach to rancor,
and indeed with even some cordiality. He shook hands

with me very warmly, and then presented me to those of
the guests with whom I was not acquainted. Among
those with whom I had not been on familiar terms during
the period since I returned to the asylum, I found, to my
very great astonishment, my old antagonist, Bullinger.
Gallwood brought him up to me as I sat talking to Dr.
Setbon and one of the convalescents. Bullinger's face
wore a genial smile, and he appeared to be very much
pleased to see me. He sat down by us at once and entered into conversation.

I found that Bullinger was a changed man. He had
altogether lost that air of secrecy and caution that I had
once noticed, and attributed—rightly, in great part—to
his unbalanced mind. Now he was frank and open in his
manner, meeting my eye without embarrassment, and conversing fluently and quietly on ordinary topics.

In the course of the evening, after the repast was over,
I had an opportunity for a quiet talk alone in one corner
with him. He manifested no reluctance to refer to his
unfortunate situation; but of his own accord spoke of the
unpleasant occurrence at the ball, and, with much mag-
nanimity, took all the blame upon himself.

"Happily," he said, "I am, I hope, at last relieved of
the terrible delusions that have weighed like an incubus
upon me for many weary months. I am now on the second stage of the course, and am confidently led to expect
that by the time summer is over I shall be completely restored to liberty. But how is it with yourself, Mr. Cliff?
I presume that your probation is over, is it not?"

"Not altogether," I answered. "I am, like yourself,
still in the second stage; but I also have strong hopes
that my freedom is not long delayed."

"Curious freaks those were of mine, were they not?" said Bullinger, with a laugh.

"To what do you refer?" said I, not knowing exactly how far asylum etiquette justified an acquiescence in a patient's views of a freak.

Bullinger laughed heartily.

"Do not be afraid to speak out, Mr. Cliff," he said, "I know what your opinions must be. Of course I referred to my own delusion respecting the spiders. It was all excessively real to me at the time, I assure you, and distressing also. I must blame you, Mr. Cliff—or perhaps bless you, who knows, the vagaries of the human mind are so unfathomable—for the turn you gave to my imagination. I now verily believe that it was the relief from one continual strain of thought of which you were the cause that restored me, under the skilled hands of Dr. Setbon, to mental health."

"Of which I was the cause? How so?"

"Oh, your suggestion respecting the sand fleas. You remember my undue violence, and I hope have long since pardoned it—"

"Of course."

"Well, that hint set my mind running in a new channel. In the end the current purified itself, and now I am happy to say that I feel and know myself to be a well man."

"Certainly," I said, "that is apparent."

"And are you wholly cured of your notions, Mr. Cliff?"

"In respect to the fleas?"

Bullinger laughed again heartily. "Oh, no; I understand now that your remarks before the ball were only a pretext to get rid of me. I refer to your delusion respecting Oversea, and all that."

"Oh, that?" I answered, as if the subject was a trivial one, "of course that is all over."

"I am glad to hear it, Mr. Cliff, truly glad. I am sure that you and I will sympathize. Now, I am proposing to myself a little quiet excursion into the country next week, just a run in the department for awhile to get braced up. What do you say to joining me?"

"I should like it above all things," I responded, "but I am—that is—it has been suggested—Mr. Gallwood spoke to me—"

"Oh, well, if you have another engagement—"

"It is not exactly an engagement."

"At any rate," said Bullinger, "my invitation stands open. I shall not leave for a day or two, and if you change your mind let me know."

The evening passed away very pleasantly. With several of those present I was already acquainted, and there were others with whom I became quite friendly. I found that poor Mr. Smalls' distressing condition was known to all, and his sad fate was the subject of deep commiseration.

In the course of the evening I said a word to Gallwood about him.

Gallwood was a little startled at first by my suggestion of a cure. I had discreetly said nothing as to any faith being required, and probably the man imagined that I referred to the use of some drug.

"You might try," he said, "I see no harm in that."

"Is it likely that his disease will prove immediately fatal?" I asked.

"Oh, no, he may linger on for some time yet, if the doctors only leave him alone." Gallwood smiled cynically. "I say this," he continued, "with all due respect to the profession."

CHAPTER XVIII.

GALLWOOD SMILED AGAIN.

THE next morning I took occasion to speak to Gallwood in respect to his proposition, telling him at the same time the suggestion that Bullinger had made.

Gallwood smiled.

"I suppose," said he, "that you would like to know the name of the travelling companion that I proposed for you?"

"I should, very much," I replied. "There were Mr. Humpath and ——; they both appeared to be gentlemen, but I confess I noticed that they seemed a trifle erratic."

Gallwood smiled again.

"How prone we all are to err," he said. "Neither of those you mentioned is the one; they are not even patients. The first you mentioned is a young physician from the fourth department, who has just come as an assistant to Dr. Setbon, with high recommendations, and the other is one of the recently appointed attendants."

I was very much abashed at my own want of judgment. I stammered out some reply, to the effect that I had noticed in these persons' conversation a something that appeared to me to indicate eccentricity.

"Oh, the young doctor is eccentric, I grant," replied Gallwood; "but what was it that struck you as especially odd?"

"He harped so continually upon an operation that he claimed to have recently performed—"

168

"Oh, that! why he has gained his reputation by that very operation—"

"But such a strange result!" I said, incredulously.

"Did it appear to you to be strange?" Gallwood asked, musingly.

"It did indeed."

"How so?"

"His claiming that by an operation on the brain he was enabled to alter completely the man's character seemed to be remarkable in the highest degree."

"I confess it was remarkable; but far from indicating eccentricity it is an evidence of the very highest intellect."

"And did he really, as he stated, so modify the man's character as to render him gentle, kind, and lovely in disposition who had before been stubborn and brutal?"

"He did indeed."

"Wonderful!"

"Yes, it is. The result of the operation has attracted a great deal of attention from scientists on the island."

"Wonderful," I repeated.

"Heretofore," continued Gallwood, "it has been all the other way. Such operations have not been, as you may perhaps know in a general way, uncommon; but the result has always been to impair rather than strengthen the moral faculties. The subject in this case was a confirmed drunkard, a thief by instinct, and who, for a deadly assault committed in passion, was serving out a long sentence at hard labor in the prison. He was employed in the forge room; while there, there was a terrible accident, by which several were killed and many seriously injured. This man was struck on the head by an iron pin, which pierced his skull. He was given up to die; but this young doctor performed an operation, by which, as I stated, not only was his physical health restored, but his moral health as well. He has now completely recovered, taken the pledge to totally abstain from liquor, and has signified his intention to join the church. It is said that he recognizes clearly the hand of Mathematics in what has befallen him."

"How one can be mistaken," I remarked. "I thought that young man was talking most wildly."

Gallwood smiled again.

"It requires an expert in these matters," he said, "to judge correctly."

"So it seems ; but now, Mr. Gallwood, if not either of those whom I have mentioned, who is it that is to be my companion ? "

Gallwood smiled again.

"It is Bullinger—"

"Bullinger ? "

"Yes."

"You do not mean to tell me that his cure is not complete ? "

"Well, as I told you, Mr. Cliff, he is on the second stage of the course, and therefore I have no direct right of supervision over his actions : but I have casually observed certain little things that have caused me considerable uneasiness—but, Mr. Cliff, you have not told me whether it will please you to make the trip with Bullinger."

"Of course," I answered. "I do not profess to be a judge. but it did seem to me that Bullinger had quite recovered the tone of his mind. He talked most rationally to me. In fact, we were in sympathy almost from the first words that passed between us. The very fact that he alluded so calmly to his own previous mental deficiencies was a convincing proof to my mind that all trouble was over."

" That goes some distance, I confess," responded Gallwood.

" What is the trouble, then ? " I asked, with some anxiety. " If I am to be in his society continually for any length of time I ought surely to know his weak point, in order, for his benefit, that I may be on my guard."

" Certainly : it is right you should know. What I say to you, Mr. Cliff, is of course in the strictest confidence."

" Of course."

" His old delusions," pursued Gallwood, "have completely vanished, that you remarked yourself ; but I regret to say that I have observed slight evidences—imperceptible to a non-expert, perhaps—which have led me to form the conclusion that what we call in technical language secondary symptoms are likely to supervene."

" Of what do they consist ? "

Gallwood smiled again.

" This is a recondite and abstruse matter," he said, speaking now very seriously, " but one to which it behoves you to pay diligent attention. In early youth Bullinger was admitted to the fold of the Established church, and was duly cancelled. As he approached man's estate he gave 'abundant evidence,' as the parsons say, of a radical change. He was devoted to his scientific pursuits, it is true, but he was likewise a devout attendant upon the ordinances of religion. He has been under our care here at the asylum for over a year. After he was pronounced convalescent, you remember the outbreak of which he was guilty at the ball towards yourself. Of course he had then to be placed under restraint, but still that we did not regard as a very serious matter. These things must all be taken in their bearings towards the general delusion, what ever that may be. He gradually recovered, and now that he has been placed on the second stage of the course of discipline, only one source of uneasiness remains : his views on religious matters appear to have undergone a radical change."

" In what respect ? " I inquired.

" He has become a Free-thinker," replied Gallwood.

" And is that evidence of the secondary symptoms ? "

" It would not be by itself ; that is, the holding of free opinions is no evidence of insanity. If it were," Gallwood continued, with another smile, " some of the most acute minds in the island would be considered impaired. It is not that, by any means ; it is rather the tendency to a change showing a laxity of fixed principle. In our code of medical jurisprudence, nothing is better established than that this has a direct tendency towards the condition called secondary."

" I understand."

" I knew that you would, Mr. Cliff. I was well aware that the mere statement of the case would be sufficient."

" Do you wish me to try and turn Bullinger's mind away from his new opinions ? "

" By no means," replied Gallwood, hastily ; " rather, if you can do so conscientiously, fall in with his views. In your case no harm will be done, and it may be the means of effecting a complete cure."

" I am not bigoted."

" I know you are not ; in fact—" Gallwood's voice sank to a whisper, " I have observed you very closely, Mr. Cliff, of late, and I have partially satisfied myself that you hold somewhat similar views to my own on these metaphysical subjects."

I started slightly. Could it be possible that Gallwood had perceived the absurdity of which I was so well aware?

"What are your views, Mr. Gallwood?" I asked.

Gallwood smiled again.

"I may speak to you in confidence, may I not?" he said.

"You may."

"Then I frankly avow that to me all these so-called religions are the merest vagaries. I do not believe in Mathematics, nor in Numbers, nor in the Digits, and I consider that the Arithmetic is only valuable for the principles it contains, nothing more."

I smiled in my turn.

"You see what I mean, Mr. Cliff?"

"Perfectly."

"I speak in the strictest confidence."

"Oh, I understand that."

"And you, Mr. Cliff, are not your views in accord with mine?"

I hesitated. It is true that by his frankness Gallwood had quite won my confidence; but still had I not in some measure committed myself to Oliver? I had avowed myself to be a mixed number, and I felt some doubt whether I had not thereby placed myself on record as desiring a more intimate union with the branch of the church to which he belonged.

"I can say this much, Mr. Gallwood, at all events," I said, evasively, "that what you have said at least I quite fully concur in."

"In respect to the principles contained in the Arithmetic being all there is of value in it?"

"Certainly."

"Then it seems our views do coincide. May I suggest?"

"Anything," I replied.

"Then if I were in your place I should go to Bullinger at once and accept his proposition. It is all the better that the suggestion came from him. Here," continued Gallwood, "here are tickets for a lecture to be delivered this evening at the capital by a certain noted Free-thinker. I am sure you will be interested, and it will be an excellent means of worming—I mean, ingratiating yourself with Bullinger."

"But the capital is out of the department—"

"Oh, I shall provide for that. If you will come to my office about noon I will furnish you both with passes."

"Thank you," I responded heartily, "I shall be very glad to go."

Gallwood was about turning away when it occurred to me that all his kindness deserved some further recognition. I held out my hand.

"Mr. Gallwood," I said, as he shook me by the hand kindly, "I have been greatly deceived in you. I must take this opportunity of expressing my gratitude to you for the magnanimous manner in which you have acted towards me."

Gallwood smiled again.

"Don't mention it, Mr. Cliff," he responded, hastily, "pray don't mention it."

In the evening, according to this understanding, Bullinger and I drove to the capital. Bullinger was very much delighted when he found that I had concluded to accept his invitation. During the drive I had an excellent opportunity to become better acquainted with the man, an opportunity of which I availed myself to the utmost. He gave me to understand, without directly proclaiming the fact, that he was in entire sympathy with the views of Colonel Hurtheart the lecturer. Of course I was very guarded, not affirming or denying my own position in the matter, but letting it be known that whatever my own views might be, I was tolerant of the opinions of others. I preserved a degree of reticence in all our conversation, while I endeavored to draw Bullinger out. In this I was successful, and by the time we reached the hall where the lecture was to be given I had completely acquired his confidence.

As a contrast to the report of the ceremonials of the church which I have, perhaps with too much minuteness, set down in the preceding pages, I venture to give a synopsis of Mr. Hurtheart's address. It was reported at great length in the *Free Speech* the next day; but the condensed account which I read in the *Vanitus* will be sufficient, I think, for the general reader. Rather than give my own recollection of the orator's effort I reproduce verbatim what the *Vanitus* printed:

"INQUIRENDO'S INFIDEL ORATOR.

"HE RIDICULES MATHEMATICAL CREEDS AND HIS HEARERS ROAR WITH LAUGHTER AND DELIGHT.

"THE POETRY OF BLASPHEMY.

" *Hurtheart says that all the churches and all the ministers on the island cannot crush him.*

"Mr. Hurtheart appeared last evening in Bloughem Hall before a somewhat promiscuous audience. He appears to have thriven by his recent tour to the east end, for his portly appearance certainly indicated prosperity. His round face and smooth skull fairly shone with the oil of unspiritual joy, and his whole appearance was redolent of self-satisfaction. His appearance on the platform evoked considerable applause, on the subsidence of which Mr. Hurtheart began his address. In the course of his remarks he wagged his big glossy head, and snapped his little twinkling eyes, and thumped his big pussy hand down on the cushion in front of him with quite as much unction as if he had not been employed in the unholy work to which he devotes himself. As usual, the gentleman charged a round sum for admission, thereby contriving to make his peculiar views profitable as well as sensational.

"'What is religion?' the gentleman began by asking. He paused and looked around the hall. One or two snickered, but no one responded.

"'Do you give it up?'

"The persons who had snickered before now snickered again, and it was evident also there were a few fresh snickers.

"'I see you all give it up,' said Hurtheart, 'and so do I, and so do all sensible people; but if you go to the parsons and ask them what is religion, do you think they give it up? Not much, they don't. What is very wonderful, they have all got a different answer. Now when a joker asks a conundrum usually there is only one answer; but you ask a Decimal priest what is religion and he will tell you one long yarn; you ask a Multiplier and he'll tell you another. The Adders and the Reformed Adders, the Subtractors and the Reformed Subtractors, and so on to the end of the list, they have all got a yarn to tell you.

"'If this was really a joke it would not be so bad, it

would only be foolishness ; but these people are all in serious earnest. I don't wonder much either that they are so, for these fellows are getting salaries for telling their different yarns, and a continuance of the salaries depends upon their being able to convince a sufficient number of people that the answer they give is the true answer. Of course, religion does do some good. I noticed the other day that a man was knocked down and beaten in the streets of this city. Some one said that the man who was beaten was a coward. " No," said the man, " I am not a coward, but it's against the rules of the church to fight on Thursdays ; " so you see religion has a powerful hold on society still. I suppose this same man wouldn't eat parsnips on Thursday either—unless. he was almighty hungry. (Laughter.) Over at the east end—I have just come from there, so I know—they are all Adders, and you can say what you like about the raft and the written solution—it isn't blasphemy. But I will give you a word of warning : don't say anything against the mental solution, for that's the worst kind of blasphemy. In order to know whether you are a blasphemer or not you must first be sure what department you are in.

" ' Here in this city it is blasphemy to say that Mathematics is not up there under the dome of the cathedral, hoisted up out of the way to keep him from being stolen, or perhaps from running off and getting lost. Imagine the principles of Mathematics getting lost. Now, when the priests wish to get a little Mathematics they lower him down in the raft from up there under the roof, and get a little piece, and then they hoist him back again. The Decimals and some of these other fellows have—they say they have, and we must believe them—actually appropriated—mind, I don't say stolen—pieces of Mathematics, and they go

12

round showing their breast-pins or their rings and telling us how much better off they are than we, for they have got a piece of the true raft. And they put a little glass around it—why?—to keep Mathematics from rotting. (Great laughter.)

"'The church does nothing for the island. It does nothing for you. It does nothing for me; though you may well believe it would like to. It would like to drown me; that's what it would like to do for me, if it could. (Renewed laughter.)

"' Let me read you what the Multipliers say they believe —they say so, mind you, and I am complimentary in saying that I think they lie. (Laughter.) It isn't often that one gets as good a. chance to compliment an enemy. I don't myself believe there is a Multiplier in all the island who is wicked enough actually to believe this. (Here Mr. Hurtheart read in full the Multipliers' Confession of Faith.) What do you call such stuff? I call it a libel on Mathematics. The Mathematicians are all united about one thing, apparently, however much they may differ about others. This thing that they unite upon happens, curiously enough, to be by far the most ludicrous and improbable of all their fables. They tell us that some ages ago—they do not even pretend to guess how many—this island was a desolate, uninhabited place, and that by the will of Mathematics the nine digits were sent hither from Oversea; that something happened—what no one knows —that put the digits in great peril, and that a certain individual, having some kind of intimate relationship to Mathematics, called Numbers, rescued our forefathers on the thing they call the raft, and which it is pretended came over the ocean. This absurd story is, after all, the sole basis of all this ridiculous mummery called worship,

wherein Numbers is given credit for what is in its very
nature an impossibility. I have gone myself to the cathedral and asked to be allowed to investigate this raft;
but the answer they make is about in substance this : " If
you don't get right away from here we'll send for a police-
man and have you locked up."   " But I only want to
investigate," I said.   "We shan't let you investigate,"
they answered.   " Let me prove that the raft can do as you
say," I said.   "No, you can't prove it ; you must believe it
because we say so."   " Isn't that pretty hard on me ? " I
say.   " It is the will of Mathematics," they answer. And I
want Mathematics to understand, right here and now, that
I don't believe he had any hand in getting up any such
absurdity. I don't myself believe in Mathematics; but it
is just possible that there may be one, and if so I want it
distinctly understood that I thought him a good deal better
than the Multipliers do. This creed of the Multipliers
would make a cheese laugh, and shock the moral sense
of an isosceles triangle. The Multipliers say that I
hurt their feelings when I tell them that there is no
Undersea; they don't seem to think they hurt mine when
they say I am going to Undersea, and the truth is, they
don't. I believe this—and I only believe it because I
know it, not because some one has told me it is in the
Arithmetic. I believe that there is nothing beyond ocean ;
nothing at all. Beyond the island it is all ocean, and nothing but ocean. There is no Oversea, no Undersea, but
just ocean. I should like to believe otherwise if I could,
but I can't. I suppose you think it strange that I should
say I want to believe ; but I will tell you—it will take but
a moment—why I wish I could believe in Oversea. When
I was a young man, and that is now years ago, I lost my
mother. If ever a good woman lived on this island it

was she. She spent her life going about doing good. She believed in Oversea, and expressed herself night and morning for me that I too might believe. She loved me, and I loved her. She died and was buried, and in her grave in the sacred solemn ocean our love lies deep, and dead too, forever. With her last lips she bade me seek her. Her last look, ere in the dark her sweet spirit took its eternal leave of life, was bent imploringly upon me. We parted, as I know, forever; but could a religion be found that would bring me to her, how gladly would I believe! But no; I stretch out my arms in vain towards the infinite and the lonely powers of nature; north, and south, and east, and west the stormy billows beat of the dark and dread expanse whose tempestuous lashings touch but to kill, and whose farther shores are lost to mortal vision and knowledge in the fog that never lifts, but broods perpetually over the eternal deep.'

"(There was a sound as of weeping among the audience. Like a flash the orator's pathetic mood and manner vanished, a smile stole over his rotund countenance, and in a jocular tone he resumed.) 'I will also tell you why I wish I could believe in Undersea. Two nights ago I was lecturing in this very hall, and while I was here in this very place, guileless as a lamb, some miscreant came in, went to the cloak-room where I had left them, and stole my hat and cane. It is not likely that I shall ever see that hat and cane again. It is even less likely that I shall ever see the thief. Now, if I was sure there was an Undersea there might be just a bare chance that my friend the thief would be come up with; as it is, alas! I fear he has got the best of me to all eternity.' "

It was after midnight when we drove through the great

iron gates into the court-yard of the asylum ; those same
iron gates through which, in charge of the officers of the
law, I had been driven, despondent and wretched, nearly
three months before.   It was after midnight, but there
was a light burning in Mr. Gallwood's office, and as we
drove up he opened the door and came out to us.

"Well, gentlemen," he said, politely, "how did you
enjoy the lecture ? "

"Wonderfully," answered Bullinger, "I was charmed."

"And you, Mr. Cliff ? "

"I was pleased, of course," I responded.   "Who could
fail to be otherwise ?   Mr. Hurtheart is an excellent
speaker, fluent, witty, and effective."

"But what did you think of his doctrines ? " said Gallwood, with a smile.

"As to his doctrines," I answered, "they were, it appeared to me, in the main, simple negations ; but he made
some splendid points, and stated some manifest truths in
a most convincing way."

The light from the open door shone full upon Gallwood's face.   As I bade him good-night our eyes met.

"I have enjoyed the evening exceedingly," I said ; and
without responding, Gallwood smiled again.

CHAPTER XIX.

IT had now been decided that Bullinger and I should take our journey together. When this was settled I had some conversation with Gallwood in regard to my duties towards my companion. Gallwood made it appear that I was doing the cause of humanity a service in being willing to assist in restoring the patient to mental health. He was exceedingly complimentary in all he said, and his manner emboldened me to make a farther request to be allowed to see Mr. Smalls.

"He is Oliver's friend," I said, "and if by any possibility I could benefit him, I should think myself very fortunate."

Gallwood rather evaded a direct answer.

"You will be in the vicinity of Mr. Mayland's summer house," he said, "in a day or two ; that is, if you take the route suggested by Bullinger : the line of the third department passes within a stone's throw of the door of Lunatico Cottage where poor Mr. Smalls now lies. You may have an opportunity of communicating with Oliver there. If he sanctions an interview I shall offer no opposition."

With this I was obliged to be content, and the next day Bullinger and I set out, with the same team of steers that I had previously hired. It seemed strange to me to be passing over the road (now virtually a free man) over which I had been driven in such hot haste on the first day of my

182

sojourn in the island. It was all one to Bullinger which way we went, or how fast we drove, and it may well be imagined that I did not delay. We reached the chief town of the department about the hour that in Inquirendo corresponds to our two o'clock. As it happened we took dinner at the same restaurant at which I had procured my first meal. The keeper did not recognize me, nor afterwards, as we strolled past the hat store, did the hatter or his assistant. Before we started again on our journey diligent inquiry was made respecting the location of the village, which we had found, by a map at the asylum, lay not over half a mile or so from Lunatico Cottage. We reached this village about sunset, and repairing at once to the only inn were provided with tolerably comfortable quarters.

We had our supper, and then, before it grew dark, strolled out over the hills in the direction of the boundary line between the two departments. After the heat of the day the evening air was delicious. The country was lovely in its garb of verdure, and the breeze that came up from the sea was refreshing in the extreme.

The path which we had been directed to take skirted the edge of the high bank overlooking the sea, winding in and out, up and down, and from its being well worn we judged it to be much frequented. It was not long before we came in sight of a villa, almost on the verge of the sea and elevated some forty feet or so above it. My heart beat wildly, throbbing as young hearts will, under the sweet influence of its nearness to the beloved one. Under that roof, I told myself, was Margery. Was she thinking of me, I wondered? Was there not some subtle chain that binds two loving ones so that she might be aware of my coming? It was while occupied with these meditations that a figure was observed coming from the direction of the villa. It was now fast growing dusky, but I recognized at once my friend Oliver.

Bullinger too recognized him, and as we had now reached a stout iron fence crossed by a stile, we sat down there and waited. Oliver soon approached. His face wore an expression of care and anxiety, but he welcomed us, nevertheless, with much joy. He explained that poor Mr. Smalls was in a very precarious state, and was not expected to survive the night.

"Are the doctors with him?" asked Bullinger.

"Oh, yes, they have not left him, day nor night, since he was stricken down. I am on my way now to the village for a remedy that has been prescribed." Oliver's eyes were full of tears as he continued, "Not that I have any hope that it will restore my poor friend, but only that it may possibly prolong his life, and assuage the pangs of his last moments."

"Does Mr. Smalls suffer much?" I asked.

"No," Oliver responded, languidly, "it is only a gradual wasting away of the vital powers."

"What is this remedy that you are about procuring?" asked Bullinger.

"It is a preparation called sea-powder," replied Oliver. "I am told that the scientific name for it is *sodide of chlorium*. It has been prescribed not by either Dr. Muir or Dr. Waltz, but by the young physician at the asylum, who, it seems, is a relative of Mr. Smalls. He was sent for yesterday, and only arrived this afternoon: young Dr. Humpath."

"Oh, Dr. Humpath!" said Bullinger. "I know him intimately. That is the young doctor we met at Mr. Gallwood's the other evening, Mr. Cliff."

"He has a wide reputation," continued Oliver, "and

seems confident that he may be able to effect a cure; but I have little faith myself in his ability to do so. His system is widely at variance with established usages, and the other physicians are greatly incensed at his having been called in."

"But you say they are there still?" said Bullinger.

"Yes, they have not left the house; but they have positively refused to consult with Dr. Humpath. The latter, in the short time we had together, told me that his system consisted in applying what he termed a counter-actant. This sodide of chlorium is obtained, so it is stated, in the form of a white powder from the sea itself. It is only obtained with great difficulty and much risk of life by those who make a living by procuring it. It is in consequence very expensive. Taken undiluted it is a deadly poison; but in doses of one grain in a barrel, and one drop of this solution three times a day, it is said by Dr. Humpath to be efficacious."

"What do the other doctors say respecting this mode of treatment?" asked Bullinger.

"They ridicule it; but it is poor Mrs. Smalls' desire that no means shall be left untried to save her boy. The faith-cure is also being tried; but, alas! ineffectually. Mr. Nudwink has been expressing himself since the dawn, and poor Mr. Smalls has my own pin with a piece of the true raft in it on his bosom."

Oliver's face was turned towards the sea, and Bullinger gave me a look which implied the strongest possible incredulity.

We went on for a time in silence in the direction of the village. I strongly desired to ask about Margery, but a sense of modesty forbade. At last Oliver spoke: "Would

you like to see the spot where poor Mr. Smalls met his
doom?"

Of course Bullinger and I responded in the affirmative,
and then, going a little off the path, Oliver pointed down
the steep declivity to the sandy beach below, over which
the sea calmly rose and fell.

"There," said Oliver, almost weeping, "he was walking along the shore, musing on the mystery that lay before him, and taking no note of the flight of time. While
so engaged the winds arose, and he, poor fellow, was wet
through almost before he was aware of his peril."   .

At Oliver's pathos all my interest revived in the unfortunate Mr. Smalls, and while we pursued our way towards
the village pharmacy, I asked many questions as to the
young clergyman's condition.

"It is beautiful to see him," said Oliver : "no repining,
no murmurs; all peace, content, and perfect joy. His
reliance upon Numbers and the merits of the raft is
something that I have never seen equalled. Mr. Humpath is, I am told, an unbeliever, but even he was
softened."

"Can nothing be done to save him?" I said.

"All is being done that lies in the power of mortal
man," answered Oliver.

Then, impressed with a strong sense of duty, I told Oliver
how I felt ; that I was assured I could cure Mr. Smalls
if I were only permitted to make the attempt. I was extremely guarded in all I said, and took an opportunity to
speak when Bullinger had gone to the end of the counter
to inspect a new kind of rotatory tooth-brush.

At first Oliver was very incredulous.

"What objection would there be?" I asked, anxiously.

"I don't know that there would be any special objection," said Oliver, doubtfully. " Mrs. Smalls would try anything."

"Then why should I not try?"

"There is one thing you appear to have forgotten," said Oliver. " Mr. Mayland's house is not in this department."

"What difference need that make?"

" I don't know that it would really make any. That would depend upon Mr. Gallwood."

"I don't think he would object."

" If you choose to run the risk," said Oliver, " I will arrange it."

With this, of course, I was completely satisfied. Bullinger was to be trusted, I knew, and having his promise of secrecy, and with the understanding that I was to be back at the inn before midnight, I went with Oliver across the fields to the Governor's house.

My hope, which I could not forbear cherishing, of seeing Margery was destined to be realized. In fact, she was waiting, being anxious in respect to Mr. Smalls, at the gate when Oliver and I arrived there. At first she was too much astonished at seeing me for speech. She stood looking at me with mute lips, her hands clasped. I saw by the light of the moon, now almost at the full, that she was ghastly pale.

In few words Oliver explained how it was that I was there.

At first her face lighted up, but then the shadows fell, and as we talked there by the wicket, the sun and shade of happy and sad emotions succeeded each other quickly over that soft cheek.

" Your coming so, dear John," she said, in a low whisper,

as Oliver went on into the house to prepare Mr. Smalls, "your coming thus, I fear, will lead to trouble."

I strove to comfort her. I explained that Gallwood and I were now friends, and that I was sure that now there was nothing to fear from him.

Margery seemed incredulous.

"He has written to papa," she said; "he has written about you and Mr. Bullinger. I saw the letter."

"Surely, then, you must be satisfied, dearest."

"There was nothing wrong about the letter," she answered, "but I have known Roth since I was a little girl."

"And do you not believe in his sincerity?"

Margery shuddered.

"Mathematics is good," she returned, quickly; "my trust is all in him; but oh, dear John, you should be on your guard. No one ought to know that you have been here to-night. Oliver can be trusted, I know."

"There is no need to fear, my darling," I said, reassuringly. As I spoke I kissed her fondly.

She returned the kiss soberly. "Let us hope for the best, John: but are you sure you can trust Mr. Bullinger?"

"Implicitly," I answered. "What possible motive would he have to mention the matter? Besides, is it such an important matter that I have crossed by a few yards the line of the department?"

"Oh, yes, if it were known it might be important."

"Could not your father grant permission?"

"Oh, no, no," she answered, hurriedly; "papa has no authority now. It is all in the hands of Roth Gallwood."

Her earnest manner, almost despairing, puzzled me. I could not account for her depression; the cause seemed to me a trivial one, and inadequate.

We were silent for a time as I stood with my arm around her in the deep shadow of the house, now and then pressing my lips to hers. She did not resist me, and during that brief interview my bliss was almost perfect.

" You say that you know of a remedy, dear John," she said at last, timidly ; " can you tell me what it is ? "

I longed to open my heart to my betrothed, but then there was no time. Even as she spoke we heard the sound of Oliver's footsteps approaching.

" Another time," I said, quickly—" to-morrow."

" But not here," she exclaimed, anxiously. " Oh, dear John, do not trust yourself here again. I am so worried."

In a few hurried words, as Oliver drew near, we arranged to meet on the following day on the pathway to the village overlooking the sea.

" Mr. Smalls will see you," said Oliver, coming up. " He is very low, but I have prepared him for your interview."

Oliver was now, of course, aware of the engagement that existed between myself and Margery. As I kissed her good-night without reservation he could hardly have failed to perceive that we were not wholly indifferent to each other.

" So you disregarded my advice," he said, gloomily, as we mounted the broad stairs.

" What advice ? "

" In respect to supplanting Gallwood."

" Oh, yes ; could you think that I should not have done so when it lay in my power ? "

" I sincerely hope that you will not regret it," replied Oliver, in a tone of depression.

" I do not think I shall. In fact, Gallwood is reconciled to the matter fully. We have spoken frankly, and he is reconciled."

There was no opportunity to say more, for we had now arrived at the door of Mr. Smalls' apartment. Oliver knocked gently. A light step approached, and an elderly lady, clad in deep black, appeared. Her appearance was dejected, and there were tears in her eyes. I knew, of course, that this was poor Mr. Smalls' mother. She came out into the hall, closing the door softly.

"This is Mr. Cliff," said Oliver.

The lady gave me her hand.

"My son is expecting you," she said, softly.

"How is he," asked Oliver, "since he took the drops? Is there any sign of a change?"

"None as yet. He is very low; but is now anxiously waiting for Mr. Cliff. Oh, tell me," she continued, turning to me, "have you hope? My poor boy is all I have left in the world. Oh! if you restore him to me you will earn a mother's gratitude."

"If your son will but consent to be guided by me," I answered, "he can be cured."

"You propose to try the faith-cure?" she said, inquiringly.

"It will require faith," I answered.

Mrs. Smalls sighed.

"Mr. Nudwink has made the endeavor already," she said, despondently, "but I see no change."

"Shall I go in?"

"If you please. I suppose you wish to be alone with my poor boy?"

"Yes."

"How long shall you be?"

"That I cannot tell. I shall come out at once if I see that I have convinced—I mean if I observe a change."

"Perhaps I had better go in with you for a moment,"

said Mrs. Smalls, "you may make a mistake about the bottles."

"Bottles?"

"Yes, the oil bottles. I have been very particular to procure all the kinds. Mr. Nudwink used asparagus oil at first, but to-day he tried peanut."

Perhaps my face showed the astonishment that I felt.

"Oh! we have provided other kinds," said the poor mother. "You had better let me go in and explain to you."

"No, I do not think that will be necessary," I answered. "I should rather go in alone."

"The bottles are all labelled," said Mrs. Smalls. "If you are only careful there will be no difficulty; but I know in the faith-cure it is so important to have the right kind of oil."

"I think Mr. Cliff understands that," said Oliver.

"Oh, yes," I said, lugubriously enough, "I understand."

"That is so comforting," said Mrs. Smalls, and then she opened the door and I passed in.

Upon the bed lay Mr. Smalls, his hands, white as marble, extended on the coverlid. His eyes opened feebly, and a gentle smile stole over his pale features as I approached him. He made an effort to raise his hand to meet mine, but his strength was not sufficient.

"I am very glad to see you, Mr. Cliff," he said, in a low, husky voice. "I hardly expected when we met that when next I saw you it would be upon my ocean bed."

"I have great hopes that you will yet recover," I answered, sitting down beside him.

He smiled sadly.

"The end is almost here," he said, feebly. "I regret to go for my mother's sake: but my trust is in the raft."

"I have come, Mr. Smalls," I said, earnestly, "to try and save you. I am confident, if you will only have faith in what I shall tell you, that all will yet be well."

"I have faith," said he. "I need hardly assure you that my faith is an abiding one. By the way, what oil do you use?"

"Oil?"

"Yes. Mr. Nudwink has tried both asparagus and peanut. Do you make use of either?"

"No, I do not; in fact, I—"

"My mother has provided an extensive assortment," he continued; "there they all are in bottles on that shelf."

I looked in the direction in which his eyes roved. The bottles were all of the quart size, and I saw on each a large white label: catnip oil, asparagus oil, peanut oil, corn oil, poppy oil, parsnip oil, worm oil, and a dozen more.

"I am all sticky now with the peanut oil," said Mr. Smalls. "It may appear irreverent, but I have little faith in either the oil or the expression of a slow churchman. Oliver tells me that you are only mixed as yet—"

"I have not yet been cancelled, it is true—"

"Oh, well, that is not essential. Now, not to take up too much of your time, may I trouble you to begin?"

"Mr. Smalls," I said, solemnly, "what I shall have to say will doubtless be a very great surprise to you. You must prepare yourself for a statement of fact from me that will no doubt amaze you greatly; but I assure you that nothing more than faith in what I shall tell you is essential to your recovery."

"Then you use no oil whatever?" he said, opening his eyes very wide.

" I do not."

" But is that Arithmetical ? " he asked, querulously. " I was given to understand that you had been thoroughly mixed. Oliver assured me of that."

" If you will only listen," I said, " and believe, your recovery is assured beyond a doubt."

" I have all faith in the raft, and in Numbers, and in the Arithmetic. Anything unarithmetical would be wholly contrary to my principles. It is true that I was completely soaked, but still I have faith."

" How long were you exposed to the ocean, Mr. Smalls ? "

" Oh, only for an instant."

" Then you were not covered with the sea ? "

Mr. Smalls shuddered, and then smiled wearily. " Oh, no ; if that had been the case I never should have survived till now. No, the ocean spray dashed over me once ; but that was enough. The doctors say that is almost invariably fatal."

" The doctors are all simpletons," I said, indignantly. " They don't know what they are talking about. A little salt water won't hurt any one."

Mr. Smalls looked at me in amazement.

" The fact is," I continued, " that if you can only rid yourself of the idea that there is any real danger from the mere touch of sea water, your health will come back to you without further effort."

He still looked at me incredulously.

" What I am going to say, Mr. Smalls, must be confidential."

" Certainly."

" Because if it were known that I had made the statements it might get me into trouble."

13

"I understand. You may trust me."

"Mr. Smalls," I said, eagerly, leaning forward and raising my finger impressively, "your illness is all in your imagination. Many a time I have gone into the ocean, bathed in it for hours at a time, and never felt the slightest ill effect. These doctors are all humbugs. Rouse yourself. Be persuaded that all you have to do is to disabuse your mind of this idea that the mere contact with the ocean is deadly, and from that moment you are a well man."

There was a peculiar look in Mr. Smalls' eye.

"I don't doubt your good intentions, Mr. Cliff," he said feebly, sighing, "but I was under the impression that you had recovered."

CHAPTER XX.

HOW WONDERFUL ARE LOVE'S SWEET INFLUENCES.

ACCORDING to her promise, Margery met me on the path by the sea at the appointed time.

I had no difficulty in persuading Bullinger that we could employ our time to good advantage for a few days in the village. He readily fell into my views in this respect, much more readily than I had anticipated, for he was of a nervous, restless disposition, ever eager to be moving.

My mind greatly relieved by his compliance, I went forth to meet Margery, feeling that in her sweet society I could almost wholly forget my troubles.

Together we sought a sheltered nook in a recess of the crags that hung over the ocean, which now lay blue and placid before us as far as the eye could reach.

How sweet it is to have the bosom made a heaven by the rainbow smile of love. How glorious is youth in its first passion. How lovely all the landscape. How hopeful the future. How immeasurable the charm of the present. In the sweet mutual delight of eye to eye, and lip to lip, and heart to heart responsive, it was long before we began to think and forgot to dream.

It was Margery who first recalled our wandering fancies.

"Mr. Smalls is so much better this morning," she said.

My heart bounded.

"Is he better? Oh, I am so glad. Did Oliver tell you?"

"Yes, Oliver and his mother."

Was it possible, I thought, that, after all, I had convinced him, notwithstanding his apparent incredulity? But if so, why had he manifested distress after my narrative? Was it feigning? Had he requested me to leave him that he might meditate upon what I had told him? Certainly his words and manner the previous evening had not been such as to inspire me with any confidence that such was the case.

"Tell me exactly how he is, Margery," I said, anxiously. "Tell me exactly what it is that you were told."

Margery blushed.

"They were all very glad indeed that poor Mr. Smalls was better; but—but—"

"Is it any secret?"

"No, no secret, John; but, I think—I am almost sure that they do not think that it was you who cured him."

"Do they think it was the drops?"

"Yes, John, they think it was the drops."

Margery looked very sober as she said this; perhaps she thought that it would hurt my feelings to know that my own efforts had been ineffectual.

"Can you not tell me exactly what occurred?"

"Yes," she responded, hesitating, "I could, but—"

"I wish you would."

"It may worry you, John."

"To know the truth ought not to worry any one," I answered, philosophically.

"But yet," she said, archly, and with perhaps even more philosophy than my own, "it is more often the truth that worries us than that which is false."

"At any rate, tell me," said I.

"It has worried me too, John, a little."

"That is quite another thing," I said, promptly. "If it will worry you to tell me, I ought not to ask it."

"I am only worried for your sake."

"For my sake?"

"Yes, lest you should be vexed."

I laughed, not, I fear, very pleasantly. "I am used to vexations by this time," I said. "A little more or less vexation can do me no especial harm."

"Perhaps, after all, you ought to know," she said, very gravely. "This is what I heard: after you left Mr. Smalls' room, he sent for his mother and Oliver almost immediately. They found him sitting up in bed. He seemed to have strangely recovered his strength, and what was more strange, he was laughing immoderately."

"Laughing?"

"Yes, they both said he was laughing uncontrollably."

"Well, what did he say?"

I began to feel some anxiety.

"It was a long time before he would say a word in respect to what took place between himself and you, and when he did speak it was only to declare that what had passed was altogether confidential."

I drew a long breath of relief. I felt that I had, perhaps, been imprudent in my frankness; but, after all, Mr. Smalls had respected the confidence I had reposed in him.

"Of course," continued Margery, "his mother was very much delighted at finding his strength so much greater, and at first she attributed it all to you; but this morning she told me that her son had convinced her that it was the drops. Dr. Humpath is delighted. He says that it is undoubtedly the drops."

"And is he really so much better?"

"Yes, he is sitting up this morning. When I left the house he and Oliver were out on the balcony under the awning."

"Did you find out what it was that he was laughing at?" I asked, rather dolorously.

"No, he would not speak of that; all he would say was that what you had told him was so comical."

Margery looked at me in a peculiar manner, half doubtful whether to weep or to laugh. I confess that what she said caused me some chagrin, and yet I certainly had no cause to anticipate anything but chagrin, and perhaps I ought to have been grateful that the emotion was not a more serious one.

"I am very glad he is better," I said. "Whether it was the drops or what I told him, I am very glad indeed that he is better."

Margery's face was very sober, and her voice low and almost trembling as she said, "What was it that you told him, dear John?"

I hesitated—very naturally I hesitated.

"Will you not tell your Margery, John?" she asked, looking up pleadingly in my face. "I ought to know; for your good I ought to know."

"It would only worry you, my darling," I said, caressing her.

"Yet ought I not to share your troubles? Ought you not to confide them all to me? Why should it worry me to hear what it was you said? Am I not to be your own, your wife?"

How could I resist such pleading?

"Promise, dearest," I said, earnestly, "promise, what-

ever it may be that I shall tell you, that you will love me
still—"

"Love you?" she interrupted, passionately, "my own,
the love I have for you is not of that kind which departs.
No, now and ever I am yours till the ocean rolls above us."

"Thank God!" I exclaimed, fervently.

"What did you say?" she asked, "I did not understand
what it was you said."

"I am grateful," I answered, "grateful to that good
power that ever keeps those who are faithful in his keeping."

"To Mathematics," she said, dreamily, "and to Numbers."

Was it wrong that I responded, "Yes"?

Margery looked at me with her pleading, eloquent eyes,
and under their serene influence I began my narration.
It is not needful to say that it was with some trepidation.
I can hardly define the feeling. My faith in Margery
was, in some sense, akin to that which I had asked of Mr.
Smalls as a condition for bringing him back to health. I
trusted and confided absolutely and fully in her. I held
nothing back in my heart, and so held nothing back in
giving her my confidence.

"You remember, dearest," I said, "that when I was
first brought to the asylum my malady was supposed
to be—"

"Why refer to that now, John?" she said, earnestly,
"why distress yourself by referring to that unhappy time?
Is it not enough that all those troubles are now of the
past?"

"No, it is not enough," I answered, gloomily, "for in
the statement of what has gone before lies the confidence
that I shall give to you."

She folded her hands before her. She looked out wistfully over the sea.

" I shall listen, then, John," she said. " However much it may pain me, I shall listen."

" My trouble," I continued, "was supposed to be a mania of a very peculiar type ; not only was I seemingly oblivious of all that had preceded in my life, but certain remarkable fancies were supposed to beset me. Among these—"

"Supposed, John !" said Margery, questioningly.

"Supposed," I replied, " that is the right word. After all, in spite of what has passed, and in spite of the misfortunes that beset me even yet, I must now speak the truth to you; to you, my own dearest Margery, as I would to my own soul. I must ask of you a belief in me, a faith in me that true love should not withhold. What I shall have to tell you, darling, is only this : that all I said then, and which has been deemed but raving, was sober, serious earnest. Among those supposed fancies was one statement which I made, coherently enough, but which was considered too marvellous for consideration, to the effect that I had come to this island from another country across the sea ; a country vaster by far than this, and far more wonderful, a land of which Inquirendo knew nothing. No one believed me, and I was hurried, as you know, within the walls of the asylum, which, dark and dismal as it was, your dear self made glorious. It was all true, Margery, all true ; to me the ocean has no terror—often have I sailed out over it ; often have I bathed in it, floated upon it, and breasted its waves, not fearing them ; for I had power over them, strong to destroy as they were.

" I came from no part of this island, darling : my home is in that other land, which I have had to deny. To secure release from the bonds of the law I have forced myself to pretend to be that which I am not. Until last night I have made a pretence of being cured. But when I heard of that young man, lying needlessly at the point of death, I could refrain no longer; I saw his poor mother grieving without cause, and I resolved to speak. I knew that the touch of the salt sea spray had no power to kill. It is true that the ocean does destroy, but not by so gentle a touch. It was to give him that knowledge, that faith— which to me was knowledge—that I spoke. It seems that he did not believe me. Ah, Margery, I well know that it is a strange, an incredible story; but it is true. Inquirendo is not the only country. There is a far mightier, more wonderful one, of which I am a citizen. I came here in a boat—something like the raft of which you know."

As I said these words I looked in Margery's eyes. She sat mute and motionless; but there was a strange expression on her lovely face.

"It is hard to ask, I know; but, dearest, can you not believe me?"

As I spoke I took both Margery's hands in mine and looked beseechingly in her eyes. The lids drooped, her hands grew cold in my tender clasp, the rosy light had faded from her face, and her form trembled.

"Is it too much to ask, darling," I repeated, "that you should have faith in me?"

Her lips moved, she trembled violently. "What can I say?" she faltered. "Oh, John, I do love you dearly," and then with sudden impulse she threw her arms about me, and with her head upon my breast, burst into an agony of tears.

I soothed and petted her; but I could not console.

"I know you love me," I said, whisperingly, "I know that, dearest; but does not perfect love cast out fear? '

She looked up now into my eyes.

"Yes, indeed, John, all fear; though all the island should forsake you, yet will I be always true."

"Can you not understand what I have told you, Margery?"

"How can I?—oh, dear John, how can I?"

"Can you not have faith in me?"

"Yes, indeed, I do have faith in *you*."

"Only believe," I said, fervently, "only believe what I have told you. Can you not do that?"

"Oh, John," she repeated, almost with a wail of anguish, "how can I?—oh, how can I?"

"What I have told you is true, Margery," I said, perhaps a little reproachfully. "You cannot think that I would deceive you?"

"Oh, no, I do not think that," she cried; "I do trust you as much as I love you."

"Then why—"

She interrupted me with passionate caresses, showering kisses upon my lips; but the tears, meanwhile, still streamed down her pallid cheeks, and her form shook with the most intense emotion.

"Spare me, John," she cried, "oh, spare me. Do not, for my sake, speak again to living soul of these things. Trust me and I will trust you; but, oh, speak not again of those awful mysteries. Oh, for my sake, John, for dear Margery's sake, never let such words cross your lips again."

She looked at me more appealingly. "Promise me, dear, promise your Margery, won't you?"

Such was her earnestness and fervor that I knew be-

yond all doubt that I had failed in establishing in my
dear girl's mind faith in the facts which I had told her;
yet even as I was aware of my utter failure, I felt an exultant glow warm my very soul as I felt the profound
assurance of the height and depth and vastness of her
love, of the love that had been able to overcome all doubt
of me. In refusing credence to my story it was not I that
she scorned; still she believed in me, and the bonds of
the love-tie between us were not only unbroken, but in
the very honesty of her nature that revolted from the unknown, and from that which appeared incredible, were in
that hour knit more closely. Out of very doubt and distrust of a fact, faith in me was shown to be the firmer.

Oh, love, how wonderful are thy sweet influences, thy
chain how strong! I looked down upon my darling, lying
upon my breast, all faithfulness, asking of me but one
thing: that I should thenceforth be silent as to the truth.
What else could I do but give her the assurance that she
asked. "From this hour, Margery," I said, "until you
release me, no word of what I have told you shall ever
pass my lips."

How rejoiced she was. How she thanked me, saying
that she did believe me with all her soul; but that I must
forgive her, if she could not understand.

When, awhile afterward, I was alone, I thought earnestly of the meaning of her words, and, more than that,
of the meaning of her glorious love, that had been able to
disregard every worldly thought.

And, pondering still over the circumstances of my forlorn condition, there seemed to come a voice out of the
blue heavens above me, whispering a sweet lesson of
faith.

How often, in my own city, I had thoughtlessly listened

to service and sermon.   How it had all failed to impress
me.   How I had more than once turned away from theology, and sought rest, and yet not finding it, in philosophy.
Here at last, in this peculiar country, by the touch of a
woman's hand, by a whisper from her sweet lips, and by
the light of her eyes, I learned a new lesson, for, even in
the very denying of my story, she had accepted me.

CHAPTER XXI.

THE SCIENCE OF NUMBERS.

AFTER our supper in the evening Bullinger and I had a confidential talk. I had learned to like him exceedingly. Even in the short period of our intimacy, he had shown himself to be gentlemanly, quiet, and retiring; not at all prone to insist upon his own views, and courteous in being willing to accord due deference to those of others. From one thing to another, our conversation came gradually around to the subject of Mr. Smalls' illness, and Bullinger expressed himself as having no confidence whatever in the faith-cure.

"Of course I tell you this, Mr. Cliff," he said, smiling, " with due deference to your own opinion in the matter ; but I should like to know, as I have found you something of a philosopher, on what basis you rest your hope of having cured Mr. Smalls."

I hesitated before replying. Mr. Bullinger had certainly been very frank indeed with me, and yet I felt that I must use caution. If my own Margery could not be persuaded, I knew well enough how useless it would be to attempt to convince even a man of scientific habits of thought.

" Suppose," I replied, evading a full answer, " suppose that you were suffering from a nervous disorder that had in it, in reality, no element of danger, do you not think the statement of a physician that you were likely to die might have a very deleterious effect upon your system ? "

" Undoubtedly."

" It might even kill you, if you were told that you were doomed, even if otherwise you were in no immediate danger ? "

" Possibly."

" Then, if a disastrous effect could be produced by faith in bad news, why could not a beneficial effect be produced by good news ? "

" It might ; very likely it would. I never thought of the faith-cure in that light before."

" No, I presume not ; but here is something analogous to the recent operation of Dr. Humpath."

" I catch your meaning ; but how about the oil ? "

I then explained to Bullinger that the use of oil formed no part of my cure.

" I never thought of it in that light before," Bullinger repeated, " but when I think it over, there does appear to be really something in it. I remember that there was an experiment made in this same direction by Dr. Humpath, in the hospital at the prison. He sent word to all the patients that he would administer a very powerful emetic, and he then gave them each a powder that consisted of harmless flour and sugar. The result was, that one hundred and four out of one hundred and ten were deathly sick, and of the remaining six, five were badly nauseated. The only one who was not affected was a stubborn fellow, who always wanted more than his share of everything, and who got hold of a double dose."

" That showed the power of mind over matter."

" Certainly."

" Then," said I, " you can see my point. If I could only convince Mr. Smalls that he was really in no danger, he would be likely to recover, would he not ? "

"Of course ; but your difficulty would be in this case—
and doubtless was, if you will pardon my apparent incredulity—to convince him. I should very much like to know
how the attempt was made. Anything you may say to me,
I, of course, regard as strictly confidential."

"The course I took was perfectly simple, although, perhaps, in this case, ineffectual. I strove to persuade him
that there was no actual fatality in the touch of the
spray."

"Ah, Mr. Cliff, I fear you found that impossible."

"I must confess that he seemed incredulous."

"And why not? Is anything better established than
that the least touch is serious, and to be wet through as
he was is almost certain death?"

"It is all a mistake," I said, emphatically.

"What is a mistake?"

"That the sea is so noxious."

"Well, Mr. Cliff," said Bullinger, laughingly, "you are
a very droll fellow. Did you talk as earnestly to Mr.
Smalls as you are now talking to me?"

"Certainly; even more so."

"Then I wonder somewhat that he did not feel like
believing you; I do, indeed."

"But it is true; I can convince you of it. As a philosopher you ought to be willing to make an experiment.
Come, it is bright moonlight; the sea is less than a mile
away; let us go down to the shore. I will take along a
couple of towels. You can stand on the shore, out of
reach of danger, and I will go in up to my neck."

I looked at Bullinger very seriously when I made this
proposition. All the answer he made was to lean back in
his chair against the wall and give way to a hearty burst
of laughter.

"Capital, capital!" he exclaimed, clapping his hands,
"you can counterfeit seriousness better than any man I
ever met in my life. Come to think of it, I do believe it
was you cured him, after all."

"Do you?" I asked, eagerly.

"Yes, I do, upon my word I do. You talked as if you
were actually in earnest. Suppose I had taken you seriously, and gone with you as you proposed, what would
have been the result?"

"The result would have been as I said. I should have
demonstrated to your satisfaction that the sea had no
power to harm me by its touch."

"Well, Mr. Cliff, you are droll. Positively, you ought
to be upon the stage. I haven't enjoyed a joke so in years.
No wonder Mr. Smalls is better. Oh, I am a convert to
your views. I don't believe in Dr. Muir, nor Dr. Waltz,
nor Humpath, either; and as for Nudwink, he is an old
idiot; but if there's any virtue in a good hearty laugh,
that story of yours ought to cure a dead man. Did
Smalls laugh at you?"

"Not while I was in the room," I answered, rather
chagrined, "but I am told he did afterwards."

Bullinger went off into another explosion of merriment.

"No wonder, Mr. Cliff, no wonder. Oh, I give you all
the credit now. You saved him."

"But," said I, "joking apart; suppose some inhabitant
of another place than this, who knew things to be fact
which we common mortals regard as only fancy and foolishness; suppose he should come and enlighten us, ought
we not to believe him?"

"On the supposition that there exists any other race
than our own, I should say, undoubtedly, yes; but as there
happens to be no other race, and the evidence is positive

that this island is all there is to the universe, such speculations appear to me to be quite profitless."

"Then you are of the same opinion respecting all these
things as the lecturer that we heard at the capital?"

"Oh, yes; no sensible man could hold a contrary opinion."

"And you do not believe there is any such thing as religion?"

"All mere foolishness."

"But even Mr. Hurtheart himself said that it would
gladden him to really know that there was a true religion.
Would it not you also?"

"That is mere idle speculation. I thought he marred
the effect of his lecture by introducing that absurd hy-
pothesis."

"Do you not believe in Mathematics?"

"Just as far as Hurtheart believes, no further."

"And of course you do not believe in the Arithmetic?"

Bullinger smiled. "There is one on the table by you,
Mr. Cliff," he said; "run your eye over it and see if there
is anything in it worthy of being believed."

I took up the Arithmetic.

"Suppose," I said, "for the sake of argument, that
this superior person came, and taking this book was able
to show conclusively to a philosopher like yourself that
there was really merit in it, merit of a different kind, perhaps, from what you expected to find, but still undeniable
merit; in that case you would be compelled to believe,
would you not?"

"If it amuses you to make that supposition, Mr. Cliff,
I see no objection."

"But what is your answer?"

14

"I suppose I should believe anything that could be proved. I certainly shall believe in nothing else."

"Now let us take a look at this Arithmetic," I said, opening the volume at the first page. "I am of the opinion that there is, after all, something valuable in it. Imagine that I make a pretence of being that superior person, and in that capacity am making the endeavor to demonstrate my views."

"All right," said Bullinger; "you are certainly exceedingly amusing."

"In the first place," said I, "what does the Arithmetic say of itself?—that it is the science of Numbers?"

"I am sick of hearing about Numbers," said Bullinger—"just sick. Well, what next does it say, anything about the raft?"

"Not as I see."

"No, it doesn't; that's in the Commentary, but the parsons all say they find it in the Arithmetic."

"No, there is nothing about the raft in it, that is very positive."

"That's what I said; anyway, all it does say is trash."

"Are you very sure," I asked, seriously, "that you thoroughly understand what is said?"

"I ought to," responded Bullinger, with a little sarcastic emphasis, "I have been over the Four Ground Rules till I know them almost by heart."

"Recently?"

He looked at me to see if I had taken my turn in being sarcastic. As I had, indeed, I could not keep my face straight.

"I don't wonder you laugh," said Bullinger. "No, not very recently. I referred to the time when I was a boy. I did, however, read the whole book over after I heard

Hurtheart the first time, just to enjoy the good points he made."

"And did you enjoy them?"

"Yes, indeed I did; they were excellent."

"Tell me some of them?"

"About that very science of Numbers. Now what could be more utterly absurd than that? The word science means truth known. How then can it be applied to that which is utterly unknown. Numbers, the parsons tell us, was an individual who got shoved off a thing called a raft, and by that means saved all our lives, or will save them, or can save them, or something, no one really knows what. Here the Arithmetic starts out by a manifest absurdity: it says it is the known truth of an unknown thing. I leave it to you, Mr. Cliff, if that wasn't an excellent point?"

"Hurtheart may be very witty," I replied, "and I have no doubt he is an exceedingly able man; but let us see how accurate he is."

"Agreed," said Bullinger, promptly; "apply any test you like. If the Arithmetic can stand it Hurtheart can."

"In the first place, in this book Numbers doesn't mean a man—"

"That's exactly what the parsons say," interrupted Bullinger. "They say he was a man and yet wasn't, but had some relation to Mathematics, all of which is absurd. He either was a man or he wasn't a man; that's common sense—that's nature."

"I said in this book Numbers isn't a man, and when it talks about the science of numbers it means the principles of computing one, two, three, and so on."

"That's figures," said Bullinger, ironically, "not numbers."

"But in this case the two mean the same thing."

"Oh, come, Mr. Cliff, that's bosh."

"A unit," said I, quoting, "is one thing of a kind."

"Well, can your superior person that you talk about explain that?"

"Easily."

"How?"

"A unit is one thing; as one dog, one stone."

Bullinger smiled cynically.

"All the commentators explain that as: 'one of a kind disposition.' And it appears to me that this reading is reasonable."

"My experience is," said I, a little impatiently, "that there are plenty of reasonable things in the wrong place, and so are only foolishness. This is one of them."

"But the commentators?"

"The commentators are all wrong."

Bullinger shrugged his shoulders.

"Go on," said he, "go on to the next verse."

"A number," said I, reading, "is a unit or a collection of units."

"Well," said Bullinger, "what does the superior person say to that?"

I explained. Bullinger listened, with an attempt at politeness. My explanation appeared to me to be perfectly logical, and I was also of the opinion that it ought to have been to my friend. Still it did not appear to be.

"A number," said he, in that provoking tone of self-satisfaction that grates so upon a logical person's mind when an ignoramus pretends to knowledge, "a number stands midway in point of holiness—at least, this is the church's account of the matter—between a unit and an integer. A number is one who is in doubt—not quite

convinced, but who is willing to be employed about churc!
work : as, for instance, as noted in that verse."

"How ? "

" In taking up a collection—"

I could not help laughing.

" 'That appears to me to be perfectly ridiculous."

" So it does to me," exclaimed Bullinger, "the whole
thing appears absurd to me. The trouble with you is, Mr.
Cliff, that you do not understand these things as I do. I
have been through this whole subject, made a study of it in
fact, and I tell you as the result of my experience that it
is all the merest nonsense. What is the use of trying to
prove a thing that can't be proved? That whole book from
beginning to end is nothing but trash."

" But I want to show you that there really is something
in it—something worth studying."

" I am afraid you will fail. The parsons have been
trying to convince me for years, and they haven't done it
yet."

"But don't you see that this book, after all, is scientific
in its nature ? "

" No, I do not," answered Bullinger, rather shortly.

" Let me call your attention to this verse," said I, turning over the page. " In the mental solution the successive steps are determined mentally—"

"Oh, do spare me, Mr. Cliff," said he, energetically,
" what is the use of going over and over the same old arguments. I have heard them till I am worn out with
them. I suppose you will be saying next that there is virtue in the written solution as well—"

" Indeed there is—"

" Well, all I have got to say is, I do not believe it."

"Not only virtue, but the utmost science," I continued.

" If you would only disembarrass your mind of all preconceived opinions the matter would become clear."

" Mr. Cliff," said Bullinger, " I see very plainly the tendency of your mind ; you have good parts, but what you
lack is experience.   Now if there is one strong point that
I possess it is this very one that you have mentioned : the
faculty of divesting myself of all prejudice.   I make it a
rigid rule to believe nothing that cannot be proved."

" That is the very point.   I wish to prove to you that in
this Arithmetic is something of real value—"

"Oh, I am willing to admit that," he answered, quickly.
and with a patronizing air, " I admit that, cheerfully.   It
is better to be a unit than a cipher."

" Of course it is," I said, hastily, " it is better to be
something than nothing."

" Ah, now you are getting beyond your depth."

" Indeed I am not.   I only want to explain."

" Go on then," said Bullinger, wearily.

" Here in the Arithmetic," I went on, being now rather
on my metal to overcome the man's obstinacy, " it speaks
of nine characters called significant—"

"Of course, the digits."

"And it also speaks of naught or cipher."

" Yes ; as the parsons say, the unconverted—"

" Not at all.   Pardon me for being so persistent. but I
wish you to divest yourself of the idea that this is an ethical work, so called. and simply regard it as scientific."

" Isn't that asking rather too much ? "

" No, it is never asking too much that one should believe a simple truth, although I admit that it is these same
simple truths that are sometimes the most difficult to understand."

" Well, what have you to say respecting the digits and the cipher ? "

" Only this, that a cipher has a value."

" A cipher a value ? " exclaimed Bullinger, amazed.

" Not by itself—"

" Oh ! "

" But dependent upon its place—"

" Why, its place is undersea, or hell, as the vulgar say—"

" But," said I, a little impatiently, " this is no ethical question. This whole book is only a scientific work about figures—"

" Oh, that I can't believe."

" Why not ?—can't you see ? "

" No, I can't. Why should one trouble one's mind about such abstractions when so many weightier matters claim attention ? "

" But can you not see ? Here, let me show you." I took out paper and pencil and wrote down a figure one, thus : 1. " That is one, is it not ? "

" Certainly," replied Bullinger.

" Now I write a cipher after it—"

" Well, what of that ? "

" In this case the cipher has a value."

The same superior cynical smile that had previously irritated me stole over Bullinger's features.

" What value ? " he asked.

" In that case, ten ; and generally the cipher's value depends wholly upon its distance from the decimal point."

Bullinger threw his head back and laughed aloud. " You must really excuse me, Mr. Cliff; I do not wish to seem impolite, but upon my word all your argument has only brought you round to the Decimals. You are only reasoning in a circle—"

"But," said I, "let me explain to you what is meant by the decimal point."

"Haven't we had about enough of this?" said Bullinger, stifling a yawn, "I am awfully tired and sleepy; suppose we retire."

"Very well," I responded, with some moroseness, "if you are not disposed to be convinced—"

"Oh, I have been very much interested, Mr. Cliff. You argue very ingeniously, but really, I can't be expected to believe impossibilities."

So, with some trifling coolness between us, Bullinger and I retired to our rooms.

CHAPTER XXII.

MR. SMALLS grew gradually better from that day. The two learned physicians from the capital—who had, however, gone back in disgust when Dr. Humpath had been called in—ascribed his cure solely to their nauseous doses. Dr. Humpath took great credit to himself, and insisted that it was the judicious use of the sea-powder drops; but while the two schools of medicine wrangled, Mr. Nudwink openly declared that to Numbers and the peanut oil the praise was due. Mrs. Smalls and Oliver were too delighted at the change to care greatly how it had been effected; but neither, of course, gave me the least credit; and they could scarcely be expected to do so, as Mr. Smalls had been true to his word, and I, of course, had not spoken.

Oliver came over to the village in the afternoon of the day whereon I had told Margery the truth respecting myself. Bullinger and I were sitting on the piazza on the main street, and it was there that Oliver handed me a letter from Margery. My first letter from her. How dear the handwriting was, the delicate strokes of the pen that she had held. I excused myself, and going to my own room, in solitude I read what she had written. Perhaps I had feared trouble; but there was no need that I should. The note was a short one, and as loving as I could have wished.

217

"Papa wishes me to write," so the note ran. "Of course, dear John, he knows nothing of your having been here; but he has received a pass for you from Roth Gallwood, which I enclose. Papa wishes me to say that he will be glad to see you and also Mr. Bullinger at any time." This was all the information that the letter contained. The passes were enclosed, and as I read them, renewed hope sprang up in my heart. I went down again to the piazza. Oliver knew that the passes had been sent, and had been telling Bullinger.

"Come over at any time," said Oliver, as he went away, "we shall all be glad to see you."

Much to my joy, it was Bullinger who, himself, suggested that we should tarry awhile in the village, and it was also his proposition that we should walk over to Lunatico Cottage that evening.

It was after dark when we arrived there, and Margery and her father were in the parlor, with Oliver and Mrs. Smalls and her son. The latter had not, of course, recovered his strength, but the faint glow of returning health was on his cheeks, and he welcomed me very cordially.

The Governor was also very kind, and Margery seemed to be content to have me with her. Though she said but little, I found, from time to time, that her eyes rested upon mine, with the happy light in them of an assured and assuring love.

We talked for a time upon indifferent subjects until, at last, the conversation became confined, almost exclusively, to Mr. Mayland and Bullinger, who had taken up the subject of the faith-cure. For a time the discussion was an abstract one, no especial reference being made to Mr. Smalls' recovery. While the two were talking in

a very animated way, there was a knock at the door, and
to my chagrin and vexation, Mr. Nudwink appeared.

He greeted the others with sanctimonious politeness,
and bowed stiffly to me.

" Do not let me interrupt your conversation," he said,
as he dropped into a chair. " Pray make no stranger of
me."

" Mr. Bullinger and I were having a little argument
respecting the faith-cure," said the Governor, with his
usual pleasant smile.

" Proceed," said Mr. Nudwink, with a wave of his
hand.

" And I had declared my opinion, very positively,
against it," said Bullinger.

Nudwink smiled. As he waved his hand in the direction of Mr. Smalls, he observed, calmly, " How is it possible to doubt in the presence of our dear friend, who,
in his own person, is a living example of its wonderful
efficacy ? "

" I deny, most emphatically," said Bullinger, a little
warmly, " that Mr. Smalls' cure was due to the exercise
of faith."

" As to that, I express no opinion," said Mr. Mayland.

" To what, then, was it due ? " demanded Nudwink,
aroused in defence of what he regarded as his own work.

" Natural causes," responded Bullinger, emphatically.
" Natural causes only ; aided, I am willing to admit, very
possibly, by medicine."

" The drops," I suggested, with, perhaps, a little satir-
ical emphasis.

Mr. Nudwink turned and looked at me, with no very
pleasant expression.

" The drops had nothing to do with it," he observed,

adding, with a significant nod, "nor I presume, Mr. Cliff,
had you."

Had I? What did he mean by that remark? I felt the
warm blood dyeing my cheek. I glanced towards Oliver;
he had turned his head away, and Margery had bent
down over the work in her lap, through which her skilful
fingers were plying, but her cheeks were tinged with the
deepest crimson.

I returned Nudwink's look as calmly as I could, and,
in a moment, he resumed, speaking very deliberately.
"Before I left the asylum, Mr. Cliff, I heard, incidentally,
that you had suggested the idea of some faith-cure of
your own devising. This suggestion, of itself, coming
from a layman, would be in the highest degree surprising,
but from one like yourself, entertaining the opinions you
do, it is, I might say, almost blasphemous. A person
who avows himself openly a believer in the pernicious
errors of Hurtheart is not surely fitted to prate of faith."

Mr. Mayland's eyes were fixed upon me inquiringly.
Margery looked up quickly, distress pictured on her face.
Oliver turned suddenly around in great amazement, and,
for a moment, there was complete silence. I regretted
having mentioned the drops; but I was about to reply
when Bullinger interposed.

"That is hardly fair, Mr. Nudwink," said he. "Mr.
Cliff and I, it is true, attended Mr. Hurtheart's lecture,
and we both were much pleased; but was not Mr. Cliff
justified if he knew or thought he knew of a remedy for
Mr. Smalls' illness in making an effort to cure him?"

Nudwink's eyes opened.

"You say that Mr. Cliff did try;—how is that, Mr.
Smalls?"

Mr. Smalls made no reply. Margery raised her head

suddenly ; her quick wit came to my rescue. " It is time
that Mr. Smalls retired," she said, promptly. " I am sure
he must feel exhausted. Is it not so, Mr. Smalls ? " she
said, coming toward him. His mother, too, easily made
anxious, now united in the persuasion that her son should
retire.

This diversion availed for a time to distract Mr. Nudwink's attention from me ; but after Mr. Smalls had left
the room, that disagreeable person returned persistently
to the subject.

" There seems to be a misapprehension about all this,"
said Nudwink ; " may I be permitted to ask the question,
to which I could get no response from Mr. Smalls ? Perhaps you can inform me, Governor ? "

" As to that," responded Mr. Mayland, " I know absolutely nothing."

" How is it, Oliver ? "

This persistence was, it may be imagined, intolerably
disagreeable to me. I saw, of course, that Oliver was also
vexed. My usual impetuosity got the better of my prudence, as it had on so many other occasions.

" Mr. Nudwink," I said, shortly and emphatically, " there
is no need for you to put these questions to others when
I am present myself to answer them."

" You heard my question," said he, coldly ; " if you
choose you may answer."

" My answer is that I did make the effort to cure Mr.
Smalls."

" Ah ! you did ? "

" I did."

" When was this attempt made ? "

" It was made last night."

" Last night ! " exclaimed Mr. Nudwink, in a tone of

assumed horror. " Why, sir, last night you had no permit. How is that ? "

Mr. Mayland now looked at me in great surprise. Poor Margery and Oliver were both much distressed. " Is it worth while," said the latter, " to pursue the subject further? Mr. Cliff has a pass now, and that surely should suffice in any event."

"Very well," said Nudwink, " I shall say nothing further now."

His tone, and the expression in his eye as he glanced at me, were both very sinister and significant. It was not long before he took himself away. When he had gone, Mr. Mayland turned to me.

" It is a disagreeable matter, Mr. Cliff," he said, kindly, " but one that for your own sake should be cleared up at once. Did I understand you rightly in respect to your having been here at this house last night ? "

" Oh, papa," said Margery, " why need anything more be said about that ? "

" I ask the question for Mr. Cliff's sake."

" Yes, Mr. Mayland," I said, " I was here at your house last night."

" For the purpose of trying a faith-cure ? "

" Faith was certainly an element," I answered.

" It is a great pity that you came without a pass."

" Well, but, papa," said Margery, " he has a pass now."

The Governor said nothing; but he appeared dissatisfied.

" Mr. Gallwood knew that it was my intention to try to cure Mr. Smalls," I said.

" But still you had no pass at the time ? "

" No, I did not then."

" It was very ill-advised. Of course I cannot tell what

Gallwood may do, but I very much fear that Mr. Nudwink will deem it his duty to report what he has learned."

"I fear so," said Oliver.

"I confess that it does not seem to me to be a serious matter," I said. "Surely Mr. Gallwood will not think it amiss when the explanation is made."

But for some reason the Governor and Oliver as well as Margery seemed to regard the occurrence as very serious. I had little opportunity to talk alone with Margery, but she contrived to whisper, as I took her chilly hand in mine for an instant at the door, "Oh, John, how could you let Mr. Nudwink know that you were here; he is so conscientious."

Bullinger chattered incessantly all the way back to the village; yet, though I replied from time to time, I was thinking of what had taken place that evening, and, above all, of what Margery had said. It did not appear to me that the word conscientious was the most fitting to apply to Nudwink. Perhaps I was prejudiced, but certainly that did not appear to be the most appropriate word.

The next day, quite early, two men in that blue uniform which I had learned to dislike so heartily, appeared at the inn, and unceremoniously demanded an interview. My mind misgave me, but of course I acceded, and going down to the parlor of the inn I there found the two officials and the landlord. The latter was in some trepidation, and looked at me with an expression of great pity. One of the officers stepped forward and handed me a document. I opened it and read what purported to be a requisition or order to deliver myself up to the custody of the constituted authority of the sun court. The paper was signed by "Bounce, justice," and to it was attached by a ribbon a ponderous wax seal. There did not appear

to be any statement of the nature of the offence of which
I was charged, and I very naturally requested this information of the policemen. They either could not or
would not comply, and only intimated that their duty in
the premises was solely to convey me forthwith to the
capital, where I would be arraigned and given an opportunity to plead. Further than this they would say nothing, although they were very civil, and, one of them being present all the time, I was given ample time to
pack my valise. Poor Mr. Bullinger appeared very much
annoyed, and before I could dissuade him, he started out
across the fields towards the Governor's house.

Despite my earnest remonstrance the officials would
not wait for his return. They declared, no doubt with
entire truth, that their orders were imperative to arrest
me forthwith and proceed with all due speed towards the
capital. A fleet team of steers bore us quickly across the
country. That night we stopped at a little wayside inn,
where, much to my surprise, I was left for the night quite
unguarded, and the next morning very early we resumed
our journey. We pursued the same poorly macadamized
highway which had now become so distasteful to me, and it
was not very long after day-break before the terrible tur-
rets·of the asylum loomed up through the fog in front of
us. Instead of entering those grim gates as on the former
occasion, the steers were driven rapidly by. We passed
the gateway also of that lovely garden sacred to the first
glimpse of my own sweet Margery, and sacred also to
our happy betrothal. As we rolled swiftly past the angle
of the asylum, there was a sudden sound overhead ; a window in the turret had been hastily raised. Involuntarily
I cast my eyes upward, and there in the casement, looking

down, sat Nudwink and Gallwood.   The latter, seeing that
I had observed him, bowed politely : "Good-day, Mr.
Cliff," said he, with a peculiar smile, " are you having a
pleasant ride ? "

15

CHAPTER XXIII.

IN due time we reached the capital, and I was conducted
at once into the presence of the justice of the sun
court. The moment our eyes met I recognized in this
individual the person whom I had met the first morning of
my arrival in the island, and from whom I obtained the
information that it was called Inquirendo; and the tip-
staff by his side was none other than the man Mike who
had been so handy with the cobble-stones. They both
knew me at once : the judge started nervously—it was
evident that I had on that occasion given him a considerable shock—and Mike put on a broad grin, which was
even more repulsive than his savage demeanor had been
when, at the judge's appeal, he had bidden me " be aff."
However, his nervousness did not prevent the judge from
going through his duties with much alacrity. As to the
details of these duties, the forms of the arraignment, and
the plea that I entered on my own behalf of " not guilty,"
it is not needful to amplify. Let it suffice that on the
complaint of the Reverend Mr. Nudwink I was charged
with being *non compos*. When this charge was read by a
court officer I felt a cold shiver run over me, and yet at
the time I had little apprehension that there would be difficulty in clearing myself. When the proceedings were
over I was remanded to the custody of an officer, and

taken at once to a cell in the prison attached to the sun court. Although it was a cell, and its dimensions were not large, yet I did not find it an uncomfortable apartment. I was allowed all the indulgence that was compatible with security during the week that elapsed before my trial; and had it not been for the load of anxiety that burdened me so heavily, I might even have been contented with my books, and the prospect of busy life from the window, both of which indulgences I was permitted to enjoy.

The day after my incarceration a letter came from Margery; a letter that was heart-breaking in its depth of despair and agony. She seemed utterly overwhelmed by the misfortune that had befallen us, for in her heart I was now linked indissolubly with her destiny. One comfort I derived from this letter: she was to leave Lunatico Cottage at once. Her father, so she wrote, had decided to return to the asylum, and her mother and herself should come to the capital as soon as it could be arranged. After that I waited in mournful expectancy, and in the afternoon of the third day I saw Margery and her mother in the cell, the prison rules not permitting me to leave it.

It was a very dreary interview: Mrs. Mayland wept and grieved even more than Margery, who, with a strength of resolution that I had hardly given her credit for, bore up and strove to comfort me. Yet after all there was little to be said in the way of comfort. I had by this time come to a realizing sense of the peril that I was in; but of its actual nature and of the crushing weight of the evidence against me I remained in ignorance until the trial began. The sad days that intervened were cheered by Margery's presence, and the time passed in her sweet society was not without its sunshine. On the Sabbath before the trial I was permitted to attend religious ser-

vices in the lower hall of the prison. From the peculiar
circumstances of my incarceration I was allowed privileges
not accorded to the rest, having a seat assigned to me a
little apart from the petty criminals, who filled the body
of the hall. The services happened that day to be conducted according to the methods of the Multipliers, it being
the law, or at least the custom, that each sect in turn was
allowed to worship in all the public institutions. The
preacher was a young man, and of no especial ability, but
his presentation of the cardinal doctrine of his creed, the
death of Numbers upon the raft, was so full of pleading
pathos that my eyes overflowed. Though I knew how
garbled was the truth in his mind, and how foolish all his
preaching, yet in his deep earnestness there was nothing
garbled, nor in his impassioned utterances, nor in his holy
faith was there foolishness. Straight from the heart the
words came, and as they affected others in one way, so in
another they affected me.

The next day the trial began. Although there was a
much greater degree of ceremony than had been the case
at my previous trial before the convalescent court, yet the
proceedings were in all respects similar. As on that occasion a crier had proclaimed the court open, so it was now
proclaimed. The judge, whose name, I was told, was
Knowitz, sat in the solemn dignity of decorum upon an
elevated bench, and there was an air of gloom over all
present. As before, the writ under seal was exhibited, and
I was then asked whether I desired to conduct my own
defence. I was told in response to my question that matters of law were involved as well as of fact, so I claimed
the privilege of counsel, and one was forthwith assigned
to me, with whom I conferred apart for a short time, while
a dead silence was preserved in the court-room. At the

end of our consultation my counsel rose and stated that we were ready to proceed.

"Read the indictment," said Judge Knowitz, in a crisp, business-like voice, and a crier or clerk, stepping briskly forward, held up a document, and read in a loud voice as follows :—

" Know all men by these presents, that it having come to the knowledge of the Hon. Justus Knowitz, one of the justices of the Sun Court, that John Cliff, a convalescent on the second stage of the course of discipline, is believed to be incurable, and has given just, proper, and reasonable grounds to the Reverend Jabez Nudwink to so believe him, to the extent that the said Nudwink hath, in due form of law, presented him as an incurable, and hath, and now doth, on behalf of himself and of his fellow citizens, demand, that due course of law in such case made and provided shall be had, to the end that the safety of all citizens of Inquirendo shall be protected as against the said convalescent, John Cliff, as aforesaid. Now, therefore, the Sun Court, by virtue of its duly constituted authority, doth arraign the said John Cliff as aforesaid, and doth call upon him to answer to the charge duly filed against him by the Reverend Jabez Nudwink as aforesaid, to wit : the charge of being incurable.

" Witness our hand, and the seal of the Sun Court, this — day of August ——.

" Justus Knowitz.

" By the Court,   [seal.]
          " Michael Tierney, Scribe."

When the clerk had finished reading, the judge addressed me by name. I rose, and looked him in the eye.

"Mr. Cliff," said the judge, with great gravity, "the general charge to which you are now called upon to plead, is the charge of being incurable. What have you to say in this regard? Are you guilty or not guilty?"

"Not guilty," I responded, promptly.

"You may sit down," said the judge.

I did so, and his Honor proceeded at some length to explain the law of my case. The substance of what he said was, that the law regarded the safety of the citizen as an individual as wholly subordinate to that of society, and that, therefore, no habitual criminal, or hopelessly diseased person, or mental incurable, should regard it as in the nature of a hardship that society took due measures to rid itself of a burden.

"The retaining of an individual upon the island," said the court, "after the determination of the fact of incurableness, whether physically, morally, or mentally, would constitute in itself a crime. You are, if guilty, no longer a citizen, but mere surplus population, and society is not only justified, but bound to rid itself of you."

The judge then proceeded to inform me, that it was my right to present my own case through my counsel, and that to enable me to prepare for such presentation a recess would be taken till afternoon.

Court thereupon adjourned, and my counsel and I had quite a lengthy conference in one of the jury rooms. Francis Dash, my lawyer, was a man of about fifty years of age, tall, spare even to emaciation, with prominent features and a cadaverous complexion; his hair was very sparse, but what there was of it was of a tawny hue; a scrawny beard, and a still scrawnier mustache were rather appendages than adornments to his visage. Although Mr. Dash was by no means a handsome man, he made up

in legal acumen what he lacked in beauty. In the course
of the hour that we spent in the jury room he gave abundant evidence that his sky-blue eyes were quite capable of
reading character; though—as Solomon might have remarked, without losing caste as a sage—no eyes, sky-blue
or any other color, can always gauge motives. Mr. Dash
asked me a great many questions—short, snappy, prompt,
decisive questions, to most of which I responded with
alacrity. He expressed no particular surprise when I
told him that I had no special home; and he only lifted
his brows a trifle when I added, thinking it best to be
frank, " At least, on the island."

" Better tell me the *whole* truth, Mr. Cliff," he remarked,
monotonously, beginning to pare his nails. " I can defend
you, of course, without that, but as a general rule it is
better to confide in your lawyer."

Margery had not released me from my promise, but I
thought it best to tell Mr. Dash the whole story. He
listened at first with great interest when I spoke of my
father's country villa at Far Rockaway, and of the house
in Park Avenue. His light eyes opened when I explained
the glories of the great city, and the attractions of Coney
Island. They opened wider yet when, thinking that he was
entertained, I mentioned certain facts connected with our
New York civilization. I think his first look of incredulity appeared when I alluded to the elevated road—it was
either then, or when I casually mentioned the dispropor-
tion between the cost of making water gas and the price
at which it was sold to consumers. Mr. Dash's face expressed not only incredulity, but amazement, when I related the circumstances of my arrival upon the island.
Incredulous, and amazed as he was, the eminent counsel
listened in silence to all I had to say, and then remarked

placidly, " Was it for the expression of these views that
you were first confined in the asylum ? "

I acknowledged that it was.

" How did it happen that you became convalescent ?
Were your views modified ? "

" Views ! they were not views—"

" What then ? " said Mr. Dash.

" Facts."

" Then, in deference to you, allow me to put the
question in another form : were your facts modified ? "

" The facts could not be modified," I answered, " but, in
deference to the prevailing sentiments and bigotry of the
populace, I modified my statement of them."

" To suit the emergency ? "

" Precisely."

" In that you were wise, Mr. Cliff.   I need not say that
while I abhor all lying, and should not advise that this
course of prevarication be pursued in the interests of
morals, yet, as your counsel. I feel bound to tell you that
if you are as frank with Judge Knowitz as you have, very
properly, been with me, you will be convicted, to a dead
certainty."

" But suppose I could prove that what I have said was
true ? "

" State the nature of your proposed proof."

" If I could be given the time, and the proper appliances,"
I responded, " I could build a coffer-dam around my boat.
I feel convinced I could raise her, and when I had once
done that, if I sailed round the island once or twice in
her, I suppose that would be abundant proof ; would it
not ? "

Mr. Dash nodded his head.

" Ample, I should say."

"Then why not suggest that to the judge?" said I, now quite eager to have my veracity put to the test.

Mr. Dash went on paring his finger-nails, but made no reply.

"Do you see what I mean?" I asked.

"Yes."

"What do you think of the suggestion?"

"There are forty things in the way of carrying it out practically," Mr. Dash responded, shutting up his knife: "the first one is that it is impossible. I will mention the others some time when we have more leisure."

"But why is it impossible? A man on trial as I am ought to be given every opportunity to defend himself. I have plenty of money. I would cheerfully bear all the expense of the coffer-dam. You have yourself admitted that the proof that I have suggested would be ample. If I did what I know I can do, all doubts of my sanity would be at an end."

"Very likely; but I should hesitate to mention the matter to the judge; and if you will be guided by me, Mr. Cliff, you will leave all the details of your defence to myself."

In this, though loath to do so, I was obliged to acquiesce, and when we returned to the court-room after the recess Mr. Dash made my defence for me. He began by reading the commitment papers, whereby I was first sent to the asylum; the report of Dr. Setbon and his associates, made at several distinct periods; the record of the trial before the convalescent court, and the findings therein; then laying down these documents on the table in front of him, Mr. Dash took off his glasses, and in a soft, low voice, calm and distinct, he began his statement of my case in his own way. He admitted very frankly

the fact of previous aberration and loss of memory, and
also admitted that the memory of remote events was still
impaired ; but he insisted with much vigor that this constituted no impediment whatever to my performance of
all duties of citizenship. He went over the whole story
of my life since my first arrest the day of my arrival upon
the island. He insisted that I belonged to the highly respectable family of the Ycliffes, and that it rather behooved the court to remand me forthwith to the Governor's
charge with a view to liberty, than that I should even be
called upon to undergo the pain of hearing frivolous evidence on a charge so palpably absurd as that which had
been made by Mr. Nudwink. In all that he said Mr.
Dash kept tight hold of the truth, but it must be admitted
that he squeezed it very hard. He complimented me by
saying that I was a philosopher, and in this manner endeavored to account for my enthusiasm respecting the
faith-cure.

"The only point," said Mr. Dash, "as to which my
client has erred in even the slightest degree is that, in the
interests of science and humanity, and under the supposition that he had verbal authority for so doing from Acting-
Governor Gallwood, he crossed the boundary of the third
department on the night when Mr. Smalls lay, as all supposed, dying. That he did err he admits, but that his
erring was criminal we do utterly deny, and now in conclusion I move the court to dismiss the case, and to remand my client to the custody of the governor of the asylum."

"Motion denied," said the judge, promptly.

"I take an exception," said Mr. Dash, who thereupon
sat down, and the court proceeded to reiterate the law so
far as it pertained to my case. In this statement I

learned little that was new to me ; but I confess that the repeated references to my supposed incurable condition of lunacy jarred upon my feelings, and the words ' *non compos* ' also, which were frequently used, were not reassuring. At the conclusion of these remarks the prosecutor got upon his feet. This person, whom I had observed diligently pouring over some papers and whispering in one corner with Nudwink, was a sinister-faced man, past his prime, but alert, and quick, and wiry. He stepped forward and began a violent harangue.

CHAPTER XXIV.

INCONSISTENCY AND CONTUMACY.

THE furious attack which this man saw fit to make upon me I shall not here repeat. He distorted everything that my own lawyer had said on my behalf, and as Mr. Dash had already done something (of course in my interest) in the way of distortion, by the time the other had finished there was very little left of the facts. He outlined in brief the course that the prosecution proposed to take, by saying that the time of the court would not be taken up by irrelevant or redundant testimony.

"We introduce," said he, "simply to make the issue clear, the records in Mr. Cliff's case; but we do not consider it necessary to offer testimony in any respects beyond two salient points, which I briefly indicate. The first point is the admitted one of leaving the third department while on the second stage of the course of discipline, and the second point is the persistent and sacrilegious attempts on Mr. Cliff's part to place peculiar constructions upon the Arithmetic. These two matters, taken together, will prove conclusively to your Honor's mind that entire absence of consistency without which, as all authorities agree, no man is sane. These peculiar constructions to which I allude are of such an extraordinary character that I might perhaps be justified in relying upon them alone to prove my case; but complicated as

the accused's statements have been with an abnormal vas-
cillation respecting religious belief, it can easily be shown
that the claim the state now makes of non composity is
well taken.

"Society demands safety," he shouted. "Society requires of constituted authority immunity from danger.
Society demands that it should not be exposed to the danger attendant upon the presence on this island of one
whose whole course indicates a vexatious determination
to unsettle the minds of men. We shall make such a presentation of facts that your Honor cannot fail to be convinced of this person's total unfitness for citizenship, and,
in consequence, of life."

There was a short interval of silence, and then, in response to an intimation from the prosecutor, the crier
called the first witness :

"Roth Gallwood."

I looked hastily round, hearing a step behind me, and
perceived that upon the benches in the rear of the room
were quite a number of persons whom I had not before
observed. From the midst of these Gallwood advanced
and took the witness-chair. I regarded him intently.
He seemed care-worn and indeed dejected. He looked
at me with a pained expression, and in testifying his answers were given with evident or apparent reluctance.

The usual preliminary questions were asked respecting
the witness' occupation, and opportunities of information
in regard to my condition.

"Did you ever have any conversation with Mr. Cliff
in respect to Mr. Smalls ? " continued the attorney.

"I did."

"State the substance of this conversation."

Gallwood did so.

" What did Mr. Cliff say respecting his ability to use the so-called faith-cure ? "

" He said that if he were allowed to try he could cure Mr. Smalls."

" Did he tell you the precise means he intended to employ ? "

" He only said, in general terms, the faith-cure."

" Did he say what kind of oil he wished to use ? "

" He did not."

" Did he say anything about oil ? "

" Not a word."

" This conversation took place, as you have stated, a short time before the journey began. Did Mr. Cliff know that his course lay in the direction of Lunatico Villa ? "

" He did."

" How do you know this ? "

" I explained that fact to him, and was careful at the same time to impress upon him the necessity of procuring a pass before seeing Mr. Smalls." The prosecutor looked significantly at the judge when this reply was made.

" Did he ask you for a pass ? "

" He did not."

" And you are positive that he clearly understood the need there was of one ? "

" Perfectly positive."

" Previous to the time of this conversation had any pass been issued to Mr. Cliff ? "

" There had been a pass issued."

" For what purpose? "

" To attend a lecture."

" Where ? "

" Here in the capital."

" Whose lecture was it ? "

" Mr. Hurtheart's."

" The Free-thinker ? "

" Yes."

" Your Honor will please note that answer."

Judge Knowitz bowed very gravely.

" Did he attend that lecture ? "

" He did."

" Was he accompanied by any one ? "

" Yes, by Mr. Bullinger."

" When they returned from that lecture did you see and speak to Mr. Cliff ? "

" I did."

" In respect to the subject-matter of the lecture ? "

" Yes."

" Did Mr. Cliff express any opinion respecting the truth of what Mr. Hurtheart said ? "

" He did. He stated that he approved of Mr. Hurt-heart's doctrine."

" Did it appear to you at all strange that Mr. Cliff should say this, and at the same time advocate the use of the faith-cure with Mr. Smalls ? "

" It did ; it seemed to me very extraordinary."

" What did it indicate to your mind ? "

" Inconsistency," Gallwood responded, dolefully.

" You are, of course, aware of the serious nature of your reply ? "

" I am," answered Gallwood. " I should be glad to reply differently, but I am unable to do so."

" And you state this, in view of your large experience, as a fact, do you ? "

" I do."

"Did you at any time issue a pass to Mr. Cliff to visit Lunatico Villa?"

"I did."

"In response to a request of his?"

"No; in deference to a request from Miss Margery Mayland. This was at once complied with. I sent a messenger to Lunatico Cottage instantly with passes for both Mr. Bullinger and Mr. Cliff."

"On the night of the twenty-third of August had this pass left your hands?"

"It had not. It was sent the next morning early."

"Then in case Mr. Cliff had been outside of the third department on the night of the twenty-third of August it would have been in violation of parole as a second-course convalescent?"

"Certainly."

"As an expert in these matters, Mr. Gallwood, what would such conduct indicate?"

"Contumacy," he responded, solemnly.

"What, as an expert, do you say respecting the testimony of insane jurisprudence on the question of proof touching cases like Mr. Cliff's? What, I mean, are the salient features of an incurable?"

"Inconsistency and contumacy," replied Gallwood, without moving a muscle.

The attorney cast a glance in the direction of the bench. The judge nodded his head.

"I wish to put a hypothetical question, Mr. Gallwood. On the supposition that a person on the second stage of the course of discipline had, in a religious conversation with an integer (he himself, the lunatic, being a cipher), expressed himself as being a mixed number, and by so expressing himself, identified himself with a religious body;

and that thereafter he (the lunatic) desired to and did attend a lecture by a Free-thinker, and at the close of the lecture declared in effect that the lecturer's arguments were sound ; also, on the supposition that this same lunatic did, contemporaneously with these latter declarations, proclaim his belief in a faith-cure, but without mentioning the word oil ; also, on the supposition that the lunatic, aware of the necessity of a pass to leave the third department, did nevertheless go outside the department without such pass, and this, too, with knowledge prepense, what, in your opinion as an expert, was this man's mind as to sanity ? "

Mr. Gallwood drew a long breath.

" Need I reply to that question? " he said, solemnly.

" In the interests of justice," replied the prosecutor, " I require an answer."

" He was incurable," said Gallwood, slowly.

" Was he therefore in your opinion *non compos ?* "

" He was."

" That will do."

Gallwood retired, and a moment after the crier announced, "Mr. Oliver."

Poor Oliver made his way slowly towards the witness-chair, and his depression of spirits was very evident. He looked furtively at me, and I saw that his eyes were full.

In response to the attorney's questions, Oliver related the circumstances of our first acquaintance, and in as few words as possible he described our journey around the island.

" There are a few points," said the attorney, " that I desire to bring out, Mr. Oliver. In the first place, on your first acquaintance, to your knowledge, did or did not Mr. Cliff manifest a very deep interest in religious matters ? "

16

" He did—a deep interest."

" In any special denomination ? "

" In all at first ; or, rather, to be exact, in any; that is, he showed a spirit of enquiry."

" Did this spirit of enquiry result in Mr. Cliff's mind being fixed regarding any special church ? "

" His remarks led me to believe so."

" Towards what church did he manifest an inclination ? "

" The Decimals."

" Did he say so absolutely ? "

" He did."

" What was his exact language, as near as you can recall it ? "

" He told me that he felt assured that a cipher's value depended upon its place in reference to the decimal point."

" Ah ! " Again the attorney cast his sinister eye towards the judge. The latter, as before, by a nod intimated that he comprehended the force of the reply.

" Did Mr. Cliff ever intimate to you," continued the prosecutor, " his desire or wish to connect himself with the Decimals ? "

" Not directly—no, sir."

" Indirectly then ? "

" I fear I must reply that he did."

" By something that he said ? "

" Yes."

" What was it that he said that led you to form the conclusion you have stated ? "

" Mr. Cliff told me one morning while we were on our journey that he felt like a mixed number."

" That he felt *like* a mixed number ! Are you not prepared to say that he stated that he actually was a mixed number?"

"No," responded Oliver, shaking his head, "I am almost sure he did not say that."

"Almost sure, you say; then there is a doubt in your mind between those two statements. You are not quite sure whether he said he *was* a mixed number or was only *like* a mixed number?"

"No, I am not sure."

As Oliver gave this answer he sighed deeply.

"On the twenty-third of August last, in the evening, where were you?"

"At Mr. Mayland's villa, Lunatico."

"Why were you there?"

"I had been sent for by my friend, Mr. Smalls, who was supposed to be dying of sea-sickness."

"Who besides yourself, so far as you know, were present at that house on that evening?"

Oliver mentioned the names, including my own.

"What took place that evening in reference to the faith-cure proposed by Mr. Cliff? Relate, as briefly as you can, all the circumstances."

Oliver told the story of his meeting with me, and of my introduction to Mrs. Smalls, and then stated that Mr. Smalls being willing, I was left for a time alone with him. It appeared to be with great reluctance that Oliver told of his subsequent interview with Mr. Smalls, and how hilarious the sick man was; but the attorney persisted till all the truth was brought out.

"Did Mr. Smalls explain the cause of his mirth?"

"He did not."

"One question more: did you warn Mr. Cliff that evening that he had better not enter Mr. Mayland's house, or cross the boundary separating the third from the second department without a pass?"

"I did."

"That will do."

Oliver stepped down.   Then one after another, Mr. Mayland, Dr. Setbon, and Drs. Humpath, Muir and Waltz were called.   Their statements were mostly medical, each being asked the hypothetical question propounded to Gallwood, and all replied in a similar manner, although Dr. Setbon testified with great reluctance.   I could see from the expression on Mr. Dash's face that he was much dissatisfied.   Mr. Mayland was the only one who qualified his answer in the least, and he only to the extent of saying that there might be some doubt as to contumacy.   He admitted fully the inconsistency, and that it alone would be considered as strong presumptive evidence of non composmentiveness.

Mr. Mayland's examination being over the court adjourned until the following day, when the Reverend Mr. Nudwink was called upon to testify.

CHAPTER XXV.

FRESH shaven and smooth, unctuous, oily, and sleek, in spite of his attenuated form, Mr. Nudwink took his seat in the witness-chair with an expression of sanctimonious hypocrisy that I should have revolted from had I been simply an indifferent spectator of the trial instead of being the one whose life was in peril. It was hardly to be wondered at that I felt some aversion for this man, and that in describing him I should be tempted to depart from the calmness of a reporter, and indulge myself in some little vituperation. But I can say now, honestly, that I have not retouched to his prejudice the photograph which that day was impressed upon a retentive memory. He was dressed from head to foot in a suit of sombre black, except that at his throat he had a green sea-color tie ; his hair was brushed sleekly—parted near the middle—behind his ears, and being long, though scanty, twisted up at the ends like fish-hooks ; his yellow, cadaverous skin was drawn tightly over bony jaws, and above a long, thin nose his green eyes looked in unholy hate upon me, his victim. His thin, pale lips opened like the mouth of a cat-fish as he responded to the questions that were propounded.

" Your name ? "

He gave it.

" Your occupation ? "

" Clergyman of the Establishment."

" Where do you officiate ? "

" Ahem ! At this present time I still minister—I trust acceptably—to the unfortunates at the asylum, and I have also, until within the last few days, striven to edify the little flock—grown greatly under my pastorate—at the adjoining village. But I deem it needful to state that I have only recently accepted a call, given with much unanimity, from a congregation whose place of worship is in this city—St. Proper Fractions."

" Highly complimentary," said the prosecutor.

" I so regard it, though not to any poor ability that I may possess as a pulpit orator, but rather to my devotion to the truth as it is in Numbers."

" You are acquainted with the accused? "

" I am."

" Have your opportunities of knowing his character intimately been ample or the reverse ? "

" Ample."

" Have you had conversations with him upon religious subjects from time to time ? "

" I have. The first of such conversations occurred before he was—mistakenly, as I now think—placed upon the course of discipline. I asked—"

Mr. Dash rose to his feet hastily.

" I object," said he, " I object to any matters being introduced which are already made the subject of previous investigation and which are matters of record."

This objection was the cause of a little wrangle, but was sustained by the judge.

" How recently was the last conversation ? "

" That occurred on the evening of the day that Mr. Smalls recovered."

" Where did it take place ? "

" At Lunatico, Mr. Mayland's summer house."

" Who were present ? "

Nudwink gave the desired information.

" Be so good as to state the nature of this conversation."

" There was very little said. Some reference was made to the subject of the remarkable cure effected by me—or, rather, through my instrumentality—of Mr. Smalls. Mr. Cliff arrogantly professed to have essayed a faith-cure of his own."

" Ah ! he did. Was any mention made by him of the time when this futile attempt was made—"

" I object," exclaimed Mr. Dash, earning his money.

" State your objection," said the judge.

" I object to counsel's assumption that Mr. Cliff's alleged faith-cure was futile. I ask to have the word futile stricken out."

" Strike it out," said the judge, laconically.

The attorney repeated his question, dropping the interdicted word.

" Mr. Cliff stated," Nudwink responded, " that this attempt was made the previous evening."

" Did he say where it was made ? "

" He admitted that he made it at Lunatico Villa."

" Did he say anything respecting his method ? "

" He did not."

" Of your own knowledge, Mr. Nudwink, can you say whether Mr. Cliff had a permit to visit Lunatico Villa at the time he admitted having been there ? "

" He had no permit."

" That will do, sir."

Nudwink squirmed a little in his chair, and his fishy mouth opened again :

"May I be permitted to say a word?"

The judge bowed.

"Lest my motives be misunderstood," said Nudwink, "I desire to state that I am only actuated in all this matter by a sincere regard for my duty to society."

"We do not doubt that, Mr. Nudwink," said the judge.

"And not only to society," continued the chaplain, "but likewise to my poor misguided young friend, whom I have striven with unceasingly, yet, I grieve to say, unavailingly. I am only a follower of the raft, but I trust that the old leaven has been thoroughly purged away. Though he has treated me with the utmost contumely, yet I bear him no malice whatever. Though he has done me a cruel wrong —and yet, not me, but the truths I represent—still I cherish none but the very kindliest, most affectionate feelings towards him. If it shall please Mathematics—if it be so ordered in his inscrutable ways—to take the soul of this our unfortunate brother home I can only regard it as a dispensation, and myself as the humble instrument. I say this lest, peradventure, there should be those who might falsely accuse me of compassing his death. I know —none better—how full the island is of iniquity, and how prone we all are to err; but I feel that in all this I have done my sacred duty, not only to society, but also to him. As a proof of my sincerity I here offer my own ministrations. I shall charge him nothing, although I might legally do so, he being no longer under my direct spiritual control; but I am happy to be able to state that sordid considerations are now the merest nothing to me, my stipend being much larger from St. Proper Fractions than it was previously as chaplain; although, in justice to myself, I must say that this fact had no influence in determining my course; I had a single eye to the advancement of the cause of Numbers, which I felt could be better done on a wider field of usefulness."

"Your motives are in the highest degree commendable," said the judge, with another profound bow. "The court appreciates your position, and exonerates you, fully."

Nudwink listened to this with a smirk of intense satisfaction, and then glided, eel-like, out of the witness-chair.

His place was taken at the call of the crier by the Reverend Mr. Smalls.

Mr. Smalls' appearance presented a strong contrast in many respects to that of Mr. Nudwink. Both were rather tall, both spare, both bony, both pale, and both smooth-looking and serious. But in the quiet, sober, sorrowful dignity of Mr. Smalls, in the delicate whiteness of his face and hands, and in the sedate glance of his gray eyes, there was something that spoke of a real and vital grace and glory within; that peace passing all understanding, which only belongs to a purified heart. Mr. Smalls responded to the usual questions politely and without hesitation, while yet his manner was dejected and forlorn. He related briefly how he had first met me at the funeral, and then told of his illness and recovery.

"You were attended by several physicians, were you not?"

"I was," Mr. Smalls replied, naming them.

"Do you regard your cure as having been effected by either of these gentlemen?"

"I do not.".

When this reply was made there was a noise behind me. Involuntarily I glanced around and saw Dr. Humpath making his way, apparently in a state of some perturbation, towards the door. The prosecutor paid no attention to this interruption, but proceeded with his enquiries.

"By whom do you consider your cure to have been made?" he asked.

"It was the will of Mathematics," Mr. Smalls responded, solemnly. "As to the means, I prefer not to speak."

"It is with great regret that I feel compelled to press the question." said the attorney, deferentially.

I leaned over and whispered to my counsel. For the first time in our intercourse he seemed to regard a suggestion of mine as worthy of his attention. He was up on his feet in a moment.

"I object," he said. "I object to that question."

"On what ground?" asked the judge, while the prosecutor looked at him with the utmost astonishment.

"On the ground that the answer will, if given, involve a privileged communication."

"If you can sustain your claim that Mr. Smalls' reply will necessarily involve such a privileged communication the motion must be granted."

Then Mr. Dash made an argument, the substance of which was that no matter what Mr. Smalls' reply might be it would involve matters of confidence between patient and physician, or if that ground was considered untenable, between a dying man, or one supposed to be dying, and his spiritual adviser. The argument was long and learned, and when Mr. Dash had finished, the prosecutor had an opportunity to reply. Of this he instantly availed himself, and quoted quite as many authorities in his own favor as Mr. Dash had in his. While they were talking some one handed Judge Knowitz a letter. This he opened and read, and then wrote a brief reply. He was in the act of licking the gum of the envelope when the attorney finished.

" Motion denied," said the judge, rubbing the envelope with his thumb. "Answer the question, Mr. Smalls."

" I take an exception to that ruling," said Mr. Dash, emphatically, as he sat down ; and then Mr. Smalls, with evident reluctance, replied, " I believe that, in the unsearchable and mysterious will of Mathematics, Mr. Cliff was the instrument, humanly speaking, of my cure."

This answer caused a manifest stir on the back benches ; the attorney looked blank, my own counsel astonished, and the amazement of the judge was evident. At first I hardly comprehended what had been said. Was it possible, after all, that I had produced the impression that I had so ardently desired to make, and which I had regarded as having so hopelessly failed in ? I listened with breathless interest to all that followed.

" You say, Mr. Smalls," continued the puzzled attorney, " that you believe Mr. Cliff to have been instrumental in curing you ? "

" I believe it to have been in consequence of his visit that I did recover."

" Did he attempt the faith-cure ? "

Mr. Smalls was thoughtful.

" He so stated.   Mr. Cliff spoke of his conference as a faith-cure."

" You are not willing to state positively that it was a faith-cure ? "

" That I would not be willing to state."

" Was the element of faith involved ? "

" So Mr. Cliff said."

" But can you not answer of your own knowledge ? "

" No, I can only repeat what he said."

" That is very singular," said the attorney, more puzzled than ever. " What oil did Mr. Cliff use? Perhaps that may guide us somewhat."

Mr. Smalls now appeared painfully embarrassed. At last he said, speaking in a very low tone : " Mr Cliff used no oil."

" What ! " exclaimed the attorney, " a pretended faith-cure and no oil ! How is that ? "

" I cannot tell," replied Mr. Smalls, feebly.

" Was oil provided ? "

" Oh, yes."

" In abundance ? "

" Certainly ; my mother attended to that."

" All kinds ? "

" Yes : all kinds."

" And he made no attempt to use oil in any way ? "

" No : he made no attempt whatever."

" What did he say ? I mean what was his mode of expression ? "

" He sat down beside me, and began—"

" Well ? "

" Is it absolutely necessary that I should make this statement ? Is there no way that I can be excused from the narration ? It is painful in the extreme."

" It is your duty under the circumstances, Mr. Smalls," said the attorney. " I regret to require it, but the interests of justice and the good of society demand that this matter should be fully elucidated."

" Mr. Cliff began to tell me a most interesting romance."

" A romance ? "

" Yes ; or a narrative."

" What was its purport ? "

" He put it in the form of a personal experience. He related very graphically what he stated were the facts

respecting ocean ; that across the ocean was a country
similar to our own island, though vastly larger and more
beautiful, and that he himself was a resident of that country, and had been brought hither on something—that—"
Mr. Smalls hesitated.

" Brought hither how ? "

" In what he called a boat."

" A boat !   What is that ?"

" I do not know," replied Mr. Smalls, gloomily.   " Mr.
Cliff attempted to explain, but I could not understand
him."

" What was the nature of his explanation ? "

" He said that this boat was—was—like—"

" Like what ? "

Mr. Smalls took out his handkerchief.   " He said it
was—like—the raft."

There was a deep silence, in the midst of which I heard
a hoarse voice on the bench behind me whispering, " Atro-
cious blasphemy."   I knew the voice.   It was Nudwink
who had spoken.   At last the attorney recovered himself
and proceeded.

" What else did Mr. Cliff say to you that evening ? "

" He told me that I need not fear ; that if I would only
believe that the touch of the ocean spray could not harm
me that I would instantly recover ; and then he went on
to state that he had repeatedly been, as I understood him,
covered by the ocean ; that he had done something in it
—swam was, if I recollect right, the word—and that it
was a mistaken notion that sea-sickness was in any way a
dangerous disease."

" Did you believe him, Mr. Smalls ? "

The witness smiled sadly.

" How could I ? " he answered, shaking his head.

" How long was Mr. Cliff with you ? "

" About an hour."

" And then did he go away ? "

" He left the house."

" What effect did this singular narrative have upon
you ? "

" For some time after Mr. Cliff left, I perhaps ought,
as a clergyman, to be ashamed, but I gave myself up to
unrestrained mirth. The story had been related with
such seriousness that the grotesque and, in truth, almost
sacrilegious absurdity was altogether too much for me to
resist. I laughed immoderately, and when my mother
and Oliver entered the room, they found me sitting up
in bed ; the excitement had actually brought back my
strength."

" Then you attribute your recovery to the effect produced upon your system by the excitement attendant
upon this narrative ? "

" I do ; I must say that I attribute it chiefly to that."

" It was a very comical story," said the attorney,
gravely.

" It would all be comical," answered Mr. Smalls, with
a sigh, "if it were not so sad."

" Was it a stratagem, do you think, Mr. Smalls, intended to produce the very excitement which resulted,
as you say, in your restoration to health ? "

" I might have thought so, but—but—that is—if I had
not known—"

The attorney smiled a cold, hard, sarcastic, unfeeling
smile. " You need say no more, Mr. Smalls, I understand fully how you feel. That will be all."

Mr. Smalls then stepped down, and soon after the
court adjourned. I was visited that evening again by

Oliver, who brought messages of love from Margery. "Cheer up, Mr. Cliff," he said, "cheer up; all is not lost by any means yet. I have had a long interview with Mr. Dash, and he has great hopes that the line of defence which he proposes to take will be successful."

"What line is that?" I asked.

"He would not divulge it. He said that it would be made known in due time."

"There is only one defence," said I, with some irritation, thinking with what scant ceremony Mr. Dash had put my views and wishes aside.

Oliver said nothing. As he went away, he handed me a paper. "I brought this in for you to read; perhaps it may interest you to read an account of your trial, particularly as there is nothing in it but what is favorable to your case."

I was in no mood for literature, but when the gas was lighted I looked over the journal, and inadvertently my eyes rested upon this in the advertising supplement, all in the largest type:

"READ THE FUNNICOLLUM! READ THE FUNNICOLLUM! *Startling developments in the trial of Mr. Cliff before the Sun Court.*

GET THE FUNNICOLLUM AND LIVE! *A witness testifies that laughter restored him to health.*

BUY THE FUNNICOLLUM! *Dying and restored to life.*

BUY THE FUNNICOLLUM! *Brought back from the brink of the grave.*

BUY THE FUNNICOLLUM !

Better than physic.   Cheaper than doctors.
Sure cure every time.

————

·   BUY THE FUNNICOLLUM !
All newsdealers keep it on hand.   Price only one farthing.
Only known cure for sea-sickness.   No family can afford
to do without it.   Physicians deny its virtues, but
this is a recommendation.   Undertakers are
all indignant, but the invalids are content.

————

BUY THE FUNNICOLLUM !
If your newsdealer does not have it, forward the price to
publishers, and it will be sent, post-paid."

In all my misery and perplexity I had yet preserved
a sense of humor ; but I felt in no mood for laughter
now.   Would the *Funnicollum* avail to save me from the
dreadful doom towards which my persecutors were hurrying me ?   Alas ! no.   What terrible irony there was in the
gibes and slurs of these agnostic islanders.   The only
things they were positively certain about were the very
ones of which they were, indeed, the most lamentably
ignorant.   Enemies and friends alike refused to credit,
for one instant, the solemn assurance that I was not mad.
And more, they alike turned deafly away, not only from
my protestations, but from my offers of proof.   How easy
it would be to convince these people that what I had
said respecting the salt sea which they called death was
all true.   I told Oliver that night all that I had related
to Mr. Dash, and begged him by his friendship, and by
the love he professed, to hear me ; begged him with

tears, and he had deigned me only the response of
sympathy. Oh! how hollow is sympathy alone when the
helping hand is withheld. Yet, bitterly as I grieved, I
could not blame Oliver, for I was now convinced that he,
too, deemed me mad.

As I lay on my pallet, wakeful, almost till the dawn,
how these dreadful thoughts racked and ravened upon
me. Then I thought of my own dear Margery. It had
been several days since I had seen her. Was it possible
that she could be ill? How heartless it had been of me
not to question Oliver more closely. Messages of love
he had, indeed, brought; messages which I had, without
effort, committed to memory—for love learns easily by
heart—and they did, indeed, comfort me. I revolved in
my mind the events of the day in the court-room, striving
to extract some little comfort out of all that dreadful
trial, and going over and over the testimony against me,
bit by bit. Alas! it was all against me. Even Oliver
and Mr. Smalls, grateful as the latter was to me, had
been forced to witness against me. Was there no hope?
I gnashed my teeth and cursed: I cursed Nudwink, the
professional hypocrite, and I cursed Gallwood, the specious villain, through whose sinister devices I saw plainly,
though he had striven to disguise them. There was no
hope. When the strength of my passion subsided I lay
for awhile in a state of torpor, glaring into the darkness,
till at last I slept. When I awoke it was broad day, and
I heard the sound of the matin chimes of the cathedral,
floating downward from the great tower that loomed up
through the foggy morning, as I looked out over the city
roused from its night's repose.

It was yet quite early. I dressed myself and sat at the
barred casement, listening to the sonorous music of the

17

chimes, and thinking, thinking, not the wild anguish of the dreadful thoughts of the night, but the calmer whisperings of returning day: the good and the bad; the cold and the heat; the day and night; the foul and fair. How they chase and change with one another. How they alternate in the sad, gay, sweet, bitter world about us, and in our own hearts as well. So thinking, the bad and the bitter, and the chill of night glided away. I thought of my own dear love, my Margery, and—the chimes still sweetly swaying sonorous melody—the tears filled my eyes. I thought of my mother, and then I fell upon my knees, there by the window facing the east, and with clasped hands, and shut eyes streaming with despairing tears, I prayed unto that good father of us all, who holds death, like the sea, in his hollowed hand. Comforted, I at last opened my eyes, and the sun, risen from the sea, smiled at me, reflected from every turret and tower of all the city.

CHAPTER XXVI.

BULLINGER was the last witness examined by the prosecution. He testified to the fact of his incarceration and subsequent release upon the course of discipline, and also (this was new to me) that he was free, having passed the examination before the convalescent court, in this case consisting solely of Gallwood, and was now restored to the full rights of citizenship. The examination proceeded.

"While you were on the second stage of the course of discipline," said the attorney, "were you detailed as acting assistant-superintendent at any time?"

"I was."

"By commission under seal?"

"Yes."

"Have you that commission with you?"

Bullinger produced a document. The attorney took it, and, after a careful perusal, handed it to the court. His Honor read it, and then it was read aloud, after being duly marked for identification by the clerk.

The commission ran thus:

"ASYLUM OF INQUIRENDO.

" *To all to whom these presents shall come, Greeting :*

"By virtue of the authority conferred upon me as assistant-governor (now acting as governor of the asylum), I hereby designate and appoint Richard Bullinger, **a** convalescent on the second stage of the course of

259

discipline, to be an acting assistant-superintendent, with
all the powers of said office, for the term of two months
from the date hereof; and he, the said Bullinger, is
hereby authorized and empowered to act as such officer,
and is hereby detailed on special duty with one of the
convalescents, also upon the said second stage of the
course of discipline, to wit : with one John Cliff, a sus-
pect. It is hereby made the duty and sole task of the
said Bullinger to well and truly perform his said obligations respecting said Cliff, to the end that the peace of
the island may be preserved, and all needful information
duly had by this asylum and its constituted authorities.

"In testimony whereof, I have hereunto
[SEAL]   signed my name as acting governor of
the asylum, and affixed the seal thereof.

"ROTH GALLWOOD.

"*Acting Governor.*"

I listened to the reading of this rascally document with
a mingling of astonishment and indignation. Before the
clerk had finished, the purport of the villany was apparent. I leaned over and whispered to my counsel, telling
him the facts as I knew them.

"Did you have a commission to watch Bullinger ? " he
asked, coldly.

"Mr. Gallwood gave me authority," I replied.

"Verbal authority?"

"Yes."

"Perfectly valueless," said Mr. Dash ; "a commission,
to be of any binding validity, must be in writing and
have affixed to it the seal of the asylum."

"But I was not aware of that fact," I interposed, "my
action was in perfect good faith—"

"No doubt, no doubt, Mr. Cliff. I am not disputing

your good faith; but you must remember the maxim of the law, that ignorance thereof excuses no man."

I turned away in great disgust, and Bullinger, not without some manifest embarrassment, continued telling how he had accompanied me to the village on the coast, and had (this was the purport of it all) acted as a spy from first to last upon my actions.

"Did you ever have any private conversation with Mr. Cliff respecting his views on death?"

"I did," responded Bullinger.

"Relate what passed between you."

Bullinger told the substance of my proposition to demonstrate to him the harmlessness of the salt water, by going down to the beach and taking a plunge.

There was an audible snicker upon some of the back benches, the attorney chuckled, Bullinger himself smiled, and even the sedate judge so far forgot his dignity as to give utterance to a laugh which, however, he promptly suppressed. My own counsel turned savagely round and glared at me contemptuously. Then shaking his shoulders vigorously, he resumed his impassive demeanor.

"Was this said jokingly, Mr. Bullinger?" inquired the attorney.

"On the contrary, it was said with great seriousness."

"How did the subject arise?"

"It was in reference to Mr. Smalls."

"Did he speak of the faith-cure?"

"Yes; it was on that special subject that Mr. Cliff was speaking. He said that his faith-cure consisted solely in convincing Mr. Smalls that there was in reality no danger to be apprehended from the sea."

"In this same conversation, was any other subject introduced?"

"Oh, yes."

"Any subject whereon the views expressed by Mr. Cliff were of a dangerous character?"

"Yes."

"What was that subject?"

"He began talking about the Arithmetic."

"What did he say?"

"He said a great deal that was wild and extravagant, and that indicated manifest unsoundness of intellect. Perhaps the most extraordinary thing that he said was that the Arithmetic was not a work teaching morals; but was, in fact—as I understood him—a scientific treatise."

"Scientific?" said the attorney, with a pitying smile, "how did he explain that?"

Mr. Bullinger also smiled.

"I hardly think what he said could be called an explanation," said he.

"Perhaps not. What was his attempt at an explanation?"

"He said a great deal about Numbers and figures being the same, and then he went on to say that our methods of computation were all wrong, and that this book was nothing but an account of a better way. All he said was so wild that I can hardly pretend to relate precisely what he did say One thing I remember distinctly: he said that a cipher had a value—that it was nothing, and yet had a value. Of course I manifested some incredulity, and he went on about putting a cipher after one, which, he said, made ten."

"The Arch ten?" .

"He only said ten; but I suppose he meant the Arch ten."

"Did you not think that absurd?"

"Of course."

"Did he say anything further?"

"He maundered on, mixing things up terribly; said that Numbers was not a man, and finally, after all his absurdities, finished by declaring that the value of a cipher depended entirely upon its distance from the decimal point."

"Well," said the attorney, "that was orthodox, or, at least, good decimal doctrine; was it not?"

"Certainly, so far as that went."

"Can you recall anything further bearing upon the subject of Mr. Cliff's eccentricities—to use a mild term?"

"That appears to be all."

"Then that will be sufficient, Mr. Bullinger."

The witness stepped down, and, after turning over his papers for several minutes, the attorney intimated that the case for the prosecution had closed.

Mr. Dash arose.

In his address which followed he was very learned, very dignified, very earnest, and very emphatic; but he was very far from satisfying me. He concluded by stating that he rested his case upon an ancient maxim of law, which he would briefly state in legal language as *the defensus jokandi;* and that he would not take up the time of the court, but would forthwith call his witnesses. A conference between Mr. Dash and the clerk was then held, some papers passed, and the latter called for "Dr. Scatterbrain."

A tall, pompous, austere individual, with glasses and scanty gray hair, and a benevolent expression of countenance in spite of his austerity, took the chair.

After the usual formula, Mr. Dash put the following interrogatory: "On the supposition that a person on the

second stage of the course of discipline had a friend
suffering from sea-sickness, and that this friend was lying
ill in a house outside of, but near the boundary of, and
adjacent to the third department; that this invalid was
an integer, having a belief in a faith-cure, and that the
person first herein referred to was desirous of effecting
a cure of his said friend, the integer; also, on the further
supposition, that the said person on the said course of
discipline did cross the limits of the third department,
and did visit his said friend and related an amusing
story, and that the said friend, being an integer, did
laugh immoderately and did subsequently recover; also,
on the supposition that the said person on the said course
of discipline did afterwards, in conversation, but before
the complete and entire cure of the said sea-sick person
was effected, tell again the same or a similar humorous
story—a story so wild and improbable as to preclude the
thought of seriousness; what, in view of all these facts
and conditions as hereinbefore stated, what was the
state of mind of the said person on said second stage
of said course of discipline, as regards sanity?"

There was a profound stillness.

Dr. Scatterbrain rubbed his forehead for an instant,
reflectively.

"I did not quite catch the import of a portion of the
query; please state it again."

Mr. Dash braced himself.

"On the supposition—" he began; and to save time
I may as well state that he went through with the question again from beginning to end. This time the witness
had his answer ready:

"The man was unquestionably sane."

The rest of the morning hour was devoted to an exam-

ination of sundry other eminent doctors, with whom, it is
to be presumed, Mr. Dash had previously put himself in
communication. The same hypothetical question was
asked of each, and the same response in substance was
in every case elicited. In several instances the question
had to be repeated, so that after a time it became tiresome, and I was, moreover, fully persuaded that Mr.
Dash was not pursuing the proper course in my defence.

At the noon recess, I intimated as much to him. Mr.
Dash was of an irascible disposition.

"Good Mathematics!" he exclaimed, testily, "what
do you know about law?"

I admitted meekly that I did not know much.

"And yet you presume to dictate to me."

"Oh, no, I only suggest."

"A suggestion is often covert dictation," said Mr.
Dash, epigrammatically. "Rely upon it, Mr. Cliff, I am
making the only possible defence : the *defensus jokandi*,
or, as it is termed colloquially, the plea of emotional
sanity, is the only one that the court can be made to
listen to, and, I must tell you, Mr. Cliff, the result of
even this is very doubtful." Mr. Dash, it was evident,
took a gloomy view of the case, and, it may as well be
· confessed, so also did I.

"When am I to be examined, Mr. Dash?" I asked,
just before the court re-opened.

"Not at all, Mr. Cliff," he responded, emphatically,
"not at all; it would be the height of folly."

We all filed into the court-room soon after, and the
tiresome examination of the doctors was again begun.

At the end of an hour Mr. Dash had finished, and
very tired he sat down, after making a motion that the
arguments should be deferred until the next day.

The judge very promptly denied the motion, and between the speech of the attorney, a string of meaningless nonsense and vituperation, and that of Mr. Dash, who only left out the vituperation, the remainder of the afternoon was wasted.

The judge was manifestly vexed that the case could not have been closed that day (I learned afterwards that his wife's mother was stopping with him, and that he had, on this account, arranged to take a run into the fifth department). He made one or two efforts to stop the flow of Mr. Dash's eloquence, and several suggestions that he should confine himself to the subject.

These interruptions had only the effect to nettle my counsel, who prolonged his harangue until it was too late for the judge to start on his journey. I may be in error; I do not wish even to appear to be doing an injustice to Judge Knowitz, who stands deservedly high in the estimation of the legal fraternity of Inquirendo; but perhaps it is calculated to destroy the delicate balance of the faculties so necessary in a jurist, to pass any length of time in company with a mother-in-law; although, as one of Inquirendo's poets sweetly sings, "it depends entirely upon the character of the mother-in-law."

The next morning, promptly on time, the judge took his seat upon the bench, and after some preliminaries he began his opinion.

"The court," he said, "sitting as a court of equity, and empowered to try matters of fact as well as matters of law, has first to consider its own limitations. These limitations naturally divide themselves into three co-ordinate branches: limitations applied to the accused; those which apply to the law as law; and those which apply solely to the mind of the court itself. Equity is the correction of that wherein the law is deficient. Now in this case it does not appear—no attempt has been made to make it appear —that the law is in any wise deficient. On the contrary, it seems to be admitted that, so far as the law extends, there is no imperfection or deficiency whatsoever. The law describes the exact crime which the accused has been shown to have committed. The accused does not deny the facts, and his counsel has made no pretence of denying them for him. The law imposes a penalty, and prescribes the mode of execution of said penalty fully. Thus far there is no doubt or hesitation in the mind of the court. If the court is, under the law, bound to render his decision according to the law, then the court has no alternative but to render the only judgment that the law permits ; that judgment would be then of necessity : Guilty of noncompos-mentiveness, and the penalty thereof would be, as a matter of law, death.

"But—" here the judge made a very impressive pause and looked around the court-room over the top of his spec-tacles benignantly ; so much so indeed that I took heart and began to think, after all, that it was just possible that his Honor might be wise enough, or simple enough, to let me off easy.

"But," he repeated, emphatically, " the court is debarred from rendering a decision of this character upon the sole question of law. Why ? Simply because an issue of equity is set up in the answer to the state's complaint, and in that issue a plea is advanced, which the court is bound to con-sider, however extravagant, and in a statutory sense obso-lete, that defence may be. This plea is, to state it briefly, the *defensus jokandi*, or, as it is now more commonly termed, the plea of emotional sanity. I say that this plea is obsolete, as there is no instance on record of its having been advanced for many years. In effect, this plea, if sustained by the evidence, is a complete bar to further proceedings, and the court would have no alternative but to release the accused. The eminent counsel who now defends Mr. Cliff has done wisely in presenting it, inasmuch as it was beyond doubt the only tenable plea in Mr. Cliff's case "—my spirits rose—" if *any* were tenable," the judge added, after a pause, in a low tone, and again my heart sank.

"'The court has made allusion to certain limitations," continued the judge. " Two have been considered : those applying to the law and those applying to the court itself. It remains now only to consider those which have direct application to the accused, and these are but two in number : the alleged contumacy; evinced, if at all, by Mr. Cliff's leaving the third department without a pass ; and inconsistency, in making a pretence of being a mixed number or like a mixed number, for the two terms are synonymous, and feigning to perform a faith-cure while admitting that his convictions coincided with those of Mr. Hurtheart. The court disregards the evidence touching the subject of death and the Arithmetic as having no bearing whatever upon the case, and confines itself entirely to a consideration of the two subjects, contumacy and inconsistency. Was Mr. Cliff contumacious ? This depends upon the state of his mind at the time. An act may be perfectly innocent and yet contrary to statute. The question to be considered in this instance is : What was the state of Mr. Cliff's mind at the time that he went to Lunatico Villa ? Did he go there under the assured conviction that he was acting rightly, and for the good of humanity, or was it through a contumacious disregard of authority that he visited Mr. Smalls ?

"After much anxious deliberation, and having all the time in view the good of society as a whole, the court is constrained to pass judgment on this specification in favor of the accused. He was not contumacious."

My heart gave a great bound of joy, and there were some evidences of satisfaction upon the benches back of me ; but these being promptly suppressed, the judge continued : " In arriving at this decision in this respect no attention whatever is paid to the ways and means—in the case of the alleged faith-cure—by which Mr. Cliff is asserted to have tried to put his benevolent object into practice. It is sufficient for the court that there was a benevolent object in view, and as the whole spirit of Iquirendian law has the good of the public for its underlying motive, this assumption is clearly justified.

" Let us now advance to a consideration of the second specification : inconsistency. Was Mr. Cliff inconsistent ? The controlling evidence here is that of Mr. Cliff's friend, Mr. Oliver, who has testified in unmistakable terms to certain declarations made by the accused, having reference to his mixed condition. and also the testimony of another friend, Mr. Gallwood, to whose distinct and positive declaration I desire to draw attention. The question was asked : ' Did Mr. Cliff express any opinion respecting the truth of what Mr. Hurtheart said ? A. He did ; he stated that he approved of Mr. Hurtheart's doctrine.'

" Neither of these declarations has been controverted, and they therefore stand in their full force. On this subject of inconsistency, there is one portion of the proof that adds weight to the conviction in the mind of the court ; it is this, that Mr. Cliff did not propose to use oil of any kind in his so-called faith-cure, although it is a matter of record that oil in abundance and of all kinds had been provided.

"As an answer to the charges against him, the accused, through his counsel, attempted to set up the defence of emotional sanity—'that all he did was a joke, and that all he said was in fun.' The answer to this is, that the proof does not come up to it, and in the second place it would not be a good defence if it did. The accused attempted to establish the *defensus jokandi*, and failed. It is true, instances were hypothetically established, most ingeniously, whereby several learned physicians were made to testify affirmatively as to their belief in Mr. Cliff's sanity; but this in the meaning of the statute does not constitute a good defence. It is the opinion of the court, therefore, that Mr. Cliff has been clearly guilty of inconsistency, and therefore the court does pronounce him of the charge of noncomposmentiveness—guilty."

I was shocked; but, after all that the judge had previously said, not greatly surprised. I did not think that his Honor had been very tender to my feelings in raising my hopes at times, only immediately after to shatter them. The judgment had now been pronounced, and at least I was relieved from the anxiety attendant upon uncertainty.

The attorney at once moved for sentence.; but Mr. Dash had been almost equally spry in his motion for a new trial.

The judge decided to hear my counsel's motion first.

"Do you ask for a new trial on the ground of newly-discovered evidence?" said the judge.

"No, your Honor," replied Mr. Dash, promptly, "on the ground that your Honor's decision is contrary to the weight of evidence, and on the further ground that your Honor erred in not admitting evidence touching the matter of death and of the Arithmetic. We hold that your Honor's mind ought to have been influenced by the conversations on these two topics, as in his extravagant utterances Mr. Cliff was plainly only in fun; and that thereby the *defensus jokandi* was established beyond a reasonable doubt."

Mr. Dash then sat down, and the attorney replied in a long, verbose and tiresome argument.

When he concluded, the judge instantly denied a new trial, and at once the attorney renewed his motion for sentence.

This was granted, and the clerk, stepping forward, called upon me to stand up, which I did, and was then asked if I had anything to say why the sentence of the court should not be pronounced. Before I could reply Mr. Dash sprang up and answered for me: "My client appeals to the General Term, but has nothing further to say now."

I beckoned to him hastily. "What is the reason that I cannot make my offer now?" I asked.

"What offer?"

"About my boat."

"Bosh!" exclaimed Mr. Dash, irritably, "I don't like trifling."

"If I were allowed to build a coffer—" I was going on, but my counsel turned away angrily. I was angry myself at his indifference, and finished the sentence for my own satisfaction.

"Damn!" I said.

The judge now reached under his desk, brought forth and donned a great green cap (green being the color of the sea), and in a solemn voice sentenced me to death, fixing the day of my execution, and commending my soul to Mathematics.

CHAPTER XXVII.

"TO THE UNKNOWN GOD."

ONLY ten days now intervened between me and the hereafter; only ten between life and death. I was conducted back to my desolate cell, where in alternate agony and apathy the night passed sleepless over me. Day dawned again, the first of the terrible ten, each one of which was to be fuller and yet more full of bitterness; and yet not so, for with Margery's coming, and the consolation her dear presence brought, hope revived. In due course of law Mr. Dash filed his bill of exceptions, and made his appeal to the General Term. Judge Bounce heard the arguments and took the papers; but the day after handed down his opinion, and that opinion was adverse. Judge Knowitz's rulings were sustained in every particular. Oliver was with me often. Dr. Setbon also came, and once Mr. Smalls visited me. This was the second day after the judgment had been pronounced. Oliver came with him, and the two with gentle exhortations strove to lift my thoughts to a consideration of what they regarded as my soul's safety. They both earnestly implored me to submit myself to the ministrations of the church and to allow the rite of cancellation to be administered.

They brought Arithmetics and read passages from these and the commentaries, and implored me to take heed lest I should be a castaway. I earnestly sympathized with them in their well meant efforts, and yet I could not bring myself to pretend a belief that I did not feel. They brought paper, and ink, and pens, and when at last they left me it was with an expression of strong desire that I would write down the confession of my sins that they deemed essential, and thereby prepare the written solution as a prelude to the last solemn ordinance. Much as I desired to please my friends I could not bring myself to do this. It is true that I saw in it no sin, and yet my conscience revolted from an act that I could not but regard as almost blasphemous. They went away greatly troubled for my spiritual welfare, and tearfully expressing a hope that I might be led in the way of truth.

The next day was the Sabbath. I was awakened early by the usual matin chorus of the cathedral bells. The morning wore on, and at the customary hour I received a summons to attend service in the hall below. As I took my seat I saw to my great horror that the hypocritical Nudwink was the officiating minister. I implored the attendant to allow me to return to my cell, but he was inflexible. He could not disregard his orders, he declared. It was my last Sabbath upon the island, and it behoved me to think upon my latter end. So, in great horror, I sat through that awful service and that awful sermon. With singular poor taste, as I thought, Nudwink selected as his text what he claimed was a fitting and appropriate passage : " Cut off the ciphers from the right of the Divisor." He had a poor delivery, but there was plenty of it such as it was. He was tremendously emphatic, and swung his arms, and shouted, and pounded the cushions in a truly orthodox way. He made one or two pointed references to myself which I felt might have been omitted without offence, and whenever he did so I became the target for the eyes of all present. I sat bolt upright through all that awful two hours, and when at last the discourse was over it was with a feeling of unutterable relief that I was permitted to be alone once more. Hardly had I seated myself by the grated window, when there was a rap at my cell door, the bolts were shot back, the door swung open, and there by the side of my sombre-visaged jailer stood the yet more sad-faced Nudwink.   I was not pleased to see him.   Doubtless my manner indicated as much, perhaps more; for Nudwink did not advance beyond the door-sill.

"My poor misguided young friend," said Nudwink, lachrymosely, "I have deemed it my bounden duty to make one last effort on your behalf.   To that end I have sought you here.   May I be permitted to call your attention to the fact that this is your last Sabbath upon the island?"

"I have had my attention called to that fact several times," I responded, irritably.   "I have no means handy to prevent your calling it again."

"I feel concerned for your welfare, young man, deeply concerned.   Can I not persuade you to give over your frivolity and to fix your mind upon a consideration of the truth?"

"Nudwink," said I, turning round and glaring at him, "you are a confounded old scamp."

"Persecuted for Mathematics' sake," murmured Nudwink, "yet must I not be weary.   Mr. Cliff!"

"Well."

"Will nothing move you?"

"I wish something would move you," I muttered. Then a thought struck me.   "Come in, Nudwink," I added aloud, "don't stand there in the draft."

Nudwink crossed the threshold. Quick as lightning I got up and made a bolt for him. I raised my leg. Nudwink was spry, but by good luck I managed to give him, as he turned to flee, one hearty kick in that portion of his person which I shall designate (I was something of a yachtsman) the starboard quarter. Unfortunately I was only provided with slippers; but no act of my life gave me more real satisfaction than that kick.

Nudwink skipped nimbly out of the door, which the attendant promptly shut after him, and I was vexed by the foulness of his hypocritical professions no more.

That evening, at dusk, I saw once more my Margery. With many sobs, clinging to me, she told of the illness that had kept her from my side.

" Ill! have you been ill, my darling ? " I said, and looking in her tear-stained face I saw how pale she was.

"Yes, I have been ill, dear John ; but I have sent you messages every day : Oliver brought them, did he not?"

" Oh, yes, Oliver has been very kind ; still I have wondered, dearest, why you did not come."

" I made Oliver promise that he would say nothing of my having been ill; but I am better now, dear. I could not let this Sabbath pass without coming to you. I want to ask you, my own, for my sake to try and prepare for the—the—" she broke out into bitter sobs : then throwing her arms about me she wailed, "Oh, how can I bear to part with you, my darling love. We must meet again. There is a better land than this, John, where there will be no more parting. Shall we not meet there ? "

"Ah ! I hope so, dearest Margery. It is my fondest hope that in that better country we may meet again."

" But how can we meet if you are not prepared?"

" I trust I am prepared," I said, fervently.

She wept again.

"Why should you grieve, darling?" I said, pressing my lips to her cheek. "This world is full of sorrow. In that other happier home we two may be again together."

Margery shuddered visibly.

"Yet Oliver tells me, John, that you will not be cancelled."

"Cancellation is that of the heart," I responded.

"Are you a Multiplier, John?" she asked, looking up into my eyes. "If so, I can send Mr. Straitlace. I know him; he would gladly come. And yet," she added, casting down her eyes, "I understood that you told Oliver you were a mixed number. I did hope that you were. If you would only be cancelled what a great joy I should feel."

"Dearest," I said, greatly troubled, "I would do anything for your sake."

"Can you not do that one thing?" she exclaimed. "Can you not realize that if you are not cancelled we shall never meet again?"

I made a motion towards the table. "There, dearest, are the paper, and pens, and ink which Oliver and Mr. Smalls left for me. It was hard to resist their importunities; how much harder is it to resist yours."

"Can you not believe in the written solution?"

"No, darling, I cannot, and never can."

"But that matters not; the mental solution will avail. Mr. Nudwink—"

"Do not mention that odious fellow's name," I said, perhaps a little sharply: "he is a villain."

"Oh, no, John, he is an earnest, consistent mathematician. He is always going about doing good. Has he not been to you? He promised that he would come and labor with you. Has he not done so?"

"Yes, he was here after the service this morning," I answered, ruefully, "but I think it was I who did all the labor—"

"Would you not listen to him, John?"

"Oh, yes, I listened."

"Could he not touch your heart?"

"Dearest, it is you alone who can touch my heart. I feel the most profound assurance that no cancellation or solution will avail for me. And yet I trust that in the other happier land we shall be always together."

· "Do you not believe in the raft, dear John?" she asked, sorrowfully. "Can you not trust to its saving power?"

I made no reply. What could I say? With patient pleading Margery besought me to give my heart to Numbers, to rely upon the raft as my only hope, and to submit to the rite of cancellation. She implored me with earnest words and streaming eyes to give her the promise that she asked, that we might meet again.

"But we shall meet again, my own darling," I said.

She turned her head away. The tears streamed unrestrained down her cheeks as she said, "Oh, no, dear John, unless you believe and are cancelled we shall never meet again, never in all eternity."

So speaking, with one bitter sob she threw her arms about me passionately and hid her face upon my breast. "Never, never, never," she moaned, "never through all the endless ages."

In a moment such as this we live a lifetime. Pressing the convulsed, despairing form of my beloved to my heart, my feelings were agonized indeed. To her it was all so real; the misery of the moment to her but a foretaste of the dread forever. What was there I could say for her comfort? As she lay upon my breast, nerveless, hopeless, speechless, motionless, save for a tremor of wretchedness that at intervals shook her form, my thoughts took a wide range. The many modes of worships of which I had been a witness passed in a vague pageant before me. Sect after sect, creed after creed, doctrine after doctrine ; each and all, as I knew, vain and hollow, false and foolish ; not one that was not a mere travesty of truth, of even that poor measure of the truth that the Infinite Father had given to this lone island. Backward, still backward my thoughts strayed, away, far away from Inquirendo, till once more in my own country it was a Sabbath day, and I listened to words of faith—of my own faith as they fell from earnest lips—no more earnest than those of Margery—saying, " Come unto me, all ye that labor and are heavy laden, and I will give you rest." Had I then gone to him ? Did I in my desolation go even now ? Words that I had listened to almost unheeding I now recalled with a pang. I saw again the reverent, white-haired old pastor as he stood pleading with his flock, pleading with me to give my heart to the dear Lord, who had given His life for me. A strange, new emotion filled me. I seemed impressed with a new and profound conviction. I heard again the voice of that aged preacher as he told of the mission of that apostle selected to be a messenger to the Gentiles. It seemed to ring in my ears, that cry from the cloud filled with light, " Saul, Saul, why persecutest thou me ? "

Again I beheld a vision : that same Saul of Tarsus, now transformed by the power of the voice from Heaven, standing erect, clothed on with the might of faith—an imposing, towering figure, despite his bent and fragile frame, —standing with uncovered head and lifted arm upon the martial hill in Athens, declaring that as he passed by he

had beheld an altar with the inscription : " To the Unknown God," and I heard him plainly say, " Whom therefore ye ignorantly worship him declare I unto you." My
heart thus filled to overflowing, my thoughts burst their
bonds, and I spoke.

There lying upon my breast, with deep, earnest words,
Margery listened to the story of my own faith, the faith of
my childhood that I had so long neglected. I told her of
the vain pretence that I knew all the island creeds to be,
and of that sweet sacred story of the crucified Son of God
who had visited the world to save the souls of sinful men.
We all speak eloquently when we feel deeply, and the
depth of my feeling then was as of one at the very doors
of death. I finished at last. It is a short story and easy
to be told. Margery had not moved nor spoken, she had
lain almost motionless.

" Do you not see, darling," I said, " that this is, this
must be true ? "

" It is a lovely story," she answered, " oh, it is a sweet
story ; but it is only our better story, our own dear truth.
Yours is the poem, John ; ours is the reality."

" Can you not understand ? " I said, mournfully.

" Oh, yes, indeed I understand," she answered ; " but—
oh, why, dearest, when you see so well the beauty can you
not also believe the truth ? There is no other name but
Numbers ; there is no other hope but in the raft. Forget the poem, John ; forget it for my sake. It is only a
poem, after all. How could it be aught else ? It is a delusion, John. My own, can you not see how all that you
have said is delusion ? Forgive me that I must speak.
Your Margery loves you ; she would not now say a word
to hurt or trouble you. Oh, darling, forget the vision ; remember only the fact. It was Numbers only who died for

you. It is only the raft that can save you. Beyond this narrow island there is the sweet Oversea country; the raft can bear you thither. I have faith. I know that I shall go there. Will you not then try to believe that you may meet your Margery there?"

"There is a land beyond the ocean, Margery; it is no delusion."

"Yes, I know, dear John, there is that land."

"But I have been there, Margery; I came from that country beyond the ocean."

She looked up pityingly into my face. She laid her soft finger gently upon my lips. "Oh, hush, dear John," she said, softly, "oh, hush, it pains me so."

"I do not wish to pain you, Margery, but all that I have said is true."

She was silent. Her eyes fell before mine. A listless, mute sorrow seemed to possess her.

"We shall meet again, Margery. Fear not, we shall meet."

She shook her head. "Never, oh, never to all eternity, John. If you will not be cancelled we shall never meet —never, never."

Her beautiful head was again bent low, and the words came in the midst of passionate sobs.

The light of the departing day had faded, the dusk had now been succeeded by the gloom of approaching night. Margery lay upon my breast for awhile, and there was silence between us, silence and grief. At last she roused herself. She sighed heavily, she laid her lips to mine, and then half withdrawing herself from me, still with her white arms about my neck, she gazed into my eyes. "It is time that I should go, dear John," she said, huskily, "but one word more I must say : it is my office, the office of the one who loves you best. The law—" she faltered.

"Say on, Margery," I said, caressingly, "nothing you can say will grieve me. Do not fear."

"The law," she continued, with trembling lips, "gives to the best beloved of one—con—condemned—"

"I understand ; condemned to die."

She hurried on, "Gives to me the right to demand one single boon that shall not extend to life. It is my right. What is it I shall ask, John ? " Her voice sank to a low whisper. "What is the one single boon that you wish me to demand of the law for you ? "

I had not been aware of this provision of Inquirendian law. At first I was at a loss for an answer. I pondered over the matter for some time in silence. Then, like a flash, it seemed, down from the dome of heaven, now deepening into a purple canopy, whereon glowed and glittered one single planet, a thought came in through the bars of my prison, came and nestled like a bird amid its sadder sister thoughts ; came like a pure dove amid the ravens of despair. Thus are great thoughts among men born, not of themselves, or from the evolution of the atoms of the brain, but sent from high heaven itself, filaments of the sacred birth robe of man's immortality, woven still in the patched and soiled and draggled garments of his later, more earthly humanity.

On the impulse of the moment I uttered a glad cry. "Thank God!" I exclaimed, in ecstasy, pressing Margery rapturously to me, feeling in that sublime instant that the two best gifts of the Creator were indeed mine—my beloved and my own life. Yes, my own life ; for hope had revived within me, and I knew now that my prayer had been answered.

Margery looked up wonderingly. "What did you say, John?" she asked, "and why is your tone so joyous?"

"Ah!" I answered, "it is no wonder that I am joyous. I feel once more the thrill of hope. Margery, I have an idea."

Margery could not shake off her depression, but she inquired very earnestly what I meant. "Have faith in me, my darling, and all shall yet be well," said I, trying to induce her to share my joy.

"Dear John, I do have faith—at least, in you."

"Only believe," I said, "only believe me, and life shall not yet be over for us."

She shook her head sadly.

"I will try, John," she said, simply. Then she looked into my eyes longingly. "I think I could do anything, believe anything, if you would only—only—"

"Only what, love?"

"Only be cancelled, John."

In the fresh vigor of the new emotions that possessed me I resolved to put my Margery to the last and greatest test of her love. What could matter now to me a mere senseless ceremony? Hypocrisy is like circumcision, a thing of the heart. The righteous man is lord also of his subterfuges.

"I will be cancelled, Margery," I broke forth, "I do consent."

She started joyfully.

"On one condition," I added, hastily.

"Tell me what it is, John; no matter what it may be, if it is in my power it shall be done."

Then I told her, in quick, short, earnest phrases, of the boon I desired.

"It shall be done," she answered.

"There is yet more to tell," I said, gloomily ; "if I am to be cancelled the condition I ask is from you alone, Margery."

"Then it is already done," she replied. "Even if it should be my death, John, you need only ask it ; whatever I can do shall be done."

"Could I ask your death, my own ? Oh, no ; what I ask is your life; your life for me, for my sake, that we may always live together ; that you should be my very own, my own wife."

"Is it that you wish to marry me, John ?"

"Yes, I do indeed wish that."

She shuddered. "What !" she exclaimed, "do you require that here in this—this prison ? Oh, John, surely you do not ask that of me ?"

"No," I answered, quickly, seeing that she had misunderstood. "No, darling, that is not what I would ask. It is that—that—" I could not trust myself to speak aloud my wish. Again I whispered low, telling all I wished to tell. At first she slightly withdrew from my embrace and appeared strangely disconcerted. "Only believe me," I said, "and all will yet be well." She turned towards me one look of love, one glorious look filling her violet eyes, and placing her little hand in mine she answered : "Death comes only a little later or a little sooner, John. It is better to die for those we love than to live on loveless. It is better to die with my beloved than to live on without him. Whether in life or death we shall not be parted. It shall be as you say, John, in all things."

My sleep was tranquil enough that night. Sometimes it happens that a great joy will make one wakeful; but with me it was not so. The next day was a busy one. It is needless to say that Mr. Smalls and Oliver were de-

lighted indeed when they heard from Margery that my
obdurate heart had, as they expressed it, been softened.
Margery had not told them the conditions, nor had she
even (this I had cautioned her about) mentioned that
there had been conditions. Mrs. Mayland came, full of
sorrowing pity for my forlorn state, and yet manifesting a
great joy that I had consented to become part of that
church which she had been taught from her youth up was
an essential condition of entrance into the joys of Oversea.

"Is it to be the written solution, John?" Mrs. Mayland
asked, and when I answered "Yes," a look of reverent
gratitude appeared upon her face; her lips trembled, and
her voice, as she told me how thankful she was.

The ceremony of cancellation took place at the hour of
vespers. Mr. Smalls wished it so, and I did not object.
There were only a few present; Mr. and Mrs. Mayland
were there, and Margery. Mr. Smalls and Oliver conducted the services, assisted by the Reverend Paul Patmos.
There was perhaps a little of that quality commonly known
as jesuitical in all this; but I felt no especial pangs of
conscience, and went through it all sedately. It was rather
a trial to write the letter from the ink of which the written
solution was made, and I am afraid in this, as in some of
the answers I gave the celebrants respecting my spiritual
condition, I must have lied. But in spite of all that casu-
ists may have to say there are lies and lies, and when one
is planning to save his life he learns to discriminate very
acutely between the two kinds : I know I did. I was
asked if I believed all the truths of the arithmetic. I replied in a ghostly voice befitting the occasion that I did.

"Do you believe in Mathematics?" said Mr. Patmos,
who conducted this portion of the ceremony.

"I do," was my answer.

" Do you believe in Numbers ? "

" Yes."

" Do you believe in the Nine Digits? "

" Yes."

" Do you unfeignedly believe in the Four Ground Rules, and do you solemnly promise to follow and be lead by them, and to abjure the hateful and hurtful devices of the Archten ? "

" I do."

" Is it your wish to become part of the visible church by the rite of cancellation and by the written solution ? "

" It is," I answered, and then having produced the letter, previously written, the ceremonies went on.

When it was all over, and with wet eyes my hand was taken by all present with murmured blessings, Margery came last of all, and whispered low," It will not be long now, my own. Be brave, as I shall be, and if not on this island, we shall be happy in Oversea together."

CHAPTER XXVIII.

THE REVISED VERSION.

WHILE I waited for the unhappy day that was to witness my execution, I had much to occupy my mind. I have heretofore stated that I was busy. Among other things, I devoted myself with some assiduity to a diligent study of the Arithmetic, having been instigated to do this on account of its giving so much pleasure to all my friends, and not so much that I really derived any great spiritual benefit therefrom. Oliver had been telling me that a council or committee had been appointed, consisting of learned men of different denominations, who had spent many months in revising the Arithmetic. On my expressing a desire to see a copy of the revised version, Oliver kindly purchased one for me, and he also brought at the same time a copy of a pamphlet by the Reverend Mr. Patmos, which, he said, would give me just the information I desired without the labor incident to an extended comparison.

Fortunately I am able to give this almost entire. It was not very lengthy, and I have merely omitted certain portions which to my mind seemed to a certain extent irrelevant.

"THE REVISED VERSION.

" BY PAUL PATMOS, Q.P.

" The laborious and careful work of the revisers is at last completed. It is a monument of judicious scholarship, and abundantly redounds to the credit of the learned gentlemen who composed the committee. The student will find many changes ; but these are chiefly orthographic, and in no instance affect doctrinal points. One of the chief difficulties which the committee had to contend with was of course the sadly defaced and mutilated condition of the great original in the cathedral. It was at one time hoped that the chief apostle would give consent to have this copy examined by the committee, who even went so far as to have a strong magnifying glass especially constructed with a view to a microscopic examination of those particular passages as to which there was known to be doubt. But, from a reverent sense of their responsibility in the matter, neither the apostle nor the scribes could be induced to permit this, and the sacred volume was therefore inspected by a telescope erected on the roof of James Brower's stove store opposite the south window of the cathedral. The leaves of the Arithmetic were opened from time to time by a blindfold boy, the motions of whose hands were directed by a priest, duly delegated. All this was of course according to the principles of the canon law, and it must be understood that we have no word of blame for the prelate or his assistants. In fact, it may be doubted whether the work would have been any better performed even had the committee had that access to the sacred original which they desired. The roof of Mr.

Brower's stove store was in many respects eligibly situated, and the telescope was of McGuiness' make, and one of his latest and best. Besides this favorable view of the great original, the committee had the advantage of the early version, printed, it is said, in the time of Henry Huit, and also of the James King's edition, later on.

" Hence the revisers have been able to do the subject full justice. They have retained many of the old readings in bulk, and only made changes where grammar or vocabulary (better understood in modern light) seemed to imperatively demand it. That they have been eminently conservative we think all Arithmetical scholars will admit ; but we are of the opinion also that it must be admitted that these radical changes which were made were such as modern scholarship imperatively demanded. Some of the most bitter opposition to the Arithmetic as a whole has come from those who, not comprehending it in its spirit and truth, have sought to find flaws in matters of mere verbiage. One of the most common modes of attack from infidels has been to take up particular passages where the sense was in some degree obscure, and endeavor to put false and erroneous interpretations thereon. A few instances of this can here be given, which will serve to demonstrate clearly not only the utter futility of these so-called philosophical views, but to throw into strong relief the exceeding richness of the material in the hands of the revisers. Take the nine plus onth chapter of the First Ground Rule, for instance, sixth line, where that remarkable if apparently somewhat disconnected account occurs of the grocer and the sacks of meal, and the lady with her furniture. In James King's version it reads as follows : 'Two men start from a given point and travel in

opposite directions, one at the rate of 94 * miles a day,
the other at the rate of 47 * miles a day : how far will
they be apart at the close of the ninth day?' Scoffers
have made this passage a target for their shafts of ridicule ;
but they will be enabled to do so no more. The absurd
pretence that because such a journey, continued for nine
days, would have carried these two men both away from
the island, can no longer be maintained.

"Instead of the reading being thirty-six in the first and
twenty-eight in the second instance the powerful telescope
of McGuiness has disclosed the fact that after the nine in
the supposed 94 was a collection of fly-specks, and no
four at all. In the case of the other, formerly written 47,
the truth is even plainer : there is not a 7, but, as revealed
by the telescope, a manifest two (2), so—(the reader does
not need to be informed that 42 and 8 are synonymous)—
the whole passage should read as follows : ' Two men
start from a given point and travel in opposite directions,
one at the rate of nine miles a day ; the other at the rate
of eight miles : how far will they be apart at the close
of the ninth day?'

"What light does this interpretation throw upon the passages? In times past commentators have striven to account for what certainly appeared to be a most remarkable statement. Blushly, a high authority, at one time
endeavored to account for the seeming contradiction by the
assumption that these men, instead of proceeding in a
straight line, did actually travel in curves, and Blushly
even went so far as to indicate what appeared to him, on
arithmetical grounds, the exact curve each man took. It

* The reader will remember that by the methods of notation in vogue
among the Inquirendians these figures should be read thirty-six and
twenty-eight respectively.

19

is needless now to state that these and all similar assumptions were unwarranted by the fact, and were wholly erroneous. How simple now, viewed in the proper light, does this verse seem? The conditions are now shown to be easy of fulfilment; for no one can pretend that there are not points on the island from which two men could start and walk in a straight line the given distance.

"This has puzzled thousands of readers in the past ; but, by the mathematical work of the committee, it need do so no longer. Who knows how many souls may be suffering the torments of the drowned on account of this one faulty rendering. The reader of the new version will be glad to discover many such changes. wherein nature and revelation are brought into absolute harmony. This especial passage is of course to be taken in a peculiar sense as illustrative of the wide distance apart mankind is from a given point : to wit, the Decimal point; and the allegory is now rendered perfect by its being so conclusively demonstrated to be in consonance with literal fact.

"Take another instance, where the art of computation is spoken of in James King's version. This has always been a stumbling-block in the way of angelical believers, who, however devoted to the traditions of the church, and ever regarding the Decimals with the warmest affection as an integral portion of the Kingdom of Numbers, yet could not concur with them in the use of pictures and statuary. Such use, however, was seen to have apparent warrant in the Arithmetic in the use of the word art in this coɪ nection. How marvellously are things brought to pass'. The revision now reads the *act* (not art), and at once all doubts are instinctively felt to be removed. It is but one more text showing the inherent necessity that exists foɪ works in a believer.

"The same word, further on (chapter 9 + 2, sec. 2 & 3), is again rendered act.

"In chapter 55 + 1 it formerly read : 'Like Numbers are confused of units of the same kind,' etc. This was supposed to mean 'put out,' or 'irritated,' and to have reference to those dissensions among integers, which are, alas! much too common; that it referred to troubles which continually arise touching new carpets, organs, modes of placing church furniture, etc. The new version hath it, 'Like Numbers are composed,' a rendering which is not only more in accordance with the remainder of the teachings of the word, but is more fully adapted to the comprehension of the unlearned and ignorant. Composed in this sense means quiet, resigned, docile.

"Yet another instance. In Book 4, chap. 9, it formerly read, 'A man earns 55 pounds a month, and pays 7 pounds for house rent, and 37 pounds for current expenses : how much will he save ?' *

"This passage has always been regarded by Arithmeticians as especially replete with error, and for many years, in all our orthodox pulpits, it has not been considered as inspired, and pastors have warned their flocks against placing too much reliance upon it. It was argued that no man ever did earn as much as twenty-five pounds in a single month; that in fact there were not a dozen fortunes in the island whose income approached this amount. The moral, of course, was evident ; the man did not save anything; in fact he lost. This loss is typical of the loss of the soul, and also of the great danger there

---

* The reader must bear in mind that these figures are taken literally from Mr. Patmos' essay. 55 is, according to their notation, 25 ; 7 is the same, but 37 is 21. This accounts for the discrepancy. The man saved 11 pounds.—ED.

is in large wealth. This has been understood, but still the entire chapter was felt to be misleading. Particularly was this the case in reference to the currents. Great care has been exercised, diligent and trustworthy investigation made from time to time, and the prevailing opinion is undoubtedly that in no one year did the value of the current crop exceed 63 * pounds. These misstatements tended to invalidate the context. In the new version the whole matter is made clear. In the original it was discovered that there were certain marks, half erased and almost undecipherable, between the two 5's. After much patient study these marks were found to be beyond a doubt a * sign, so that the second 5 is redundant or expressive of assurance. The man did earn 5 pounds and no more. His paying 7 pounds for house rent was great recklessness, and 37 pounds for expenses criminal extravagance. The revisers also became satisfied that the word which has always heretofore been rendered current was in reality 'certain,' and, as amended, the chapter presents none of the old difficulties. We pass on now to a few of the points where the revisers have not altogether succeeded in clearing away the old stumbling-blocks.

" In that remarkable chapter of the second book (Chap. 9+5) it states, ' In the Roman method numbers are expressed by means of seven capital letters.' Thus far all is clear ; but immediately after follows this most confusing passage, 'Viz.: IVXLCDM.' It was greatly to have been desired that this could have been settled satisfactorily ; but still we do not wish to be captious or hypercritical.

" The committee have availed themselves of the able and

* 18 pounds.—ED.

exhaustive treatises of Pawk and Crullers, and also of the more profound work of X. E. Geesis relating thereto.

"Pawk, it will be remembered, reasoning from analogy, has taken the ground that the word 'viz' is simply a root, and that what follows has reference to a period antedating the historical period. There are grounds for thinking that he was at least on the right track, as philologists agree that there never was a time within the memory of man when vowels were not used, and it will be noted that in this entire passage there is not a single vowel; all the sounds are guttural.

"Crullers takes a widely different view, asserting as he does that these consonants are notes of music, or directions to the musicians by whom this portion of the Arithmetic was sung.

"Geesis, as is well known, has gone over the entire ground taken by both Pawk and Crullers, and has arrived at the conclusion that the mysterious characters are neither more nor less than a name, and he therefore separates the passage into two parts, thus: IVIX LICKIDOM.

"The committee have taken a medium course, and in a measure incorporated into their translation all of these conflicting views. They have departed entirely from the old version, rejecting the root word, 'viz,' and substituting therefor the word 'namely,' which analogy clearly authorized them to do. By making this substitution no direct name is mentioned, yet it is manifest that they had in mind the name IVIX LICKIDOM—the name, or the one name—meaning, of course, Numbers. We do not object to this rendering on philological grounds; on the contrary, the committee is deserving of very great praise for the result, as evincing not only profound learning, but a spiritual insight into the meaning of what must still be regarded as enigmatic. What we do say, however, is simply this, and we think all candid persons must admit the truth of the criticism, that in making the alteration the committee showed more learning than regard for the time-honored traditions of our fathers. How many souls now in glory have been comforted by the words which the committee have now wholly eliminated. How many, by that one portion of the Arithmetic, have been brought to the raft. What tender memories linger about the word 'viz,' memories of home and a mother's tender care. How sweetly does its plaintive melody sound in the ears of a believer. But now all this is changed; and although, as we have said above, great credit is due the committee, yet we feel that in making the substitution they have detracted somewhat from the general merit of the revision. There are other passages also to which attention might be called did our space admit, but these must suffice for the present. The work, as gotten up by Spell & Hyphen, under the auspices of the committee, is a marvel of mechanical execution, and is furnished to subscribers at the extremely low price of one penny. It is understood that a paper edition will shortly be published. There is little doubt that the new version will very shortly be adopted by all the orthodox denominations, as it has already been by the establishment."

"How do you like the new version?" Oliver asked that evening.

I did not think it worth while to enter into any details, but I left Oliver to infer that I was on the whole well satisfied.

"You read what Dr. Patmos said respecting the use of the comprehensive word 'namely'?"

"Yes."

"Did that meet with your approval?"

"The sense seemed to be materially changed."

"But for the better; did it not strike you so?"

"I think the letters ought to have been kept as they were," I said, after some hesitation.

This Oliver would not admit; in fact, he was very pronounced in his views that the revision was admirably made, and that the new version was a vast improvement over the old.

CHAPTER XXIX.

THE next day and the following days until the one fixed for the execution I was very busy. I had many things to arrange.

My property I wished to divide among the charitable institutions of the island; but when I signified my wishes in this respect I was rather astonished to find that the law forbade such a disposition by a noncomposed person. Oliver kindly brought me the statute book, and I read the clause myself. The substance of it was that where property was thus left it either descended to next of kin, according to common law (which was the same with the Inquirendians as with us) or escheated to the crown.

This state of the law was not satisfactory to me. I expressed my dissatisfaction.

" I don't see how you can get round it," said Oliver.

Then I showed Oliver the list of bequests that I proposed to make.

" Four shillings to Festus Idler ? " said he, in a tone of some surprise.

" Yes," I said, " he seems to be doing a good work."

" Is that quite consistent with your new character as an integer so close to the decimal point ? "

" I don't see why not. Charity is the same, no matter what the distance from the decimal point."

" Still, it is unusual. However, it does not matter now; the law utterly forbids it."

" And is there no way to get round the law?" I asked.
Having had some experiences with our own board of Alder-
men it was perhaps natural that I asked the question.

"I know of none," replied Oliver.

In the evening Mr. Dash called. I stated the case to
him and asked his advice as a lawyer. At first he shook
his head, but when, running his eyes down the list, it
lighted upon the name of Festus Idler, he began to take
an interest directly. Even the greatest men in the island
of Inquirendo or elsewhere are prone to take interest in
what benefits them personally. Mr. Dash said nothing at
the time as to his intimate relations with Mr. Idler, but
I discovered afterwards that they were cousins, and that
Mr. Dash was a great believer in the gentleman's doctrines.

" I see you have given a pound each to St. Complex
Fractions and to Mr. Smalls' church of 'Our Dividend.'"

"Yes," I responded.

"Idler is doing a good work," said Mr. Dash, musingly,
"why not make it a whole pound to him?"

" I could do so."

"If I were in your place I would. Possibly, if you did
so, I might fix it with the crown. He has the right to
relinquish the state's claim in certain cases."

" But would he?"

" I think he would; the fact is, Mr. Cliff, the crown is
a brother-in-law of Idler's. Of course, such things do unconsciously have weight."

I made the change, Mr. Dash drew up the will as
amended, and the next day came with the information
that the crown had granted a dispensation.

With the will and other matters I was fully employed,

and the time passed all too quickly, until at last the sun
arose on the day upon which I had been doomed to die.

Beside myself there were two others—noncomposed persons—who were to suffer on that day. One was (so I was
told) a raving maniac, and the other was in a condition
of idiocy. The case of this latter was one of peculiar ag-
gravation, and, as I regarded it, of some hardship. He
was a boy of about eighteen, whose parents, very unjustifi-
ably, had concealed from the authorities the fact of his
condition. They had kept him closely guarded, and as
they lived in a secluded portion of the fourth department,
it had only recently been known that he existed. He was
his parents' only child, and, strange as it may appear, they
were devotedly attached to him, and resisted the officers of
the law frantically. The law, however, was explicit as to
such cases, and I found the sentiment of the public was
strongly against the parents.

How an incident like this would have pleased Mr.
Malthus.

The day, as I have said, at last dawned. I forego any
lengthy description of our journey to the coast, and shall
only mention that during it all Oliver and Mr. Smalls
sat by my side, cheering me constantly with appropriate
selections from the Arithmetic.

We stood silent at the iron door, on the verge of the
steep crag overlooking the calm, slow-heaving sea below.
Above, the summer sky of the early September morning
hung, flecked by fleecy clouds ; the fields, in waving bloom
of verdure, spread out, treeless but beautiful, on every
side, save one, where the dark green ocean (type of the
eternity that rolls its boundless billows round the world)
lazily rocked in placid content. The waters and fields of
grain were alike stirred by the soft breeze that from far

seaward fanned my fevered cheek. So, from beyond the dreadful deep of the grave come sweet, refreshing influences, brightening our planet and clothing it in the immortal verdure of eternal hope. And as the sea breeze comes from whither we know not, and blows its gentle breath at the bidding of the warm land, so from the hearts of men warm thoughts arise, and the cool, refreshing winds from the great deep steal in, an answer to our prayer. By my side stood my dearest and best friends. These were, first and dearest, my Margery, next were Oliver and Mr. Smalls, and Margery's father and mother. As chief mourners they were all clad from head to foot in the solemn white vesture, the type of their grief for the dying. There were tears in all those eyes, and farewell words were spoken with hushed and husky voices. By my side through all that dread ordeal, my Margery stood : at times her eyes sought mine with wistful, painful meaning ; at times her hand stole out and clasped my own, and at times, as she joined in the awful responses, her lips trembled and her voice refused to fulfil its office. It was a solemn, dreadful funeral service. The ritual of the Established Church for the burial of the dead was recited, and chanted in unison by a choir of surpliced children. Mr. Smalls had asked the favor from the crown of conducting this ceremonial, and the pitiful privilege had been granted to him. Oliver had proposed to assist, but his emotions had been too overpowering. He, as well as Mr. Mayland, joined occasionally in the responses, but their voices were all the time quivering with subdued sobs and sad thoughts.

Nudwink, I saw, was present ; but (let us hope) from motives of delicacy he did not attempt to join actively with the others of the clergy. Gallwood too was there.

I had been told (while yet in confinement at the capital)
that he had purposed withdrawing for a short period, and
secluding himself from the island until all should be over.
Being of a forgiving disposition, I sent word that it was
my last request that he should be present at my obse-
quies. It was for that reason that he was there. He appeared much affected, and kept time while the chants
were sung and the hymns, as did also Nudwink, with his
fore arm, and I observed that they kept time very accurately together. Of all the multitude, and a large crowd
had assembled, perhaps I was of all the least moved,
though I had, of course, never before attended my own
funeral. After the chants were over and the reading of
passages from the Arithmetic had ended there was a hymn,
which had been prepared by Mr. Smalls expressly for the
occasion. Copies of this hymn had been circulated among
the audience, and it was thus that I became possessed of
it. In the singing Mr. Nudwink's voice was especially
prominent, though it was Mr. Smalls who really led. The
hymn was as follows :

> " Now when the dark hour of ocean draws near,
> And I leave the sweet hopes I have cherished so here ;
> When I leave this fair island, oh, why should I care
> In the midst of the waters if Numbers be there ?
> > If Numbers be there,
> > If Numbers be there,
> In the midst of the waters, oh, why should I care ?

> " While we dwell on the island, this beautiful place,
> Oh, let us, dear integers, look for His face.
> If we seek we shall find, for the far shall come near
> And abide in our spirits, for Numbers is here.
> > For Numbers is here,
> > For Numbers is here,
> If we seek we shall find Him, for Numbers is here.

" Oh, how can I tell what that bright land shall be
That Numbers has promised forever for me ?
When I leave this dear island, oh, why should I care,
In the Oversea country, for Numbers is there.
    For Numbers is there,
    For Numbers is there,
When I leave this dear island, oh, why should I care ?

" When o'er the wild ocean my soul he shall waft,
I trust all my hope to the mystical raft.
I know only this in the midst of despair :
I shall pass through all safely, for Numbers is there.
    For Numbers is there,
    For Numbers is there,
To Oversea's glory, and Numbers is there."

The hymn ended. There was an interval of silence,
and then Mr. Paul Patmos, having mounted upon an improvised pulpit on one of the steer carts, delivered what
from the standpoint of Inquirendo opinion was a most
excellent discourse. There were some things in it to
which, very naturally, I took exception. It did not
appear to me that he made sufficient distinction between
my case and that of the lunatic on my right, who once
or twice interrupted the proceedings with a howl, or that
of the idiot on my left, who jabbered and blinked to himself all the time. I considered myself entitled to at
least a trifling consideration as in some sort belonging to
the aristocracy of non composmentiveness. In my first
year at West Point there was a young gentleman whose
name was, I think, Abbott—at any rate it began with ' A '
—who was found deficient and sent away from that exacting institution. He was in sore distress ; but his poor
father, who had come from somewhere in the wilderness
to witness a triumph, was in much sadder case.

I was over at the guard house, where the list of deficients was read off by the cadet adjutant. The old man listened to his boy's disgrace with much disquietude. Then the names having been read alphabetically he blubbered out, a smile of sad satisfaction struggling with tears : " At any rate, Johnny was head of the deficients ; that's one comfort."

So it appeared to me that if I was non compos, at least my rank as the head of the unfortunate trio ought to have been acknowledged.

Alas ! it was not, and we were all linked together in the worthy rector's mind as surplus population, by which name he did not scruple to refer to us.

The sermon, like the hymn, at last was over. Again there was silence, and then Mr. Smalls approached and asked me if there was anything I wished to say. I looked about me. Whispering together upon a rock in the rear sat Nudwink and Gallwood, close together. A thought struck me. To Oliver and Mr. Mayland I had already said farewell. Would it not be right that as an integer I should leave the island at peace with all men ? I signified my desire for a few last words with Nudwink and Gallwood. Oliver bore my message and the two approached, Nudwink with a sanctimonious expression of pretended melancholy thinly disguising his satisfaction at the final accomplishment of his foul purposes, Gallwood with his handkerchief to his face, through the folds of which I could see his eyes twinkling.

Nudwink and I clasped hands. He looked me coolly in the eye as he told me how rejoiced he felt that in my last hours I had given my heart to Mathematics by becoming an integer.

" I should have been better pleased," he observed, " if it had been my own blessed privilege to administer the rite of cancellation, and if you had used the mental solution rather than the written, which latter I cannot—being strictly Angelical—regard as other than replete with danger ; but farewell, dear brother, farewell. I am truly glad to observe that you cherish no enmity against those who in fulfilling their duty to society have unwittingly been the innocent cause of your trouble. Farewell."

So, with his eyes devoutly raised, Nudwink turned away.

"Farewell," said Gallwood, coming forward, "farewell, Mr. Cliff." Then as our hands met, he leaned forward and whispered hoarsely, through the folds of his handkerchief, which was still pressed to his face, "Who has the advantage now ?"

I saw his point directly. I sighed.

"Alas ! Mr. Gallwood," I said, "in this island advantages change about with great rapidity."

"They do indeed," responded Gallwood, "but I am truly glad to observe that you keep up your spirits under these distressing circumstances. I understand," he continued, "that you have only recently been cancelled. Your views must have undergone a considerable change since you attended Hurtheart's lecture."

"They have undergone no particular change."

"What ! no change !"

"None whatever."

"Then how did it happen that you consented to be cancelled ? "

" I did that to please Margery. '

" Oh, you did. And pray did it please her ? "

" Immensely."

" I am glad you told me that, I'll make a note of it.

While I think of it, Mr. Cliff, I may as well mention that
it will be hereafter my fondest desire to please Margery."
I sighed again.

"When I am gone, Gallwood," I said, earnestly, "and
you are in the enjoyment of all the happiness that this
island affords, spare a thought in the midst of your joy
for one who is lying—"

"Do not speak of it, Mr. Cliff. I shall be most happy
to attend to that or any other little commission that you
may suggest. Is there anything further that I can do
for you ?"

"Nothing, I believe."

"Then I shall say farewell. You have this advantage
of me, Mr. Cliff, that it will not be many minutes before
you will know whether there is any merit in the process
of cancellation."

"There I certainly have an advantage," I responded.

"Then we are both satisfied," said Gallwood. "Well, I
won't detain you any longer, as I see you have urgent
business. Good-day."

He gave my hand a grip, and with his handkerchief
pressed to his eyes he went back to the side of Nudwink.

The ceremonies, which had been suspended out of deference to my feelings, were now resumed. It had been
arranged that I should suffer last ; so the poor idiot was
brought forward first, grinning, and blinking, and utterly
unconscious of the dreadful fate that awaited him. He
even chattered with delight as he approached his coffin,
and when told to lie down therein he manifested no reluctance. He suffered himself to be placed in a reclining
posture, and offered no opposition when the lids were
closed over him and bolted tightly. There was a signal
given, and eight stalwart fellows came forward, and lifted

the enormous iron box, which must have weighed upwards
of a ton, upon their shoulders, and bore it forward, staggering, to the edge of the sea-way.

The great iron doors stood open, and I was able to
look down, with a strange interest, into my own grave.
The multitude clustered closely round the edge of the inclined plane on which the coffin was held balanced. Mr.
Smalls stood on one side and Oliver on the other, while
beside them, and directly in front of the door of the tomb,
stood—this was the Inquirendian custom—the two chief
mourners—the idiot's father and mother. There was a
short interval of silence, and then Mr. Smalls, opening
his Arithmetic, read the customary verses : " A Factor
of a number is its Divisor."

"The number above the line is called the Numerator."

"The Divisor and Quotient are factors of the Dividend."

The formula " water to water " was omitted in deference to the wishes of the parents.

Mr. Smalls ceased ; the bearers heaved, and the poor
idiot was sent, all unconscious still, to his long home in
the sea.

Then the maniac, who was struggling and howling frantically, was treated in like manner, except that to reduce
him to submission his hands were tied. The bearers bore
him to the coffin. He was forced into it. The lids were
closed and bolted securely down. Then the heavy load
was raised, and as before, staggering under the immense
weight, the men advanced to the sea-way. The solemn
ritual was proceeded with. The maniac had no mourners,
so the state provided dummies. He was not known to
have been cancelled, so the church gave him the benefit

20

of the doubt. In his case the coffin was sprinkled, and Mr. Smalls used the words "water to water." The texts were recited, the signal was given. I saw the bearers heave. I heard the rush and whir of the descending coffin, a sound of a great splash, and the ocean had swallowed the maniac.

A great horror fell upon me. It was now my turn.

"Come," said one of the attendants, not roughly or unkindly, but in a business-like way that jarred upon my nerves. I made no resistance, however, but followed him directly. I was about to lie down in the coffin, which was all prepared for me, when there was a wild cry, and poor Margery, unable longer to control herself, darted into my arms.

The attendants stopped their preparations, and the Governor came hastily forward.

"Oh, Margery, this will never do," he said, "you are forgetting yourself. Come, dearest, come with me. I know Mr. Cliff will excuse you."

"Certainly," I said, and then, as Margery relaxed her hold, I contrived to whisper in her ear: "Do not be troubled, darling, remember your promise."

"I do, I do," she responded. "Oh, John, could you think that I would forget? Rather than wed that loathsome Gallwood I would cheerfully die."

If Gallwood had heard her perhaps he would not have felt so confident of his ability to please.

Margery was led away by her father, and as I again stepped forward I saw that she had taken the place of one of my chief mourners by the side of the sea-way. The other mourner was Oliver. This had not been my doing; according to modern science they had selected themselves. I lay down in my coffin, and the lid was closed and barred

over me. It was not entirely dark, and I could plainly
hear the tremulous tones of Mr. Smalls as he recited the
touching words of the Arithmetic. The water was sprinkled; the words said. The bearers at the given signal
heaved with one accord. I felt myself moving. I heard
one wild, despairing cry and all became dark, as the iron
coffin thundered down the sea-way and plunged into the
ocean.

CHAPTER XXX.

AN APPROPRIATE OCCASION.

I TAKE this appropriate occasion to indulge in some moralizing that appears to be not only desirable but almost necessary under the circumstances. I have a friend, Mr. G. I. Cervus, who has written several books and is in his way something of a critic, who suggests that some of the details of my narrative are in the highest degree improbable. Being asked to mention those which he thinks the most difficult to believe he very promptly names two points which he regards as particularly open to this objection. He cannot conceive, he says, that a community so far advanced in the arts and sciences as the Inquirendians were could be so blind as to allow themselves to regard as sacred an arithmetic, or that they were not able to see at a glance the real character of the book. The second point which he makes is this: that although it is quite conceivable that the Almighty might be adored under the names given by the Inquirendians, yet it is not to be believed that the absurd mummeries which passed in the island for religious worship were ever made use of by a people so far advanced in culture and refinement. This critical friend, it may be as well to remark, does not affect any particular phase of dogmatic belief himself, yet being a man of very strong opinions he is tolerant of opinion, and wholly averse to saying anything that might give offence. In other words, he is exceedingly liberal in all his modes of thought. I was rather surprised that he should have selected these two points, and I told him so. We were sitting together in this gentleman's library about two weeks after my return from the island, and I had been telling him (under the strictest injunctions of secrecy) of my adventures, and had read a portion of the previous manuscript. His wife also was present, and seemed to take a deep interest in the story.

"What do you regard as the most improbable part of your narrative, John?" Mr. Cervus asked with a smile when I dissented from his views.

"The existence of such an island in the Atlantic," I responded, "so near our coast, and wholly unknown. That appears to be the most extraordinary statement that I have made, by far."

"It is rather singular."

"And yet it can be accounted for, I think, without much difficulty."

"How?"

"Have you a map of the world on Mercator's projection?"

Mr. Cervus brought the map.

"A ruler also, if you please," I said.

He brought that also.

I laid the ruler down upon the map, and traced a number of lines with my blue pencil. First from New York to Liverpool, then from New York to different European ports, and to the Mediterranean, and also lines from the capes of the Chesapeake and the mouth of the Delaware.

I called my friend's attention to the fact that there was a certain very considerable space enclosed between the

blue lines, which, crossing and recrossing in every direction elsewhere, left this space—an area several hundred
miles across in every direction—absolutely untouched.

"My idea is this," I said : "the island is not high ; probably the highest points are in the range of hills separating the eighth from the ninth department, and they cannot
possibly exceed two hundred and fifty feet. A ship would
have to come within a comparatively short distance to see
the island at all.   Now, unless driven as I was by stress
of weather out of its course, no vessel would be at all
likely to come near enough on any commercial voyage to
make the discovery.   You see by the lines I have drawn
the ordinary tracks of commerce are distinctly laid down,
and trade, as is well known, will not be diverted, unless
under exceptional circumstances, from a right line."

"Your explanation is certainly ingenious," said my
friend.   "Come and see what you think of it, Mary."

Mr. Cervus had not been very long married.   His wife
was busy crochetting.   She put her work down at her
husband's request, and came across the room to the
table, saying as she did so, "I don't know much about
such things.   I am sure you and Mr. Cliff must know
best."

My friend made the explanation.   She listened, and
nodded at intervals.

"So you see, Mary," he said, "it is not so highly
improbable, after all."

"Yes, I see," she answered : then, brightening up suddenly, "Oh, Mr. Cliff, where did you get that dear little
blue pencil?   I never saw such a cunning little pencil in all my life."

There was some more conversation respecting the pencil, and then, a promise having been exacted from me

that I would bring one just like it for her the next time I came, Mary went back to her crochetting.

"So you think that the public will not believe that the people of Inquirendo regarded the Arithmetic as sacred?"

"There is certainly an air of improbability in the idea," my friend answered. "Now, between ourselves: of course your opportunities of judging have been better than my own. How do you account for the existence of such a community and for their peculiar customs? Have you given that matter any thought?"

"Indeed I have," I replied, "very serious thought."

"If I were you," continued my friend, soberly, "I certainly should embody those views in your proposed book."

"But why? Do they not naturally suggest themselves?"

"To literary and scientific persons no doubt they do; but the great mass of mankind would, I fear, regard the whole narrative as a wild and improbable tale, unworthy of serious credence. If your object is to convince you ought certainly to explain matters more fully; especially, as you have cast your account into the form of a novel."

"It is none the less true for that reason," said I, a little indignantly.

"That may be, John; but when you are my age you will have learned that novel readers do not like to be instructed. They will look at your book simply as a story. and perhaps be interested in the love affairs of John Cliff and Margery, and wax indignant over the villany of Gallwood, and contemptuous at the hypocrisy of Nudwink; but they will totally disbelieve your statement respecting the raft and the Complex Fractions church, and all that, even if they take the trouble to read what you have written."

" Do you think so ? " I asked, gloomily.

"I know it," said Mr. Cervus, emphatically; " nine readers out of ten will skip all you have been at so much pains to write, if it gives them the slightest trouble. Take that chapter where you describe the mode of reckoning time, and so forth, and the other—one of the last you read—that sermon or editorial of Mr. Patmos' about the revised Arithmetic; no one would read that in a novel."

" I haven't time to write it all over," I said, much discouraged.

" No, I understand that; you want to bring it before the public so that you can get influence to have the Government fit out a ship."

" Yes, that is true."

" Then of course you will not have time. There are no ships in the Navy now that are fit for so long a voyage ; one will have to be built expressly for the purpose. You could not expect to have a vessel before spring."

" And you think I was unwise to call the work a novel?"

" No, I do not go as far as that. You want to influence the public, do you not ? "

" Yes."

" Then a novel is the best shape your book could take; but if you will be advised you will most certainly explain what to me—and I do not claim to be a fool—appears blind."

" If you think so," I answered, "of course I will do it; but—"

" Or else," continued Mr. Cervus, "people will take the whole thing for a joke."

" I always did hate to explain a joke," said I, a little mortified.

"You do not hate it any more than I do; but you may depend upon it in this instance, the facts being in their nature so improbable, it will be necessary to give all your reasons for the statements you have made. Even I—and of course I take your word without question—even I find it almost inconceivable that such a community exists with such peculiar customs. It is almost fabulous."

"And yet the whole thing is literally true."

"I do not doubt it. What I am speaking of is the public incredulity. Take that matter of the raft, for instance, and Numbers, how could anything be more utterly unreasonable than that such an absurdity should be an object of veneration—"

"No more absurd than the sun-worship among the Parsees and Peruvians."

"Ah," said Mr. Cervus, with a smile of superiority, "you forget that there was a physical basis for that."

"And so there is in the story of the raft."

"You surprise me. I thought you said distinctly that these people had no notion whatever of navigation."

"Nor have they."

"Then I do not see—"

"It is all plain enough. These nine original inhabitants, or digits, as they called them, were evidently on board of some vessel, which was driven out of her course and wrecked on the island, as I said in the early part of the book. This probably happened somewhere about the time of Henry the Eighth. Numbers was an individual who constructed a raft and saved these nine, and who doubtless lost his own life in preserving the others."

"But why should the raft have become an object of worship, or at least of veneration?"

"These people were all undoubtedly very much alarmed

at the peril they were in, and this incident was no doubt
impressed upon their memories ever after. They were
unable to leave the island, as there was no wood out of
which to construct a vessel."

" They had the raft."

"Certainly ; but the raft was a small affair, and besides, they probably felt themselves safer on shore. I
can only account for the presence of sheep and cattle on
the supposition that live stock constituted the cargo of
the ship and that some of them swam ashore. The seeds
—for they had vegetables, you remember, of all kinds—
were doubtless preserved in some similar way."

" But how did the strange notion that the sea was
death arise ? "

" I account for that also naturally enough. It is, I
think, undoubted that all these original inhabitants were
overwhelmed with horror and dread of the sea, and this feeling, intensified, was transmitted to their posterity. Perhaps some of their women were pregnant at the time of
the wreck. I can easily suppose that children might have
been mentally so marked that the aversion in the parents
became, in due course of nature, absolute conviction that
the touch of the sea was death. There is nothing essentially improbable in that."

" No, perhaps not ; but the singular religion still remains to be accounted for. A religion that is, I may say,
absolutely unique, differing as it does from any known
to exist in the world."

" You will think it strange, perhaps, but yet I trace the
origin directly to Christianity. It seems to me that the
tradition of the one called Angel and his associates makes
the whole matter tolerably clear. I am of the opinion
that all the original inhabitants were persons of limited

intelligence, and probably all of the lower classes, with the exception of this one called Angel, who was a skilled artisan in several directions. There may have been a weaver among the others perhaps, or a blacksmith ; certainly there must have been some persons skilled in various crafts ; but the traditions are positive that to Angel was due the so-called inventions and the working of the mines, particularly the mine of iron. That there was not a priest among them I regard as certain, otherwise there would have been transmitted many more religious phrases, words and names, to the exclusion even of principles. These, as I have noted, were almost entirely absent. I feel also assured that none of the nine had any strong religious convictions ; but that some one or more, probably of the women, as they advanced in life with young children, began to feel twinges of conscience respecting religious matters, and perhaps more for the children's sake than even for their own, when they found themselves drawing near their end they made some attempt to relate what they had learned in early life of religion. The children who heard this story (garbled as it must have been) had the story itself very firmly impressed upon their imaginations while the names were almost all forgotten. I can imagine that these children, grown in their turn to maturity, transmitted this tale, accompanied by the story as told to them of the rescue and the raft, in such a manner that the two accounts became finally blended. It would be in the highest degree natural that the Bible should have been spoken of as containing all the truths respecting religion. I suppose that the second or third generation, having been taught to read, and a smattering of simple learning having been imparted by Angel, found that copy of the Arithmetic—doubtless part of an old horn book—

on the shore washed up beyond the reach of the waves, and having never been told of any book but the Bible they assumed this to be that much valued one to which allusion had been made by their parents. Assuming all this to be true the rest is easy to understand."

"You spoke of some of the original inhabitants as workers; what do you understand by that term?"

"I give it up," said I, laughing, "bachelors perhaps."

"Your reasoning appears plausible," said Mr. Cervus, "but I see nothing in what you have stated of these people's beliefs that resembles Christianity."

"The controlling principles are identical," I responded, "although the names are, of course, widely different."

"There is one other point," said Mr. Cervus, after a pause: "is it probable that the language used by the islanders would be as pure English as appears in your narrative?"

"I have thought of that," I answered; "it really was a peculiar idiom, but not so peculiar as to be difficult of comprehension. I hate old-fashioned dialect stories myself, and therefore made no attempt to reproduce it."

"Perhaps you are right," said my friend; "but if I were you I should explain it."

"At all events," he continued, "you have certainly written a most entertaining account of your adventures. Whether your explanation of the origin of the Inquirendian religion is or is not the true one, it is certainly ingenious. Don't you think so, Mary?"

Mrs. Cervus was busy taking up a dropped stitch.

"What did you say, dear? Excuse me, I wasn't listening."

My friend repeated his question.

"Entertaining, oh, yes, indeed, very."

"What did you think of Mr. Cliff's views of the religion of the islanders?"

"What did I think?"

"Yes."

She hesitated.

"We had such a beautiful sermon last Sunday," she said, at last; "it was on that very subject."

"Oh, no, my dear, that could hardly be possible."

"Yes, it was about sending missionaries to the islands."

"But the minister knew nothing of Inquirendo."

"No, I suppose not; but they took up a collection, and I was so mortified because I found that I had left my purse in the pocket of my other dress."

"I suppose when it becomes known that there is such an island as Inquirendo," I said, "that they will be sending missionaries there."

"Oh, I hope so, I do hope so," said Mary, laying down her crochet in her lap, "and I should be glad to contribute. I think it so dreadful to be without religion. Though there seems to be a growing belief," she added, resuming the crochet-work, "that it is becoming more and more confined to the upper classes of society. Of course I cannot help feeling that this is a pity."

Mrs. Cervus was a very lovely woman; but as it happens there are many things said by lovely women that do not call for any special reply. I made none in this instance, the lady continued her diligence at the crochet-work, and soon after I took my leave.

CHAPTER XXXI.

SOME DETAILS IN RESPECT TO MY COFFIN.

LET us now return to my condemned cell, and to a somewhat more detailed narration of the events of the week preceding my execution.

In response to my request, Margery sent word by one of the servants at the hotel where she was stopping to the Governor of the Fabrican, and the day after, quite early, that person despatched one of his most skilled workmen to me, with orders to place himself at my disposal. It will perhaps be remembered that, according to Inquirendian custom, a condemned person was given the right to one single favor, and it was in consequence of this that I sent for a worker in iron.

Robert Crafts was the man's name. Although a somewhat lugubrious, yet he was not at all a disagreeable individual, and understood his business well in all its branches. What was perhaps even more to the purpose, he was possessed of an acute and discerning mind. He was a silent man, but an attentive listener, and he readily comprehended the purport of all I said to him. After we had conversed for an hour or more, he made a suggestion that found favor with me. He therefore went out into the city, and made sundry purchases of stiff, smooth paper, pencils, rulers, and a compass. When he returned, we spread out the paper on a table which I happened to have, and with the pencil, rulers, and compass, and by consult-

318

ing together, we managed to get a number of diagrams
made, with which I was well satisfied, and which Crafts
declared he understood thoroughly.   It was dark before
we had finished, but the gas was lighted, and I spent a
portion of the evening in explaining certain matters of detail that I thought were essential.   It was natural that at
first there should have been difficulty, and that I was
obliged to go over my work many times before Crafts
thoroughly understood my object.   I very soon discovered
that my preconceived notions of a design would have to
be abandoned.   I had been at much pains to fabricate a
small model in the clay which Oliver procured for me, and
this was to a certain extent an advantage ; but the explanation of this on paper, and the working out of a practical design for a practical man to reproduce in iron I found
would be a vastly more difficult process.   It was not long
before I concluded to abandon my original project entirely, and to let Crafts himself have his own way respecting the method of accomplishing my object.

My own views in the first instance had only been those
of one whose experience was limited to working in wood,
and to reproduce in another material a result was something that required no little of that quality or resultant of
qualities which (for the want of a better word) may be
called genius.   I did not possess genius.   Crafts did, and
it was not above an hour after we sat down together before
he was instructing me, not I him.   He grasped my ideas
with celerity, and when the paper and apparatus had been
procured, he it was who, by a few dexterous strokes, drawn
to a suitable scale, indicated a plan that I perceived at
once was easy and practicable.   My chief difficulty had
been the short time at our disposal, and the necessity that
I imagined existed for the making of suitable patterns.

This necessity was obviated by Crafts, who showed me conclusively that what I desired could be accomplished in wrought steel much better than in cast. As all the plates of steel were kept in stock at the Fabrican, I saw at a glance that all that was needed was a little patient ingenuity, which I now felt assured Crafts could supply. As the sea-way was six feet (using our linear measure) in each direction, broad and deep, these dimensions gave us our limits. In the end it was decided that the working drawings should be prepared, to fit our construction, which was to be five feet deep, six—or a trifle less, to allow free play—in breadth, and about sixteen feet long. I spent a portion of the afternoon in making a calculation of weights, for which I had frequent occasion to consult the arithmetic, and won great credit in this from Mr Crafts, who, being himself a rigid old Multiplier under stood the need there was, as he expressed it, of Mathematical assistance. For reasons of my own, while so employed I did not show Crafts the processes by which I arrived at my results. His own figuring had a totally different basis, and on more than one occasion I was obliged to resort to some specious arguments to convince him that certain proportions were essential. He was a rather self-willed man, but likewise open to conviction, and in the end he gave in to my views, and the plans were drawn in accord therewith. Beside the use of the paper and pencil, I was enabled to take advantage of the smooth iron of the floor of my cell, whereon we drew with chalk certain rude designs to a half scale of all the parts of our proposed work.

This, as finally agreed upon, was simple enough. There was a solid iron to be first set upright, about sixteen feet in length, the top of which was to be firmly riveted to a channel-bar, into which the plates were to be inserted, overlapping in a manner somewhat similar to the clapboards of a common frame house, although not downwards, but from front to rear. This was the suggestion of Crafts, and it is not necessary to state was satisfactory in every particular.

In front there was only one plate, at right angles to the channel-bar; then followed two overlapping; after these broader and longer, and spread slightly, were two more, and so on, each pair spreading more and more, and being longer as they progressed towards the middle, and likewise broader. After the mid point was reached there was a gradual diminishing towards the other end. The shape of the several sheets of steel may, I think, be readily imagined without the aid of a diagram.

In my instructions to Crafts the weights of these several sheets were designated very accurately (of course reduced to Inquirendian equivalents), and this accuracy was a source of considerable surprise to the man, although he good-humoredly gave way to what he no doubt considered as mere whims of a dying, or perhaps hallucinations of a non compos, person.

"In my time," said he, very positively, "I've 'ad a 'and in getting up more'n a hundred coffins for them as 'ad a fahncy in the coffin way; but I never see a gent as wos so 'andy, not to say pertikeler, as you, sir."

I laughed.

"Well, Crafts," I answered, "I suppose last dying wishes ought to be respected."

"In course, in course; I'm not a objectin'. If a gent wants a coffin built, why, I builds it. I've got nothink to say as to nothink."

"Good!" said I, emphatically.

21

"But I do say this," Crafts continued, with equal emphasis, "it's sheer waste of money to have them sheets rolled down so fine. It'll make the cost come to double. If you'd a been willin' to keep 'em 'arf a hinch, 'twould a come to no more'n nine shillin'; has it his, hit'll run hup to two pun, let 'lone the traps hinside. Hif we've got to roll 'em down to a heighth of a hinch the hexpense 'll be henormous."

I satisfied Crafts that the expense of my proposed coffin was of no moment whatever, and as the payments were guaranteed, he made no further objection. He left me with the promise to report every day as the work progressed, and this promise he faithfully fulfilled. The chief difficulty lay in the details. Beside the outer framework there were matters connected with the cover, the arrangement of the braces, and the construction of certain slots and bolts, as to which I was very particular, and I fear tried poor Mr. Crafts' patience exceedingly. Oliver was with me every day, and with true kindness of heart humored what he considered my caprices. He went back and forward to the Fabrican almost daily, and was invaluable to me; so much so that I doubt if my coffin would have been completed in time if he had not united his loving efforts to those of Crafts. The arrangement of the flexible hinges, by which it was supposed Numbers was able to get at an integer, had to be calculated with great nicety, and about this I was for a time very anxious, as the ordinary construction conflicted somewhat with my own views. However, all this was settled at last, and at the close of the ninth day after my conviction Oliver reported that the coffin was completed. He also told me that it had been arranged that I should have an opportunity to inspect it early on the following morning, when it would pass through the city on the way to the place of execution.

I was up and at my window by dawn, and not long after was much gratified by seeing the oxen coming slowly along the street followed by a great crowd. Crafts came up to my cell, and was very much gratified at the compliments I paid him for his work. Crafts had indeed carried out my instructions remarkably well. As the oxen halted in front of the window the lids were removed, and I was enabled to see distinctly all the parts of the interior. It had been divided as I had ordered into two equal parts in front, and in the rear was an open space. In the upright partition was a slab of steel, working on a pivot towards the front, and which could be raised or lowered at pleasure. The projection in the rear, about which there had been some discussion, had been most satisfactorily arranged, and Crafts had one of his workmen swing it from side to side to show me how well it worked. The hole that I had designed near the front end of the coffin had been fitted with an iron plug, but a ring had been attached to this in deference to my wishes. The poles were brought out, and at my request the two shorter ones were placed in the swivels on either side, and the longer was inserted into the hole which I have mentioned. Everything worked admirably, and I could not help expressing my unbounded gratification. The plug in this hole was not at all an essential part of the construction; but as the church rules forbade more than one opening in the coffin, I was forced to the alternative of either doing without the hole altogether, or having it made and then plugged up. As the hole was in my opinion, if not essential, at least desirable, I gave the order to have it made, and then plugged

up.   Oliver was much distressed that I was so persistent
in this matter.

"There is but one access to Mathematics," said he, "and
to an integer it seems so irreverent to even suggest the
possibility of there being more than one.   Straight is the
gate and narrow is the way," he continued, "and by mak
ing a round hole in your coffin, it would seem to be implied that a round opening was as good as a square one,
which the Arithmetic assures us in divers places is not the
case."

"But," I replied, somewhat thoughtlessly, "this coffin of
mine is sanctioned by the Arithmetic."

"How so?" asked Oliver.   "Can you point out the
passages?"

I was rather confused.   I made an evasive reply to the
effect that it would take time.

"As you have had the hole plugged," said Oliver, "it
really makes no great difference ; that is no serious obsta-
cle to your eternal well-being ; but no point is more conclusively established than this one, that in Numbers alone
is safety.   The door by which Numbers approaches the
integer is plainly indicated in the Arithmetic in divers
places."

"Yes," I said, "I understand that—"   I was about to
add that my reliance was not to be found in divers, but
rather in floaters' places, but from motives of prudence,
lest my meaning should be misapprehended by Oliver, I
refrained.

The oxen again started on their journey, and I sat down
by the window and watched them as they passed from
sight.   Oliver explained to me that as soon as they were
outside of the city they would be put to the top of their
speed, and as relays had been provided all along the route

there was no doubt whatever that the coffin would reach the place of execution at the appointed hour.

" I hope it will," I remarked ; " it would be very awkward if by any chance it should not arrive."

"Give yourself no unnecessary uneasiness," replied Oliver, sympathetically. " There is very little danger of there being any delay ; and even if there should be I have taken the precaution to order another coffin sent from the Fabrican by another route."

" But," said I, irritably, " I do not want any other coffin. I want that one."

"The other is even more expensive," said Oliver, soothingly.

I was angry, and indeed to some extent alarmed. " I don't care a copper continental," said I, with some asperity, perhaps ill-befitting my character as a newly cancelled integer.   " I want my own coffin."

" Do not excite yourself needlessly," said Oliver, calmly. "The other coffin of which I spoke could not possibly fail to satisfy even the most exacting—"

" I want my own coffin," I repeated.

"There is little doubt that it will arrive in time," said Oliver. " I knew that you would like to see it so I gave instructions that it should be brought this way.   I only spoke of the matter at all to ease your mind, lest you should think there might not be a nice coffin provided. I know some minds are so constituted that they are not satisfied unless every little detail in respect to their funeral is carried out."

" You have hit the point exactly, Oliver," I said, " I am just one of that kind."

" So," continued Oliver, "desiring to please you, I had a coffin sent the other way, so as to make sure.   It has

been waiting at the Fabrican for upwards of two years
now for a purchaser. It was built for a Mr. Mopes, who
was supposed to be wealthy, but whose estate turned out
to be much less than was expected. His heirs refused to
live up to the bargain made by the old man before he
died, and the coffin has been on hand ever since. I got
the refusal of it at a very low figure—less than cost, in
fact."

"But what makes you think that my own coffin may
possibly not be there in time?"

"I don't say it will not. Still, there was a fear that
the bridge just the other side of the asylum had not
been strengthened sufficiently to allow it to pass over in
safety. But do not be alarmed, Gallwood has promised to
see that it is shored up properly."

"Gallwood!" I stammered. "Does my safety depend
upon his exertions?"

"Why do you speak so?" said Oliver, "Gallwood takes
the very deepest possible interest in you." Then he
added in another tone, "Do not allow yourself to brood
over these things. Fix your thoughts in these your last
hours upon a consideration of your latter end."

My response to this was to pull out a memoranda that
I had made on a fly-leaf of the Arithmetic.

"What strain is the bridge of the asylum calculated to
bear?" said I.

Although Oliver was not well satisfied that I should
harp upon the subject as I did, yet he gave me the desired information. I made a quick calculation; assuming
the oxen to weigh so much, and the cart to weigh so much
more, I easily informed myself that there was a bare possibility of the whole train, coffin and all, going over safely,
even without any of Gallwood's shoring. There was not

much to spare, but still the result of my calculations was satisfactory. I knew to a pound the weight of my own coffin, and my hope was based upon the fact that I felt confident was unknown to Gallwood, that its weight was only about one-third that of the lightest made.

Not to harrow up the feelings of the reader unnecessarily I shall pass over the events of the few hours that elapsed until, in company with Oliver and Mr. Smalls, I arrived at the appointed place of execution on the coast. We had been driven over from the capital with the fleetest team of oxen, relays of which were also provided. In this way we proceeded with very great rapidity, and it was exactly at the hour that had been officially designated by the court when we drove into the midst of the assembled concourse. The idiot and the maniac, of whom mention has been made, had been sent by slower stages the previous day. Until we passed the bridge beyond the asylum I was in a state of great trepidation, and must have given some slight offence to my travelling companions, who both strove to fix my attention on certain passages of the Arithmetic, which they declared to be peculiarly adapted to my unfortunate condition. Mr. Smalls especially must at one point in the journey have had his feelings hurt, although it was entirely unintentional on my part. This was just as we were approaching the bridge and I was particularly worried lest there might have been a mishap. There was a rather long hill after leaving the asylum, and it was as we neared the summit of this incline that I was especially on the alert. I knew—because I had passed over that road several times before, and as my memory was retentive—that beyond the top of the brow ahead I should be able to look down over the valley where the bridge spanned the gorge. It was no wonder that I was anxious; but still I freely admit that I ought not to have shown my anxiety so plainly. I do not in the least wonder that Mr. Smalls felt annoyed, and I take this opportunity of apologizing to him. It was the third relay of oxen since leaving the capital, and the fourth was to be provided a short distance beyond the bridge. The hill was long; the weather was insufferably hot; not a breath of air was stirring; the oxen had come at full gallop for a long distance, and so the driver considerately allowed them to go up the hill at a walk. While the close, confined, covered vehicle was dragged slowly along Mr. Smalls improved the occasion by reading to me sundry texts which he considered suitable. One after another he drawled these out with tantalizing monotony of voice, which was an additional agony, on a par with the heat, and the dust, and the slow pace of the oxen. These latter switched their tails, and tossed their horns, and every now and then even stopped to kick a fly off their nose or ear with a hind foot.

I was very anxious, and when Mr. Smalls, seeing that my attention was wandering (for I poked my head out more than once), sighed, and said that it behooved me to make an effort to fix my attention on the pages of the word, I responded that I could do so with more cordiality after I had been assured that my coffin had passed the bridge in safety. Mr. Smalls again sighed, and taking up the Arithmetic began again :

"Twice one make two," he read.

At this instant the oxen, having arrived at the top of the incline, took up a brisk trot, and, unmindful of Mr. Smalls' feelings, of the Arithmetic, and of aught else except my coffin, I stuck my head out of the window of the carriage, and, as we reached the further bluff, looked

down over the valley. The bridge was there safe, and
there was no sign of my coffin in sight anywhere. I gave
a great sigh of relief and pulled in my head instantly.

"Go on," said I, now complaisant enough, "go on, Mr.
Smalls, I am very much interested."

Both Mr. Smalls and Oliver looked as if they did not
believe me, but the former went on :

"Twice two make four."

"That is true," said I. In my great joy that I had not
seen the oxen with my coffin stuck on the bridge, or
broken down with it in the bottom of the gorge, I felt inclined to acquiesce in anything. "That is very true. I
often felt the force of that remark."

"Do not be too hasty," said Oliver, "let Mr. Smalls
explain that passage. It is a confessedly difficult one."

"Does it need explanation?" I asked, surprised.

"Of course it does. No layman could be expected to
fully understand it in all its bearings without that kind of
instruction which a priest is alone fitted to give."

"Please explain it," said I, humbly. "I had an idea
that I understood the meaning."

"You could hardly be expected to," said Oliver.
"Some of our most esteemed integers have utterly failed
to interpret it aright."

"Please interpret it for me," said I.

"Your humility does you credit," said Mr. Smalls. "I
shall do so with great pleasure."

He then proceeded with a long homily, which I think
best on the whole to omit. The substance of the interpretation can be found in any well regulated theological
library in any civilized country in the world, and is, I think,
take it all in all, one of the most dispiriting and withal
ridiculous spectacles that this earth presents. "So you

see," said Mr. Smalls, in conclusion, " that the passage has
a very different signification from that which it appears to
bear upon the surface."

As the object of his conversation had been to demonstrate that two and two could make almost any other
number than four by making a certain proper appeal to
Mathematics I was fully persuaded that the views which
I had always held in respect to the limitations of the
Arithmetic were in the eyes of Mr. Smalls and Oliver
erroneous.

" Your explanation is probably satisfactory," said I, a
little evasively.

" Is it not perfectly so ? " said Oliver.

" I confess not altogether."

" You must remember that all these things must be
taken with faith," said Mr. Smalls.

I admitted that this was unquestionably so—if at all.

" But did you ever know of an instance where two and
two made anything else but four ? " I asked.

" Unquestionably," said Oliver, promptly.

" Many," said Mr. Smalls.

" Please give me the particulars of one."

" There is one special case that I have in my mind
now," said Mr. Smalls, musingly. " You remember, Oliver,
the Widow Meeks and her cruse of whiskey ? "

" I do," responded Oliver, " distinctly."

" Tell me about that," said I.

" There is not much to tell. It is only a simple story ;
but it illustrates the power of expression. Mrs. Meeks'
husband had died and left her with nothing but the business to rely upon as a means of support—a little retail
whiskey shop in the second ward of the capital. I had
occasion soon after the funeral to call. Mr. Meeks had

not been a kind husband. It was beautiful to see how resigned the widow was. She took me down in the cellar
and pointed with pride to a cruse in one corner. A cruse,
as is well known, contains exactly four quarts. The widow
told me how she was situated, and how hard she had
found it to make a livelihood, especially with Patsey Finnegan on the corner underselling her, so in her trouble
the widow besought Mathematics that her cruse might
thereafter contain five quarts instead of four, and," continued Mr. Smalls, in a voice choked with emotion, " her
supplication was answered. It was done."

"How do you know that?" said I.

"How do I know it!" exclaimed Mr. Smalls. "She
told me."

"And in addition to the testimony of the widow herself," added Oliver, eagerly, " there was the undoubted
evidence of the well known fact that the poor widow
was thereafter enabled to sell her whiskey so low as to
compete successfully with Finnegan, who was obliged to
withdraw wholly from business in consequence."

"Yes," said Mr. Smalls, " not only that, but Finnegan
himself had finally to admit that he was vanquished by no
power of the island, and the widow to this day ascribes
all credit to the raft and the water of the written solution."

I could not forbear making the suggestion that perhaps
water at least had something to do with it.

"You may depend upon it, Mr. Cliff," said Mr. Smalls,
earnestly, " that it did, and that this is only one of many—
I may say innumerable instances."

"You regard that as a direct intervention of Mathematics?"

"Certainly I do."

"But why should Mathematics interfere?"

"What are we, worms as we are, to question, or to pry into these things?"

"Worm as I am," I replied, "it does appear to me a little peculiar that Mathematics should interpose. Besides, wasn't it a little rough on Patsey Finnegan?"

"Not only have I known of two and two making five," continued Mr. Smalls, ignoring my last remark, "but I have even had instances come under the sphere of my observation where it made six or seven; but such, I admit, are rare."

It was with such cheerful conversation as this that Mr. Smalls and Oliver endeavored to beguile my thoughts from a consideration of the dreadful doom that lay before me, and to lift them to the blessed hopes of the Arithmetic. If it had not been for the trifling uneasiness which I still felt it is probable that I should even have been amused; but until we arrived at the grave, there was still the uncertainty respecting my coffin.

Oliver noticed that I was preoccupied, and feeling it to be his duty to do so, gently took me to task for what he said he could not but regard as vanity, and a clinging to the things of the island.

"Indeed, Oliver," said I, "you misjudge me. It is not vanity. I assure you I do not cling to the island."

"Ah, I am glad to hear you say that," said Mr. Smalls, "truly glad."

"Yes, John," added Oliver, affectionately, "we ought all to be resigned. How little it matters of what shape our coffin shall be, provided we are prepared for the last plunge."

"I wish to be prepared," I murmured, "and I do think I am."

At this instant the oxen, turning a sharp corner, brought

us in plain sight of the place of execution, and there to my unbounded joy, just unloaded in front of the grave, stood my coffin. Mr. Crafts came directly up to us.

"Well, Robert," said I, "so you got the coffin over safely, did you?"

Crafts' face became very sober.

"We did, Muster Cliff," he replied; "but if 't'ud a weighed the heft of a hounce more, we'd not 'ave made hout to 'ave done hit. Some willain 'ad been hand hundid part hof the hunderpinin'."

I looked round me, and at a distance I saw Gallwood furtively regarding me. He hung down his head, but I knew that he had been foiled again. From that moment until the last we both dissembled.

CHAPTER XXXII.

"INTO THE WORLD AT LIBERTY AGAIN."

IT will be remembered that I was left some few chapters back in a state of considerable suspense. I had succeeded, after much tribulation, in getting my way about my coffin, and, snugly ensconced within it, had been pushed down the sloping sea-way. As I felt myself moving the light was suddenly blotted out, and all was darkness, while a great cry arose from the multitude. Little time had I to moralize or to speculate; with a whir and bang the coffin shot down, jolting uneasily from side to side, but still, I was glad to see, maintaining an upright position. Suddenly there was an upheaval of the front; my feet, which had been pointed downward at such an angle that I was obliged to cling to the iron partition for support, now in a moment assumed a horizontal position, and at the same time I heard a splashing swash as my strange craft plunged into the waves. I reflected no longer; the time for action had come. With quick, impatient hands I felt in the obscurity for the slots constructed for this particular emergency, and grasping the bolts shot them back. It needed but a slight effort to rise upon my knees and throw back the lids which it had been anticipated Numbers alone would raise. The sea was shining with great brilliancy; but the eye of true love blazes brighter than the sun. Against the sides of the strange craft rippled and washed the waves of the quiet ocean, and on the deck,

with her eyes lifted to the sky, and her beautiful white
hands fervently clasped, knelt Margery. She had fulfilled
her promise to go with me on my coffin into the sea. Her
long flowing robe—the mourning robe that she had put on
for me—had slipped from her shoulders and lay all about
her. Her dress, the loose flowing dress, cut in the Inquirendian fashion low about her neck, was also of the pur-
est white. How like a sweet, fair angel she was. I went
to her, unmindful of all else, and put my arms around
her.

"Darling," I said, "we are safe at last."

"Safe," she repeated, her eyes still lifted, "safe; oh,
is this indeed death?"

"No, it is not death, Margery," I answered, "it is life.
Come, darling, look at me. See, I am no spirit. It is I,
your own John. Do you believe me now, my own?"

Slowly Margery's eyes turned earthward; and as they
did so, lost that fixed and agonized expression. She
turned towards me, sighed deeply, and at last she found
her voice.

"How did it all happen, John? Is it indeed true that
the dead can live?"

"It is true that we are living, Margery. Look yonder.
There is the island. There are your father and mother
now watching you. Here around us is the sea, the sea
that you so dreaded."

I leaned over the side of the boat, now lazily rocking
on the smooth, swelling surface of the placid deep. I
dipped my hands in the warm waters.

"See, Margery," I said, "it does not hurt me, it cannot
harm you. Come, darling, touch the waters, and see how
harmless they are."

Margery heard me. She lifted her eyes to mine, and

then, for a brief instant, upward to where, overcome with amazement and horror, her father and mother stood in the midst of a silent, terrified throng. She was still upon her knees on the deck, but her clasped hands had fallen apart, and hung nerveless by her side. The rich, rosy bloom of her cheeks had departed, and in its place was a deathly pallor. Her beautiful long brown hair, escaped from the careful coil around her shapely head, fell in twining folds about her. Her eyes moved from the shore to the sea, and then met mine, with one wild, questioning look. Her lips, ashy pale, parted, but ere she could syllable a word she fell forward into my arms overcome, in all the semblance of the death that she had sought with me, the one she loved.

But not dead; no, thank God, not dead. I had been fortunate enough in the midst of my terrible anxieties to think of all our necessities; so, hid away—the further whim of a poor lunatic—under the thwarts, by the tender care of Oliver, was a sufficient store of all needful things for the voyage homeward, and there was also water, fresh, limpid water, from a cold spring not a hundred yards from the shore. I laid my Margery tenderly upon the soft cushions of the thwart in the afterpart of the boat. I bathed her brow and lips, and not till there were signs of returning life did I leave her. But the lips grew ruddy, and a faint hue of pink tinged her sweet cheeks once more. My anxiety was over. I rose to my feet. The boat, riding like a gull on even keel, swayed to and fro, rocked by the long, peaceful waves. The gentle tide set in towards the shore, on whose marge, a hundred yards away, the little breakers rolled over like truant children clapping their playful hands. We had drifted in, and now the great iron plane, inclined at a sharp angle, dipped into the water almost beside us. I looked up; the crest of the bluff, for a long distance on either side of those awful iron doors, was lined by an awe-stricken and astonished multitude. But the current (doubtless an offset of the Gulf-stream) was drifting us slowly in. I could not, of course, be assured what treatment would be vouchsafed to ghosts in Inquirendo, so I prudently made haste to place my craft, and myself, and Margery beyond the reach of all possible peril. I brought out the longer of the three poles of which mention has been made, and jerking out the useless plug that Oliver from religious scruples had caused to be inserted, threw it into the sea. I quickly fastened the white mourning robe, and stepping my mast had, in a trice, a most serviceable sail of the leg-o'-mutton pattern. I found the tiller (one of the mysterious things that had been wrought at the Fabrican), and inserting it into the slot in the rudder, I was once more a yachtsman. A gentle breeze was rising, just enough to fill the sail. I sat down, holding the helm. Margery's supple form lay beside me. One arm was about her tenderly. With the other I brought the breeze abeam and drew away from the island.

I was delighted to observe how beautifully my boat sailed. The centre-board worked to a charm, and finding how easily she obeyed the helm I tacked about.

Along the brow of the bluff still stood, apparently stupefied, the assembled islanders. No difficulty had I in singling out the many familiar faces. There was the benign, placid Mr. Mayland and his gentle wife, towards whom my heart went out, and there also were Mr. Smalls and Oliver, looking down upon us with expressions of the utmost horror. Speechless and awe-stricken, the self-sat-

22

isfied smirks frozen upon their vicious faces, stood peer-
ing over the crag my enemies, Gallwood and Nudwink.

I sailed now close in shore. The water was deep at
this point and the bluff was low. I rose to my feet as
the boat sailed slowly past, and bowing my head to the
multitude, called in a loud voice : " Gallwood ! "

No answer came from the discomfited and wretched
man ; but I heard a sound like the sighing of the wind
through a forest. It was the awe-stricken people groaning
in terror.

" Gallwood," I repeated solemnly, " Gallwood, answer
me."

Then came a response, not indeed from Gallwood,
whose fear forbade speech, whose cadaverous lower jaw
hung on his breast, and whose eyes protruded in the extremity of horror.

There was a deep silence, and in the midst of it, as I
brought the boat's head to the wind, and held her there
motionless, a voice rose sharp and clear :

" Howly Noombers, the ghost spakes."

So saying, my early acquaintance, Mike Tierney, took
one step forward, lifting both hands, palms upward, over
his head, and as he did so, another groan burst from all
around him.

It ought to be distinctly understood that I do not in the
least blame the populace, and especially Mike, for totally
misapprehending my position. Any reader of this account
who may be inclined to do so, and who may imagine that
under similar circumstances he would be wiser, has only
to put himself in the place of an Inquirendian. This
writing is not perhaps intended for a class of readers who
are in the habit of attending public executions ; but we
all do occasionally peruse accounts more or less accurate

of such, and, as the imagination is not often particular, it may be suggested that if a staid, respectable citizen (let us say of Newark, N. J., or Poughkeepsie, N. Y.) happened, in the strict line of his duty, to be present at the untimely taking off of a criminal, who acted as I had, doubtless he would have felt as Mike did.

Imagine the culprit, the instant after the hangman had cut the rope, make a sudden ascending venture, apparently on nothing, or on a toy balloon, and go floating around overhead just within earshot.

It behooves us all to be on our guard constantly against censorious criticism. Doubtless such a circumstance would strike any citizen, staid or otherwise, as a little peculiar.

At any rate, that was the way it struck Mike, and caused him to say what he did.

However, it was not with Mike that I desired to converse. I hailed Gallwood again. He made no reply, but his jaw dropped lower still and his eyes bulged out with fright.

I was conscientious in all that I did. I pressed my advantage mercilessly.

"Gallwood," I said, "step forward."

No answer but a low groan.

"And you too, Nudwink."

Seeing that neither was disposed to move I continued, somewhat sharply. "Come, step to the edge of the bluff; I have a word to say to you."

Their knees trembled, and it was evident that they were both utterly overcome with fear. Some further incentive to action was necessary, so I added, in my most persuasive tone, "Obey me, or I shall be compelled to come ashore after you."

Nudwink shivered all over, clutched his companion by the arm, and by one impulse they made a staggering step forward.

"Do you hear me?" I asked, not over gently, as they stood on the verge of the steep slope, gazing open-eyed down upon me.

Nudwink's mouth opened, but while his teeth chattered no articulate sound could he utter. "Ye—ye—yes," stammered Gallwood, incoherently.

"Have your views been modified lately," I asked, "upon the general subject of advantages?"

"Ye—ye—yes."

"Materially modified?"

Again he stammered a pitiful assent. He appeared to be painfully embarrassed, and not in the least blaming him I forbore to add to his annoyance. Yet I was not of a mind to depart until I had expressed my views of the dastardly conduct of both these men.

"Behold," I said, "the untoward result of your plotting villany. I am free forever from all your control, and to-day I bear with me to my own home, in that better land of which I told you, all that I hold dearest and best, and of which you strove to rob me.

"I know not which of you is the greater and more infamous wretch. I weigh not the delicate balance between wilful service of the powers of evil, and hypocrisy. This I say, that you are both evil men. You, Gallwood, have thought hitherto that this ocean, that has to me no terrors, ends all, and that there was to be no reckoning for you for all your misdeeds. You, Nudwink, have crammed yourself full of idolatries, and thought to hide your soul's wickedness under a garb of specious pretence.

You are both guilty of my blood, though by a power of which you are ignorant I have found life.

"And now, farewell."

I raised my voice.

"Farewell, Oliver. Farewell, Mr. Smalls. Tell Margery's father and mother that she is safe with me. She loved me well enough to die for me, and hereafter will love me enough to live with me. Some day I hope that we shall all meet again. Farewell."

I turned the boat's head to the west. The favorable breeze freshened, the sail filled, and leaving the populace still overcome with mute horror, we skimmed away, till, as the sun went down in the flaming west, the island lay far off, a tiny, green speck, hardly distinguishable from the waves of the surrounding sea.

It was noon of a Sabbath day. Margery was now thoroughly recovered, and withal remarkably well content with my society. We had passed through the inlet and landed at the dock. A few loafers stared at us with much impudence, and all the indigenous inhabitants of Far Rockaway seemed to be curious about us. I walked up towards the village with Margery on my arm ; she, poor girl, somewhat surprised at all she saw. On the way to my father's summer cottage I passed the little church. The sexton was a man I knew. His name was Higgins. He stood at his ease outside. Even in that moment I could not help remembering how I had always envied him the privilege of attending church, and the further advantage of being able to take a run outside when things grew hot within.

I went directly up to him. "How are you, Higgins?" said I, extending my hand. He did not know me. My beard had grown sufficiently to be a complete disguise. He

shook my hand, though, very politely. "Won't you walk
in?" said he.

I hesitated. "Any special service?" I asked.

"Yes, yes," Higgins responded, promptly; "memorial
services for Mr. William Cliff's son; wild lad — well-
meaning, but wild."

POSTFACE.

"NEW YORK, *September* 20, 1885.

" MY DEAR BOY :

" Your account of adventures in the island has been read by me with great interest. Having heard from you much that you have related, of course there was little novelty in the story. But, my son, do you think it wise to enter as minutely as you have done into the details of the peculiar ceremonials that you describe ? If I did not feel thoroughly assured of your own state of heart I should have serious apprehensions on your own account. But my fear now is, that the effect upon the world of your narrative may be pernicious. The world will not know what it means, and, in order that it may be understood, I advise you to speak plainer. Do not, I beg of you, by word or pen, say anything which might obscure the truth in any mind, whether cultivated or the reverse. Remember who it was that said, ' He that is not with me is against me.' I am fully aware that the moral of all that you have written is against the outward display of religion, and against its superstitions ; but, if weak minds read it, and translate it as opposed to truth, its delicate bits of writing, and the tenderness and pathos of some of the scenes which you have depicted, will only add to the force of its supposed arguments.

" The beauty of Christianity lies in this, that the way-faring man, though a fool, need not err therein.

"When religion is the theme, its handling should be well guarded, as you would handle the name of a mother, a sister, or a wife. If you were to write what appeared to be a satire on them, surely it would be a reproach to you. How much more then should you be on your guard against bringing discredit upon revealed religion. As St. Paul says, 'All things are lawful unto me, but all things are not expedient.' Would it not be well to refrain from the exactness of description, which will, I fear, be misinterpreted by mankind. It will not be credited that you are striving to uphold the cause of Christ. The religious press in particular will, I fear, regard what you have written as irreligious, not to say sacrilegious. Such a result would, I am sure, be felt by you to be unfortunate. 'If meat make my brother to offend, I will eat no flesh while the world standeth.'

"Think over what I have said, my dear son, and soften down much of what you have written. This is a time in the world's history when our trumpet should give no uncertain sound, and I know that you would regret being the cause of any one's falling away from the faith, and that this might be the tendency of some that you have written I have good reason to believe.

"Your Attached Mother."

MY REPLY.

"New Windsor, *Sept.* 30, 1885.

"Dear Mother :

"Your letter, in respect to 'Inquirendo,' was received several days ago. I have not replied sooner, as I desired to think over the whole matter, that I might explain, in as few words as possible, my reasons for the minuteness which you regard as likely to be detrimental to the faith of the world.

"What I have written is certainly eccentric; but in the nomenclature of the islanders alone is the eccentricity. Humanity, isolated, reaches out in vain and futile longings to know as itself is known. In their unknown God, whom they called Mathematics, the Inquirendians strove to deify the sum of all truth, the body of all power. They brought a cold and formal abstraction home to their hearts by personifying this everlasting principle in Numbers, in whom resided the tangible manifestation of the infinite unknown.

"Thinking the surrounding seas unnavigable they did not understand the story of the raft. They apprehended only in part that virtue of which I *knew*.

"With us, as with the people of Inquirendo, philosophy alone is vain and foolish. Intellect is as ignorant of the meaning of things as the Inquirendians were.

"Christianity presents itself to man in two aspects: intellectually we are concerned with it as a matter of history, and in the means whereby its underlying and pervading principles, embodied in doctrine, are made known to the mind. Spiritually, man is concerned only with the result of its force upon his heart and life.

"We are all practically agreed as to premises, the difference lies in our conclusions, as to the formulæ in which abstract truth ought to be presented in concrete shape.

"Science habitually employs diagrams, definitions, theorems, comparisons, and symbols. The substance of religion is inherent in the heart of humanity. Its principles are eternal. Ultimate truth is as inexplicable as an axiom, and as certain; but more absurdities are uttered in the name of truth, than crimes committed in that of liberty.

All philosophical writing is but a record of varying phases of opinion. As the white light of the sun is distorted in a lens, or polarized by a refracting medium, so, by strata of opinion, the grand truths of God are refracted, bent, warped, distorted.

" Belief is an amazing word ; but the spurious kind, concerning itself with oils and the guesswork of opinion, is utterly worthless.

" True religion is not a mere assent to doctrine—a chilly, formal politeness to the Almighty. It is not the wire over which the message of hope comes from God to man, it is the message itself. It makes the filial relations sure between man and his Maker. If this relation comes by form and ceremony, or if it comes without it ; if doctrine brings it, or if philosophy brings it, or idolatry, or even infidelity, it matters not. Now I myself, dear mother, have never seen a man of whom I thought it could be said his philosophy was sufficient for him, or his idolatry, or his infidelity ; neither have I seen one whose ceremonial of itself was sufficient. But this has nothing to do with the plain statement of the fact, that if the filial relation is established that is the substance of all religion.

" Mr. Smalls (in the story) would have saved his life by faith if he had possessed the faith, and by that alone. I saved my life by my works, and showed my faith thereby.

" You caution me, dear mother, against injuring the faith of the world. I am at bitter enmity with its superstitions, its bigotry, its intolerance. I am sure, that in what I have written I have upheld its faith, by showing the nature of the real thing. It is unfortunately at the present day the wayfaring man who is not a fool who is most apt to err. If there were no hypocrites within the churches there would be no infidels without. To intellect alone the ordinary spurious faith is mere cant and sham.

" I have attempted no demonstration of other matters on which my narrative touches ; these must be left to some future occasion ; but I may say to you, that I believe the existence of God to be as certain as that the principles of Mathematics exist ; man's immortality as assured as that the sea is capable of being navigated, and the Bible as certainly contains the truth as the Arithmetic.

" One fact only has been demonstrated : the existence and the reality of faith. To believe, and not to pretend, is the moral of all that I have written, and to show that underlying all form, and all ceremony, and all history is something vital and eternal, and that in the divine story of Christianity (of which my narrative may be considered in some degree an allegory) is to be found the truth brought home to the heart by means and by a symbol worthy of a God.

" With much love.

" YOUR ATTACHED SON."

Twentieth Century Publishing Co.

PARTIAL LIST OF

RATIONALISTIC WORKS.

The Religion of Humanity. 12mo, cloth extra. $1.50.

A History of Trancendentalism in New England. Octavo, with portrait of the author. Cloth. extra, $2.50. " Masterly in matter, treatment and style." —[N. Y. Tribune.

The Cradle of the Christ. A Study of Primitive Christianity. 8vo., cloth extra. $1.75. " Marked by all those elements of strong intellectuality, refined culture, mental honesty, and skill in argument, which are so prominent in all h's previous works."—[New Bedford Mercury.

Gardener, Helen H. Men, Women, and Gods. With an introduction by Col. R. G. Ingersoll. Paper, 50 cents; cloth, $1.

Gibbon, Edward. History of Christianity. Cloth, 864 pages. Many illustrations ; $1.50.

Graves, Kersey. Bible of Bibles; or, Twenty-seven "Divine Revelations." Containing a description of twenty-seven Bibles, and an exposition of two thousand biblical errors in science, history, morals, religion, and general events. Cloth, $1.75.

Greg. W.R. Creed of Christiandom. Its foundation contrasted with its superstructure. 399 pages, $1.50.

Half-Hours with Some Ancient and Modern Celebrated Freethinkers : Thomas Hobbs, Lord Bolingbroke, Condorcet, Spinoza, Anthony Collins, Descartes, M. de Voltaire, John Toland, Comte de Volney, Charles Blount, Percy Bysshe Shelley, Claude A. Helvetius, Francis Wright, Darusmont, Zeno, Epicurus, Mathew Tindal, David Hume, Dr. Thomas Burnet, Thomas Paine, Baptiste de Mirabaud, Baron de Holbach, Robert Taylor, Joseph Barker. By " Iconoclast," Collins, and Watts Cloth, 75c.

Hogan, William [25 years a confessing priest]. Popery Dissected. 50 cents; cloth, 75c.

Janes, Lewis G. A Study of Primitive Christianity. Revised edition. 319 pages; 8vo, cloth, gilt-top, $1.50. Treats of the natural evolution of the Christian religion, according to the historical method.

Jamieson, W. F. The Clergy a Source of Danger to the American Republic. $1.75.

Jamieson-Ditzler Debate. Christianity and Liberalism. 50c.; cloth, 75c.

Jehovah Unveiled. Character of Jewish Deity. 35c.

Kelso, Col. J. R. Real Blasphemers. Paper, 50c.

Larned, E. C.: A Critical Analysis of Drummond's " Natural Law in the Spiritual World. ' By many thought to be the best reply yet made to Drummond's able work. 46 pages, 40c.

Legge, James. The Religions of China. Confucianism and Taoism described and compared with Christianity. $1.50.

Lux Mundi : Twelve Essays by Eleven Prominent Theological Writers. The great theological sensation of the day in England. The frank acceptance of Evolution. The ungrudging concession to modern criticism of the Old Testament. Cloth, $1.75.

Mensinga, F. Was Christ a God ? Conclusions from New Testament. $1.50.

Meslier, Jean. (A Roman Catholic priest, who abjured religious dogmas). Superstition in All Ages Paper, 50 cents; cloth. $1.

Muller, Max. Chips from a German Workshop. Vol. 1—Essays on the Science of Religion. Vol. 2—Essays on Mythology, Traditions, and Customs. Vol. 3—Essays on Literature, Biographies, and Antiquities. Volume 4—Comparative Philology. Mythology, etc. Vol. 5--On Freedom, etc. Cloth; per volume, $2 ; set, $10

Murray, Alex. S.: Manual of Mythology. With 45 plates on tinted paper, representing nearly 100 mythological subjects. Cloth, $1.75.

O'Donoghue, A. H.: Theology and Mythology. An inquiry into the claims of biblical inspiration and the supernatural element in religion. $1.

Offen, B. Legacy to Friends of Free Discussion. $1.

Oppenheim, Josie Personal Immortality and Other Papers. 75c.

Oswald, Dr. Felix L. Bible of Nature; or, the Principles of Secularism. A contribution to the religion of the future. $1.

Secret of the East. Origin of the Christian Religion. $1.

Palmer, S. Good Word for the Devil. Paper, 50c.

Peeples, J. M. Jesus: Man, Myth, or God ? 50c.; cloth, 75c.

Pedder, H.C. Issues of the Age. Modern Thought. $1.

Pillsbury, Parker. Ecclesiastical vs. Civil Liberty. God in the Federal Constitution : Man and Woman Out. Paper, 20c.; 8 copies, $1.

Popes and Their Doings. Account of Vicars of Christ and Vicegerents of God. 50c.; cloth, 75c.

Proceedings and Addresses at the Watkins Convention. Excellent speeches and essays. 400 pages. $1.

Radical Pulpit. Discourses of Advanced Thought. By O. B. Frothingham and Felix Adler. $1.

Rawlinson, Prof. Geo. Religions of the Ancient World. $1.

Reber, George. Christ of Paul; or, The Enigmas of Christianity. $2.
Therapeutæ and Essenes. Origin of Christian Doctrine and Scripture. $1.

Reade, Winwood. The Martyrdom of Man. 545 pages. Cloth, $1.75.

Renouf, P. LePage. Origin and Growth of Religion, illustrated by the Religion of Ancient Egypt. $1 50.

Revile, Prof. A. Ancient Religions of Mexico and Peru. $1.50.

Rousseau, Jean Jacques (with portrait). The Vicar of Savoy. Paper, 25 cents; cloth, 50c.
Confessions. Paper, 75 cts; cloth, $1.50.

Salter, William M. Ethical Religion. Reconstructive thought in religion on a rationalistic and moral basis. Something to make the mere iconoclast think. One of the best works in our rationalistic literature. 332 pages. Cloth, $1 50.

Scott, Thomas. English Life of Jesus. $1.50.

Slenker, Elmina D. Studying the Bible. 75c.

Spencer, Herbert. Ceremonial Institutions. Being part 4 of the Principles of Sociology. $1.50.

Stevens, H. R. Faith and Reason. An account of Christian and all prominent religions before and since Christ. Extracts from sacred books of the East. $1.50.

Strauss, D. F. Old Faith and New. A confession. $1.50.

Taylor, T. B. Old Theology Turned Upside Down, or Right Side Up. $1; cloth $1.25.

Taylor, Rev. Robert: Astro-Theological Lectures. Allegorical. $1.50.
Devil's Pulpit. Astro-Theological Sermons. $1.50.
Diegesis. Origin and Early History of Christianity. Portrait. $2.
Syntagma of the Evidences of the Christian Religion. $1.

Thirty Discussions, Bible Stories. Essays, and Lectures. 700 pages. Paper, 75c.

Truesdale, John W. Bottom Facts of Spiritualism. Claims to be a complete exposition of so-called Spiritual Manifestation. $1.50.

Underwood, B. F. The Burgess-Underwood Debate A four days' debate between B. F. Underwood and Prof. O. A. Burgess, president of the Northwestern Christian University, Indianapolis, Ind. Accurately reported. 183 pages. Cloth, 80c; paper, 50c.
Debate on the Existence of a Personal God and Inspiration of Scripture, between B. F. Underwood and Rev. J. Marples. 35c.; cloth, 60c.
Essays and Lectures. Contains most of the pamphlets found under his name, "Debates" and "Twelve Tracts" excepted. 300 pages; 60c.

THE TWENTIETH CENTURY PUBLISHING COMPANY

WILL SEND

Any Book on any Subject Published anywhere

BY ANY PUBLISHER TO ANY ADDRESS

on receipt of price. ☞ We pay the postage or expressage.

FREETHOUGHT PAMPHLETS.

Partial List of Freethought Tracts and Pamphlets published and sold by the TWENTIETH CENTURY PUBLISHING COMPANY.

Appleton, Henry. What is Freedom, and When am I Free? Being an attempt to put liberty on a rational basis, and wrest its keeping from irresponsible pretenders in Church and State. Second edition. 15c

Bakounine, Michael. God and the State. With a preface by Carlo Cafiero and Elisée Reclus. Translated by Benj. R Tucker. Seventh edition. 15c.

Barlow, W. S. Orthodox Hash, with Change of Diet. 10c.
If, Then, and When. Church Doctrines. 10c.

Birney, J. G. Churches the Bulwarks of Slavery. 15c.

Bradlaugh, Charles: A Plea for Atheism, 10 cents.

Brown, Dr. George: A Historical and Critical Review on the Sunday Question, with Replies to an Objector. 15c.

Bruno, Giordano. His Life, Works, Worth, Martyrdom; portrait and monument. Contributors: George Jacob Holyoake, Thomas Davidson, T. B. Wakeman, Karl Blind, Lydia R. Chase, Robt. G. Ingersoll, Hudson Tuttle, etc. Two pamphlets, 15c. each.

Chronicles of Simon Christianus. His manifold and wonderful adventures in the land of Cosmos. A new scripture (evidently inspired) discovered by I N. Fidel. From the English Very rich. 25 cents.

Farrington, M. Sabbath. The Sunday Question. 10c.

Grumbine, Rev. I. C. F. Evolution and Christianity. A Study. 25c.

Helvetius; or, The True Meaning of the System of Nature. Cloth, 20 cents.

Hertwig, J. G.: Sunday Laws. 10c.

Holland, F. M. Atheists and Agnostics; a protest against their disabilities before the law. A lecture before the Ingersoll Secular Society. 5c.

Holyoake. George Jacob. What Would Follow on the Effacement of Christianity. 10c.
Logic of Death. 10c. Logic of Life. 10c.

Hume, David: Essay on Miracles. 10 cents.

Ingersoll, Robert G.: Bible Idolatry. 3 cents; 30 cents per dozen, $2 per 100.
What Must We Do to be Saved? 12mo, paper, 25c.
Address on Civil Rights. Paper, 10 cents. Orthodoxy. Paper, 10 cents.
Blasphemy Argument (Trial of Reynolds.) Paper, 25 cents; cloth, 50 cents.
Crimes Against Criminals (his latest address.) Paper, 10 cents.
Ingersoll Catechized. Answers to Questions by Editor "San Franciscan." 3 cents; 30 cents per dozen.
Ingersoll on McGlynn. 3 cents; 30 cts. per dozen; $2 per hundred.
Lay Sermon. Delivered before the tenth annual congress of the American Secular Union, on the labor question. 5c.; 50c per dozen; 25 'or $1.
Limitations of Toleration. A discussion between Col. Robert G. Ingersoll, Hon. Frederic R. Condert, ex Governor Stewart L. Woodford. 25c.
Paine Vindicated. Reply to the New York "Observer." 15 cents.
Photograph (cabinet) of. 50 cents.
Truth of History. 3c.; 30c per dozen; $2 per 100.
Which Way. Lecture at the Boston Theatre, Sunday evening, January 18, 1885. Paper, 5c.
Crumbling Creeds. 3 cents. Human Rights. 3c.
Plea for Individuality and Arraignment of the Church. 5c.
The Personal Philosopher of Reason—Humboldt. 5c.
Personal Deism Denied. 5c. The Declaration of Independence. 5c.
Life and Deeds of Thomas Paine. 5c. Past and Present Gods. 5c.
Modern Thinkers. 5c. Views of the Religious Outlook. 5c.
Some Reasons Why. 5c. The Great Infidels. 5c.
Review of His Reviewers. 5c. Oration on Decoration Day. 5c.
Oration at a Child's Grave, with comment on the oration; and answers to interrogatories of eminent Indiana clergymen. 5c.
Myth and Miracle. 5c. Abraham Lincoln. 5c.
Eulogy on Roscoe Conkling. 5c. Skulls. 5c. Hell. 5c.
Geister. A German translation of Ghosts. 10c.
[A list of the larger works of Col. Ingersoll appears on another page.]

Jacobson, A.: Bible Inquirer. 148 striking selfcontradictions of the Bible, and 152 marvelous occurrences. 25 cents.

Jones, Alonzo T. Civil Government and Religion, or Christianity and the American Constitution. 25c.

Jefferson, Thomas, the Father of American Democracy: His Political, Social, and Religious Philosophy, by Gen. M. M. Trumbull. 5cc.

Lenstrand, Viktor. The God Idea. For delivering this lecture the author was sentenced to six months' imprisonment for blasphemy in Sweden. Translated from the Swedish, with an introduction by J. M. Wheeler. 10c.

Luce, H. C. Antidote Analyzed. Inconsistency of Christians. 10c.

Lyall, A. C. Relation of Witchcraft to Religion. 15c.

Muller, Max: Buddhist Nihilism. 10 cents.

Newman, Prof. F. W. Religion not History. 25c.

Nibble at Prof. John Fiske's Crumb for the Modern Symposium 10c.

Paine, Testimonials to; author of Common Sense, The Crisis, Rights of Man, English System of Finance, Age of Reason, etc. Compiled by Joseph N. Moreau. 15 cents.

Peck, J. Soul Problems. Theological Amendment. 25c.

Pellegrini, A. S. de. Mortality of the Soul, and the Immortality of its Elements. 25c.

Ptolemy, G. W. Bar. The Origin of Priestcraft, or Religion the Curse of the World. 25c.

Priest in Absolution. Criticism and Denunciation of the Confessional. 25c.

Pringle, A. The "Mail's" Theology. Reply to the Toronto "Mail." 15c. Ingersoll in Canada. 15c.

Public School Question. By Bishop McQuade and F. E. Abbott. (Catholic and Liberal.) 20c.

Putnam, S. P. Problem of the Universe and Its Scientific Solution. Criticisms of Universology. 20c. New God. 10c.

Pentecost, Hugh O.: Wanted—Men Willing to Work for a Living. 3c. Why I am Not an Agnostic. 3c. How the Church Obstructs Progress. 3c. A Bad God and a False Heaven. 3c. Thomas Paine. 3c. The Presbyterian Dilemma. 3c. Calvin's God or None. 3c. The Freethinkers' Deathbed. 3c. The Evil the Church Does. 3c. A Helpless God. 3c.

The Rag Picker of Paris.

BY FELIX PYAT.

"Better than I," wrote Victor Hugo to Felix Pyat, "you have proved the royalty of genius and the divinity of love." Paper, 50 cents. Cloth, $1.

.

Caesar's Column.

A STORY OF THE TWENTIETH CENTURY.

BY EDMUND BOISGILBERT, M. D.

Paper, 50 cents. | | Cloth, $1.25.

WORKS OF
P. J. PROUDHON.

TRANSLATED BY BENJ. R. TUCKER.

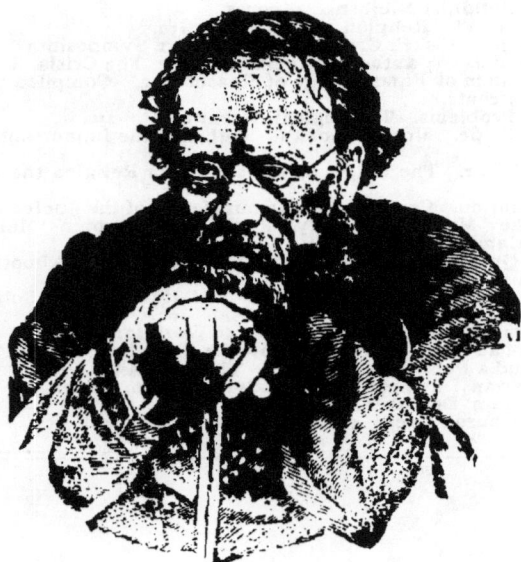

"The face which looks out from the page which fronts the title-page of this book is that of a powerful intellect filled with immense emotion; is that of a seer and enthusiast. It is the face of the man who wrote, PROPERTY IS ROBBERY."—*The Golden Rule*.

VOL. 1—WHAT IS PROPERTY?
or an Inquiry into the Principle of Right and of Government.

Prefaced by a Sketch of Proudhon's Life and Works. 500 pages. Price, cloth, $3.50; full calf, blue, gilt edges, $6.50.

Vol. 4. System of Economic Contradictions;
or, The Philosophy of Misery.

This work is one of the most celebrated written by Proudhon. 469 pages. Price, cloth, $3.50; full calf, blue, gilt edges, $6.50.

Address Twentieth Century Pub'g Co., 4 Warren street, New York.

A Strike of Millionaires

AGAINST MINERS;

—·· OR ··—

THE ·· STORY ·· OF ·· SPRING ·· VALLEY.

By HENRY D. LLOYD.

This book tells how the Spring Valley miners were starved into actual slavery. It is the story of a monstrous and inhuman crime. It deals not with theories but with facts, figures and names.

IT IS A POWERFUL AND PATHETIC BOOK.

264 Pages. Paper, 50 cents; cloth, $1. Sent post-paid to any address on receipt of price, by

Twentieth Century Publishing Co., New York.

ROBERT G. INGERSOLL'S
WRITINGS.

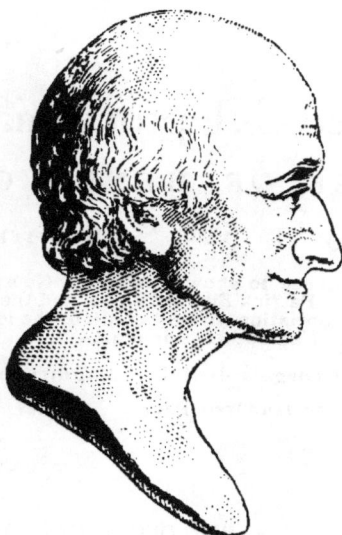

THE DAWNING.

By J. M. L. BABCOCK.

An Economic Novel that is—what the usual run of economic novels is not a veritable *novel ;* and that is at the same time a dissection of social conditions, present and prospective. Price in paper, 50 cents ; cloth, $1.

Highly commended by Hugh O. Pentecost.

Ideo - Kleptomania :

THE CASE OF HENRY GEORGE.

By J. W. Sullivan.

The author offers evidence to show that Henry George took his doctrines bodily from the works of Patrick Edward Dove, and that "Progress and Poverty" is largely an appropriation without credit of the ideas of Dove, William Godwin, Herbert Spencer and other economists.

With Henry George's denial of plagiarism, complete.

One Hundred Pages.   15 cents.

THE VERY LATEST ON PHILOSOPHICAL ANARCHISM.

Economics of Anarchy :

A Study of the Industrial Type.   By DYER D. LUM.

CONTENTS :

1. Fundamental Principles.   2. Free Land.   3. Free Labor.   4. Free Capital.
5. Free Exchange.   6. Mutual Credit.   7. Emancipation of Credit.
8. Industrial Economics.   9. Insurance, or Security.   10. Digression on Methods.
PRICE, 25 CENTS.

ECONOMIC, SOCIOLOGICAL, SCIENTIFIC,

Liberal and Radical Books.

TWENTIETH CENTURY PUBLISHING CO.,
NEW YORK.

The Modern Science Essayist.

TWENTIETH CENTURY PUBLISHING CO., New York City.

The Liberal Classics.

GIBBON.

History of Christianity.

By Edward Gibbon.   One vol., 12mo., cloth, 864 pp., profusely illustrated, $1.50.

The Vicar of Savoy.

By Jean Jacques Rousseau, with portrait.   Paper cover, 25 cents:
cloth, 50 cents.

Christian Paradoxes.

By Francis Bacon, 10 cents.

Superstition in all Ages.

By Jean Meslier, an unbelieving Monk.   Paper cover, 50 cents;
cloth, $1.00.

Volney's Ruins of Empires.

With portrait and map of Astrological Heaven of the Ancients (in
press).   Paper, 40 cents ; cloth, 75 cents.

Works of Thomas Paine.

Age of Reason. Paper, 25c; cloth, 50c.

Age of Reason and Examination of the Prophecies. Paper, 40c; cloth, 75c.

Common Sense. Written in 1776. 15c.

Crisis. Written during American Revolution. Paper, 40c; cloth, 75c.

Great Works. 8vo, 800 pages. Cloth, $3; leather, $4; morocco, gilt edges, $4.50.

Political Works: "Common Sense," "Crisis," "Rights of Man." Cloth, $1.50.

Rights of Man. Answer to Burke's Attack on French Revolution. Paper, 25c; cloth, 50c.

Theological Works: "Age of Reason," "Examination of Prophecies," etc., with Life of Paine and steel portrait, $1.50.

Paine Vindicated. Reply to New York *Observer*. By R. G. Ingersoll. With Roman Catholic canard, 15c.

SUPERSTITION IN ALL AGES.

—— BY ——

JEAN MESLIER,

AN UNBELIEVING PRIEST.

339 Pages. · Paper, 50c.; Cloth, $1.

"Glaube und Vernunft," the above work in German. Cloth, $1.

Twentieth Century Publishing Company,

NEW YORK CITY.